THE
LION'S WISDOM

A Channeled Text Toward
Awakening Human Consciousness

Uma Shankari

Dedicated to my parents who breathed life into me.

TABLE OF CONTENTS

PREFACE

This book has been a gift to me. As an ordinary person, I never expected to take such an extraordinary journey—to channel the words you are about to read. You see, the writings in this book are not my words. I am simply the medium through which the universe chose to share its message with you. It has been an awe-inspiring and completely humbling experience. I don't consider myself a writer. Aside from the occasional corporate presentation many years ago, I have written very little in my life. And, until recently, I was not an especially spiritual person, either. I was raised in a big city in India as a Hindu, though I never really felt connected to religion. For these reasons and more, I consider myself a most unlikely candidate to write about divine wisdom. Yet, here I am, introducing you to a book called *The Lion's Wisdom*. The universe does indeed work in mysterious ways.

Until I channeled this text, I never fully understood my extraordinariness. Channeling this book has changed my perception of who I am. Actually, it has changed my perception of who we all are. The spirits who wrote this book through me taught me about our innate wisdom and complete oneness as beings of Mother Earth. When we struggle with doubts and fears—as I certainly do—that's our ego at work. I've had to battle my ego relentlessly throughout the writing of this book. But when we listen to our higher selves—our souls—that is when we are able to receive truth and love. This is what the spirits have asked of me, to lend them my higher self as a vessel, so that they could share their truth and love with all of us.

The first time the spirits gave me something to write, I was astonished. To be honest, I didn't think much of it at first, as I did not understand the power within to that extent. The initial words were nothing exceptional. I just kept allowing my thoughts to flow and wrote them on the paper, until eventually it was not my thoughts that flowed. Before I knew it, I had written about five pages. When I went back and reread the contents, I was touched by what had flowed. While channeling, I had no idea what words were about to come. I simply allowed the information as it came through me. While I was writing, I had no sense of time or space. I was in a trance-like state. When I awakened, and read what I had written, I was often dumbstruck. There on the page, I found so many words and ideas. I was aware of many of the messages, but some I was not. What was amazing was, I could not have written these thoughts in the way they came through me. At times, I was given words that I had never heard or used in my life. Even though I had written the words, they were completely new to me when I read them. Many of the messages had a profound and immediate effect on me. Others were difficult for me to understand, and I had to re-read them several times.

Throughout this journey, I have experienced a cornucopia of emotions—wonder, love and joy as well as pain, fear and self-doubt. There were times I questioned whether my ego had changed any of the thoughts as they came through me. Other times, I felt like a fraud. I worried about tainting the contents with my own opinions. If my ego did slip into the message of this book in any way, I hope you will forgive me. It was not my intent. Having said that, I can assure you my physical, ego-driven self could not have written a book like this. The wisdom in·this book comes from a place of truth and love that is truly paradise. Only our higher selves have access to the type of wisdom imparted in these pages.

Like many of you, I was brought up to believe there is no magic in this world. That's why this whole experience has been so surreal. Only now, when I look back on my life, can I see that I was being prepared. I have always been a highly intuitive person. As a child, I had several unexplainable things happen in my life, though I never sought to piece them together. While I remember each experience vividly, it was easier at the time not to analyze what seemed impossible. Later, after finishing my graduate degree in Chicago, I became an engineer at a top U.S. company. It was my intuitiveness, not my skills, that helped me thrive in the corporate world. I had one manager who thought I was making up things. Over time, he began to trust me, as my intuition was proven right over and over.

In 2006, I had two clairaudient experiences. Both times I was told that a friend would be separating from their husband. In one case, the spirit told me that my friend would call in two weeks to share the news. Lo and behold, after two weeks, my friend called and said, "I am separating from my husband." All I could say was, "I know." It was an overwhelming burden, so at the end of that year I begged the spirit, "Please take it away. I don't want it." And just like that, the clairaudient experiences stopped and never came back.

For six years life seemed normal, but I wondered about the clairaudient experience. In fact, at that point I did not know that it was a clairaudient experience. Then, in 2012, I received an email from an angel reader. I did not care for such things, or believe in readings, but for some reason the email kept nagging at me. No matter how I tried to ignore it, the email kept popping up in mysterious ways. Every time I opened my inbox, the email would show up in some way. After weeks of consideration, I finally emailed the angel reader back and set up a session, even though I was still very skeptical.

On the day of our reading, she was late and disorganized, which served to further confirm my doubts. As she began the reading, I was convinced the session was going to be a waste of my time and money. But then she started sharing things about my relationship with my father—things that no stranger could ever have known. Tears began streaming down my face. When she was done, I asked her how she knew all these things. She explained that she was merely a conduit, that angels came and gave her the messages, which she in turn shared with her clients. I was fascinated. In time, my work with the angel reader led me down a path of spiritual exploration. I read *I Am the Word* by Paul Selig and learned about mediums, channellers and psychics. Selig's books also further taught me about guides, who provide authentic information about humanity and human evolution. They are an energy of divine truth, a truth that resonates with all of humanity and every creature alive.

In May of 2017, I was sitting at one of Selig's seminars, and asked the guides he was channeling about my purpose. They told me, "You want answers, but we will tell you that you are in the way of your own purpose." I wasn't sure what to make of this, so the next day I sat and meditated. Of all of Selig's books, the one that resonated with me most was the "Wisdom" chapter in his third book. It explained how to tap into your own wisdom and revealed how we are wise beyond what we have thought ourselves to be. I called upon my wisdom and meditated. I was shown a rabbi in a garden. He was so wise and gentle. He talked to me and gave me some advice. I felt at peace. The next day I decide to meditate and see what else might come through. I decided to put my pen on paper and write all the words that were given to me. As I started writing, sentences started coming through. I kept writing, and eventually it started flowing. After writing about five pages, I named the chapter, wrapped it up, and went through my day.

The next morning, I was woken up just after 5:00 am with my forearm tingling. I felt compelled to write. For the next 21 days, the same thing happened, weekends included. Trust me, I didn't care to be woken up so early on weekends, but I kept writing. One chapter after another flowed through me. When I finished the book, I had withdrawal symptoms, though I also knew that I didn't want to write for a while. The daily channeling sessions were exhilarating, but also exhausting. I needed a reprieve. I shared this with my guides, and they agreed gracefully. They were truly loving to me. They carried me when I fell. They stood by me when I questioned them. They were there for me through all the highs and lows of this amazing journey. When you read these pages, you too will experience their presence, if you allow them to be there for you.

Lovingly yours,
Uma

AUTHOR'S NOTE

*A*s you read *The Lion's Wisdom* keep in mind that the messages and experiences within its pages are non-linear. Occasionally, this might confuse you, but continue reading as in a few paragraphs you will feel reoriented.

A couple of things about the book: the terms God and Goddess are the same aspect of ourselves. They are interchangeable.

The word "rape" is used to describe the plight of Mother Earth and the magnitude of destruction at the hands of humanity. I am sensitive about the use of this word by the spirits. I understand the emotions that it will evoke for some people. I assure you that use of this word was not meant to be disrespectful or to make light of the term.

When you finish reading this book, you will understand yourself much more deeply. You might even start to participate in your life differently, for this book is a celebration of life. For some of you, this book will be transformative. For others, it will not yet resonate. That is okay. I only ask that you open yourself to the potential for transformation. As much as I am a control freak, I relinquish the need to control your experience. Of course, I want you to love this book and have revelations as a result of reading it. That's my ego seeking your approval—I know that. Each of you will have a different experience and all experiences are valid in human consciousness.

No matter what your experience, know that I am on this journey with you. I am no different than you. My trials and tribulations are similar to yours, though our paths in life are different. When we are asked to awaken—as you will be in this book—we often resist. Change is difficult. Change is unsettling. When we release our resistance, that's when the magic shows up. This book is filled with the magic that I experienced when I stopped resisting my calling, my gift. I can't imagine what my life might be like if I continued resisting and never wrote this book. It has changed my life.

Lovingly yours,
Uma

CHAPTER 1: WISDOM

*M*y wisdom, filled with truth and knowledge, leads me every day when I sit silent and listen to it. It is profound, and it is my wisdom and mine only. It does not justify. It does not argue. It has no need to prove anything. It is just what is so. It resonates with my heart, my knowing, and my being. It is my truth, my divine truth that has arisen from the depth of my being. It is the one and only truth that serves me. It is strong in its resonance. It is deep in its meaning. It is powerful in its stating. It does not waver in its authenticity. It is what is so—my wisdom, my truth. It honors me. It loves me. It cherishes me. Even when the message is not to my liking, my wisdom is still loving and kind in its tone. It does not demand, it is just wise. It is the greater truth and it is customized for me. Hence, no one—including myself—has a say in the matter, except for my wisdom, for it is wise.

My wisdom constantly contradicts the opinion of others...even mine. It knows there is more value in truth than in an opinion. An opinion may seem like a truth, but my wisdom knows it is not the same. It is something that is inexplicable. It is something that cannot be debated. It is just so, and only my being knows, since it resonates with my core like no other.

The truth in my wisdom transcends the purposes of self. It has a higher need to heal. Healing is my wisdom's main path. It may look different to others and it may look unwise to others, but it is mine and mine only. No one can add any value to my wisdom, including myself. I am filled with the confusion of everyday life, bombarded with a thousand ideas and opinions. To fit my wisdom with those would be a fool's choice, so I don't even attempt it. I simply let it be.

Sometimes I am shaken by the wisdom. It is so pure, so clear and unwavering and uncompromising in its message that I sometimes do not want to admit the truth in it. It appears harsh yet resonates with my core.

My wisdom that comes from within me, my consciousness, does not prod my mind. It is simply what is so. Yes, my wisdom is a simple one, neither to be rattled with nor debated. It is simple and plain, yet deep and courageous.

I feel like a child when my wisdom speaks. It takes me by my hands and walks me through life's beauty. It shows me things I have never seen or paid attention to. I look at life's beauty with new eyes. My life appears differently when my wisdom holds my hands. When I choose to ignore my wisdom, I am left chaotic, and inundated with opinions and judgments. Some opinions appear as wisdom, since they have been taught for generations.

When I reach out to my wisdom and hold its hands, a calmness pervades me; a clarity enshrouds me. The shift in perception is drastic. That is what my wisdom shows. I have to teach myself to hold the hands of my wisdom. I get distracted by opinions and judgments too often to notice my wisdom right by me, reaching out its hand.

I feel consoled by my wisdom. I feel comforted by my wisdom. I feel nurtured by my wisdom. Its soothing tone and voice lead me to a higher path. It diminishes my pettiness like nobody's business. It is constantly calling me to seek my higher self, to seek my divine path, to be the one who holds the light. It makes me feel the real me, the unique me, the loving me, the divine me.

My wisdom—ever present, never leaving, by my side- constantly—whispers my truth. I may not always hear it, but it is persistent in its message and voice. I have heard it many times. It is as clear as a waterfall, the ocean waves, lightning, thunder, the air, the wind. It is the truth that no one can explain or examine, for there is nothing to examine.

It may confuse others, but it clarifies me. My truth deeply resonates in my heart, in my being, in my core, clear as a lion's roar, yet gentle as a lapping wave. My wisdom is mine and only mine, and it is not to be used on others as a tool. If I do, I miss the point, for the presence of my wisdom teaches the presence of wisdom in others. It teaches me that my path, my duty, and my lessons are different from those of others. Hence, I never have to interfere, judge or teach another about their life path, duty or lessons. It is not my job, but theirs, to learn from their wisdom, ever present on their side.

Judgment is quick to show up. It is the one companion I have chosen throughout my presence. However, I find it critiquing me and others constantly, wavering me from my path of wisdom. Judgment always justifies its presence and importance, but I am unable to move forward with pride or my true self in its presence. Its chatter fills me with doubt, confusion and fear. Yet, I have had it as my companion for as long as I have known. Why would I choose to have a companion that is so unloving to me? Well, I didn't know any better. Now that I have met my wisdom, I am choosing to walk beside it, hand in hand, allowing it to show me my path and my true journey. The path is clear and my guidance sound. I am set for life with my wisdom, who is ever loving, never commanding or demanding. Its voice is as gentle as a lullaby to a baby—soothing, healing, and nourishing. It brings joy to my soul, my being, myself. It brings me back home to myself, me, my real me, free of judgment and fear. Its resonant voice deepens my faith, my love, my journey. In Its presence, I know not any worries, for it is ushering me deep into my soul to be submerged in my essence—*my* essence, *my* truth, *my*self.

The life I had led, in ignorance of my wisdom, was torturous, chaotic, and filled with desires from my ego, which knew no boundaries and ran like a beast. My wisdom's choices veered me to my path, to my truth, to my soul's journey. I was not easily convinced by my wisdom, yet my wisdom prevailed, showing me that there was a wiser path, a different journey, a different message, waiting for me to choose.

My wisdom, gentle and patient, waited beside me. It had talked to me several times, but I ignored it, since it contradicted my opinions and judgments, which I thought were my true gospel. No matter what agony was created by my judgment, I decided to stay faithful to it, until one day I could not ignore my wisdom because it became louder in my heart. I was used to having my opinions be loud and clear and dominate my life. This was new to me. It was not harsh as my opinion, but gentle and not controlling. Wisdom always appeared to be a pipe dream, and I used my rational mind as an excuse to not follow my wisdom. I was chosen by my wisdom as a special student, the one and only student, to teach the truth. My wisdom, that is so perfect, so clear and concise, knows nothing but the truth. The conciseness of my wisdom was what caught my attention. Its conciseness highlighted the profoundness in the message. I was distracted from my judgment by the mere conciseness, for my judgment was too chatty, too confusing with too many opinions—some mine, some others. There was too much information to sort through to get the clarity which I never got. My wisdom's conciseness paved the way to clarity in my life that I ached for and sought out.

Here I am, with my wisdom, on my journey, not knowing my destination, yet clear on my path. I need not worry as my wisdom guides me with love and care, which is all I need. My love, my wisdom's love, intertwined, emanating a fragrance that is hard to resist and ignore. To ignore my wisdom is to ignore my true essence. I cannot be ignored. I should not be ignored. I need not be ignored. I could not be ignored, for I was born for a purpose, a true purpose, a higher purpose that is mine and mine only, unique and beautiful and perfect for me.

I am content in this journey, the clear velvety sands felt under my feet, the lush creepers around me, the blue green water—all provide a vision of the faraway lands I am about to embark upon. My love for myself dominates me, faithful in its purpose, its divine purpose, never wavering in its journey.

I have found myself in this path with my wisdom. I never have to ask another for my true path or to lead me. My wisdom is my divine gift given to me at my birth. I lost it along the way and found it again in my despair. Ever since I found it, I can't seem to part with it. How could I? It belongs to me, for it is me and I am it, my wisdom. When my judgment surfaces again, from having been left out, my wisdom gently squeezes my hand. I have a choice, I know, to listen to my judgment or my wisdom. In the moment of choice, I am liberated by the knowing that my wisdom stands right by me, holding my hands, dissolving in my heart, my thoughts and my being.

For I found my wisdom, in its fullness, impregnated with messages from beyond my comprehension. If I am wise enough, I know what to choose. My wisdom never reprimands me when I don't listen, for it knows my true self always finds my wisdom, for it is me, and I am it.

I have learned, by feeding my insatiable judgment, that I am exhausted. I am tired because I ignore my true *self*— me, the true and real me. Judgment feeds me an intoxicating drug that keeps me in the guise of control.

It makes my movements so vapid, as I go where my judgment goes, without care for my well-being or myself.

That insatiable beast of judgment is uncontrollable, and it gets bigger and bigger as a giant that dominates me with its mere ugly presence and demonic appearance. I have learned that my judgment is a deflatable toy that has no substance; it is only vacuum. It is not real, made up of gossip, opinions and other's judgment. I was born without judgment; therefore, it can be undone as it was done.

To realize that I have dealt with this lie of judgment for no purpose is disheartening. Yet, I would have not found my wisdom without this deflatable toy. It has no form but the one I give it. I can choose for it not to dominate my life, for it is not even real.

I have played with this toy with several others. I am declaring through my wisdom that I am letting go of playing with this giant toy that was man made. It has no blood, no flesh, no life, no consciousness. It breathes with me only because I constantly resuscitate it. To know that I was resuscitating something that had no life is a joke, I realize. But what did I know? I did as I was told. For the first time, I realize I need not listen to another, for they don't know any better, just as I don't. My wisdom taught me that one of my purposes on this journey is to throw away the farce of this toy that we as humans believe in and resuscitate every day in order to keep up with the madness, the drama, the accusations. I am blessed by my divine wisdom, and never have to look at another useless toy that was manufactured by humanity. In throwing away the toy, others may see the wisdom and seek their own wisdom on their path. There may be others that are not ready for it, for their wisdom is waiting for them to feel the squeeze in their hands.

I am intrigued by the irony, by the humor of this farce with whom my hands were joined. I withdraw my support of this irony, this farce. I forge forward to seek my journey with joy, bliss and comfort. I am comforted in my knowing that I am cared for by my wisdom, my *self*, my me, my dear perfect me, my wise me—that is all I need, me on this journey. On my journey, I will be brought the right people to walk beside me. I will learn lessons with them and enjoy their camaraderie and love. I am strong in knowing that all I need is me. Yet, I can enjoy this beautiful journey with others by my side. This journey, free of the judgments and filled with wisdom, has been chosen by my soul in collaboration with my higher self. See, I am not alone. You are not alone. Do not worry about being left out. No one is, and neither are you.

Step into the puddle on your journey. It is not dirty, but rather cool and healing on your feet. Throw away your shoes, for the cool velvety sands will soothe your feet. Do not worry. When you need a shoe, it will magically appear, just as it did for Dorothy. You can pick a shiny shoe of your color of choice. It doesn't have to be the shiny red. Yes, it is a magic land that you are journeying towards. While you journey towards that magic land, remember that you are in one magic land already. You are not leaving one land for another magic land. You are exploring one magic land to another.

When your judgment surfaces laugh your heart out, for you know it is not real, and shred it with your mind's eye. It does not need a knife but your kind thoughts to yourself and to the world. If you ever miss your judgment, reach out for to your wisdom for guidance. Your ever-present guidance system, implanted in you, in your soul before you were ever born. See, you were born with it and you will die with it. It is ever present. It is older than you, wiser than you. It is your all-knowing champion, your truth, your essence, and this is your wisdom, wise one. This is your wisdom.

You are about to embark upon a journey with me in understanding how I attained this wisdom. It was not too long ago that I was anything but wise. I was someone who cared little about wisdom, in fact I cared nothing about wisdom.

Holding your hands through your journey of our wisdom,
Man

CHAPTER 2: THIEVERY

I have been told that it is okay to steal. Steal whatever you want to live a comfortable life. Look beyond your current needs and steal and hoard, so that generations to come after you will be comfortable. That is called planning for life. Not only do you think for yourself, but for your future generations that will carry your legacy. Your legacy is an important one. YOU walked the Earth, and you left a mark on Mother Earth by hoarding enough so that your future generations would have your name; your legacy would be on their lips. What a great honor for your name to be on the lips of many.

I am a father. I work hard every day, so that my future generations will lead comfortable lives, so that they don't have to suffer like my ancestors or even me. I cannot bear for my future generations to suffer. My soul will not rest in peace, not knowing if my future generations will be safe and comfortable. I make sure I provide my children with everything they need. I follow my society's direction—finding the best education, feeding them the best food, providing them with the best clothes. I was deprived of these, so I want to ensure that my children don't suffer, my grandchildren don't suffer, and my future generations don't suffer. I am investing in my children's education, so that my future generations are well cared for. I feel joy and pride in my children's growth. I teach them all that they need to know about society, getting ahead, and forging through no matter what. This is my job as a parent.

If I don't teach them values like how to make money, who will? I am buying multiple homes, so that each of my children will have a comfortable home when I die. I have so much to do before my death. I work hard every day to ensure I make more money. Money, an important factor that will save my legacy. All my children will know what a good father, grandfather, great-grand father I was by taking care of their needs well in advance. I am proud of myself for my forethought, planning and strategy. I am getting good at this. I teach my children good work ethics, discipline and morality. These are the groundwork for their survival and my survival. I better pound this into them, for my legacy and their survival depends on this. I envision a bright future for my children and my future generations.

I have come a long way. I have made enough money for generations to survive. I am proud of my accomplishments. My children respect me and fear me. I continue to work even in my old age, acquiring more, more, more and more. I have an insatiable need to hoard wealth. I like the wealth, but I like the power that it comes with it even more. I am well respected in my community, among my peers, my fellow elite. I am respected for being someone who started with nothing and grew wealth. I am known for my honesty, hard work and perseverance. I am teaching my children about the wealth I grew and continue to grow. I am here to make an imprint, to continue my legacy.

I am a mother. I will do anything to ensure that my children are taken care of. Don't ever try to harm my children. I could hurt you, if I need to protect my precious children. I love them. I adore them. I am teaching them for their future. I nourish my children with the best food. I provide the best clothes. I provide only the best for my children. Don't even try to interfere with my motherhood, for I am fierce. I will protect my children like a she-wolf. I can be a warrior, if need be, to protect my children. Of course, I teach my children several good things. I teach them to share, but by ensuring that they have enough, for one cannot share by denying oneself. I teach them careful, measured generosity. I always ensure that they have enough before sharing. I am a good mother who cares for the welfare of my children. Since I am a mother, isn't it my job to protect my children? I have seen careless mothers. I am not one of them. I like my children to play with others, but not all of them. Some children can be a bad influence on my children. I teach my children to not make friends with some children, for it is my job to protect my children, isn't it? I ensure that my children only hang out with those kids that are good at school. I don't want them to get influenced by poor performers, for I want to ensure that my children are smart and remain smart. I am a caring mother, for I care for my children's well-being.

I teach them compassion, but not at the expense of themselves. I teach them, and mostly they listen to me, but sometimes they don't. They are good at their school work, share some with others, and sometimes show compassion, but sometimes they don't. I am proud when they show compassion without getting too involved. They share some stories. I am proud of their sensitive nature, but I don't let them get carried away. It is not their job to care for everyone. It is impossible to take care of everyone. My mother taught me this when I was a child, and I relay her teachings to my children. We are good parents teaching discipline, generosity, compassion and morality to our children.

My dear readers, isn't it wonderful that my parents taught these wonderful qualities to their children, me and my siblings, so that I and my wife can teach these values to our children? We live in a society where people do try to give good values. I have lived a life of good teachings. My parents raised me well. They taught me discipline—discipline that would help me propagate our wealth and values. Values, talking about values, my parents taught such good values that I can't wait to pass them on to my own children. Values that would raise an eyebrow if you really knew the truth, but I understand my parents did it for our sake, and how can I fault them? They did it for me, for my siblings, for our future generations. They taught us the value of money. Money earned honestly, which is very important to my family.

I take pride in the honesty of my family. We always paid the right price, and all our dealings were based on our faith. But something irks me. I am not sure if I should voice it, for that would show my family in a light that is not admirable. Our legacy that we continue to create would be tarnished. We are, in reality, thieves. We have stolen every resource that is available on the planet: water, land, animals, plants and more. Here is my story that needs to be told to end our legacy, and to propagate Mother Nature's legacy. I am learning that my parents were wrong—wrong in every sense of the word. One day I was given a dream. In that dream, I was told a truth. Let me narrate it to you my dear adults, for it is an important story.

Long ago, there was a civilization, and that civilization thrived. It followed Mother Nature's plan, and in that plan was true generosity, true morality, true compassion, true discipline and true values. The most important value was respect. It was the key ingredient for thriving. It was a respect that was not given, but already present in every living creature. Every creature was respected, trusted and loved. Every creature was free to roam Mother Earth's vast expansive terrains. No one was contained, no one; not humans, not bugs, not ants, not worms, not animals, not water, not air. Nothing was contained. Every creature roamed around freely with respect to one another. No food was taken unless necessary. No water was taken unless necessary. Every creature had its rightful place and they inherently knew it. They played with each other. They shared things naturally as part of Mother Nature's plan. No one told them how. They just knew. Man was equal with all the other beings on Earth. The population of every creature was kept in balance as part of the rules of the ecosystem.

Every creature was humble and respectful of Mother Nature, and Mother Nature responded continuously with grace and abundance--an abundance one cannot comprehend. It was a paradise. A paradise such as you have never seen, never could imagine. Animals mated and produced offspring per Mother Nature's cyclical calendar. The animals knew, through their inheritance, the right times to mate and give birth. They understood life and death. They created precious life, and when death came, they accepted it with grace. Everything worked beautifully through Mother Nature's timetable. Everyone had a part in the ecological balance. No one was left out—not the monkeys, not the donkeys, not the horses, not the shrubs, not the moss, not the algae. It was a perfect, well planned ecology.

A wounded animal or human would know exactly what plants brought them cure, though no one taught them, no one. Mother Nature imprinted this knowledge on each creature at birth. There were no serious diseases, no big ailments, just the natural cycle of birth and death.

Compassion and love reigned the motherland. Respect was the predominant ingredient in the cycle. They all had an inherent wisdom. A wisdom that was not taught but inherited, inherited from Mother Earth.

All creatures lived in harmony, abundance, love, compassion, and above all, respect—a kind of respect that has been forgotten, a kind of respect that has been ignored, a kind of respect that has been lost, a kind of respect that has been suppressed, a kind of respect that has been manipulated.

Respect: the God-given right of every living creature on Mother Earth's vast plains. In the beginning, every single creation was respected for just its mere presence. Every single creation was respected for its significance. Every single creation was respected for the mere purpose of being respected. This respect continued with harmony for eons. Man was the happiest at these times. He was one with the air, water, animals, mountains, plants, bugs, worms and Mother Earth herself. He had so much respect for Mother Earth that he never had the slightest inkling to harm any of her creatures or creations. Such was life, a wonderful paradise. No one was left hungry when conditions were harsh as part of Mother Nature's natural cycle. Their wisdom taught them to move and/or to instinctively protect themselves.

Sometimes, some died--men, animals, plants, worms, bugs and so on. But they knew it was part of Mother Nature's plan. No, they didn't think God hated them and hence punished them. They knew the laws of creation inherently. They were inherently wise, and their wisdom always came through. Their mind didn't chatter since their wisdom reigned. Their wisdom was Mother Earth's wisdom. She would continue to allow her wisdom to permeate the atmosphere and the creations would absorb the wisdom into themselves. This was a perfectly orchestrated plan co-created by Mother Earth and God.

The symphony, in perfect harmony with Mother Nature's tunes and lyrics, was played by her creations and children. What a perfect rhythm they had, a rhythm that has not been heard or seen. The man who roamed this land in this rhythm eons before would be called a barbarian who is uncivilized as he followed Mother Nature's natural rhythm, respecting her creations—yes, a barbarian who is uncouth and uncivilized. If we found one today, we would want him to go to school and learn greed, disrespect and hoarding. We would also give him a suit, as he is so uncivilized that he is minimally clothed or nude.

That uncivilized man could teach us a thing or two that we are too civilized to learn. However, I heard the man talk to me in my dream. He was gorgeous: no disease, no paunch, well-toned. I offered him refreshments and food. He refused. I did not press. So here is the wisdom that he shared with me, that made me rethink all the values my parents had instilled. I realized my parents did not know or did not want to know, for that would crush their legacy, their dream.

The man said he is the happiest man alive, as he had a mother who taught him to use his own wisdom. He always called upon his wisdom when he needed an answer. He roamed Mother Earth's vast plains freely. He had seen the deserts, mountains, snow glaciers, caves, oceans, and all that Mother Earth had created. It was a joy to wander and learn the different creations of Mother Earth. In fact, he said that Father God and Mother Earth collaborated and co-created this masterpiece we call Mother Nature—Mother Nature, a divine Goddess. He said he has seen beauty that could not be fathomed by me. He decided to come into my dream to teach me a few things that he saw through his mind's eye, namely the destruction currently being caused by man.

He was here to teach me to create a different reality than the one I was taught, than the one that was dictated to me. I requested he take me to the places where he had been. In my life, I have traveled and seen beauty, but I wanted to see what he had witnessed. He said I had turned my back on Mother Nature, and that is why I could not see all her beauty. He asked me to turn around to see her beauty. He was right. What I witnessed was awe inspiring. It was nothing like what I was able to see in my everyday life.

He asked me, "Did you like what you saw?"

I was utterly dumbfounded. The words would not come out of my mouth. What I saw was a paradise that I had never witnessed before.

"Would you like to be in that paradise?" he asked.

"Yes."

"Are you willing to give up everything—your wealth and power, the legacy of your parents, and all the things you have learned so far?"

I could not answer. I stayed silent. How could I give up everything that I worked hard for, everything that was rightfully mine, everything my parents worked hard for? How could I? My parents are important to me. I thought, I cannot walk away and lead their life. Then, I thought, if it is only a dream, what is the worst that could happen, if I said yes? I could wake up in the morning like nothing had happened and go my merry way. Voila!

So, I said, "Yes. I will give up everything."

"Are you sure?" he asked again.

"Yes."

"Can you give up knowing what you have known until now?"

"I can't," I replied, "as I already have it in my brain. How can I forget something I have already learned and practiced?"

"By learning new things."

New things, I pondered, "New like what?"

"New, like wisdom."

I told him that I had heard that word but thought only spiritual people who had renounced everything could have wisdom. I also realized, in a way, he had already asked me to renounce everything.

"Okay," I said. "It is still a dream, so no harm done."

He asked me to go into my mind's eye and envision the paradise that had been shown to me. He then asked me to see things and pointed me to various aspects in this paradise. At some point, I lost his voice, and I was transported to the paradise itself. I saw a lion approach me. I was stunned with fear and wanted to run, but realized it was a dream and stayed on. The Lion licked my hands, laid next to me and looked at me with intent. It was as if he was asking me to do something. I decided to sit by him and reached out for what the man had called wisdom. In my stillness, I heard the Lion.

"Save my legacy," the Lion said clearly.

I was jolted by these words. In my life, busy making money, I had never thought of saving another being's legacy; I'd only thought about saving my own.

I noticed the Lion looked different from the ones that I had seen in my comfortable safaris in Africa. He turned his head back, and I followed his eyes. Behind him there was a pride of lions with cubs and lionesses. They were happy, healthy and lush. I looked at the Lion. He had a long mane. He was bigger than the lions I had seen on my safaris. He was very sure of himself, and not at all scared of me. He did not try to attack me. In fact, he was very gentle. It was a sight to see his beautiful pride.

"Are you ready to carry my legacy?" the Lion asked again.

I wasn't sure, since it was a huge task. I would have to leave everything to pursue something outside myself. This was not what my parents had taught me. Then, I remembered it was just a dream; why not say yes?

"Yes," I told the Lion. "I will save your legacy."

"Do you know what it takes to save my legacy?"

"No, I don't. I will need your help."

In response, this is what the Lion told me: through his wisdom, he could see his future being usurped by man, the same man that he loved and who had loved him back unconditionally. This pained him, as the man's family and his pride currently co-existed and shared everything. In fact, his cubs and the man's children played together every day. He saw in his mind's eye that one day soon man would lose his respect for the Lion's pride. In fact, all of creation and all of their legacy—including man's legacy—would be dead. He predicted that man would destroy the forest's creatures for his own comfort and deprive every living creation and creature for his own greed.

The Lion said that he knew this was not the intention of man in his current state. However, his wisdom showed him that man's change of heart was imminent. If he did not reach out to me, all would be lost. His pride would suffer. In fact, he could not even comprehend what he saw in his mind's eye. He would lose his home, his forest, his water, his food, and above all the wonderful connection he had with man. He said that this pained him, but he had faith in man. Mother Nature's wisdom had been implanted in man and would save them when the Lion went to a place of no-return. The Lion said there he would have nothing more to lose. He faced extinction.

I realized something. The ancient man I saw, who was completely and totally one with creation, Mother Earth and all living creatures, would one day be reduced to thievery without any concern or respect for his co-habitants. The Lion, through his wisdom, was seeing this thievery, plundering, and raping of his world.

Something else astonished me. This disregard for man's cohabitants had reduced him to thievery, rape, plunder and disrespect for himself and humanity. If one cannot respect another inhabitant, how can he respect another human? Man, in his current state, justifies his rape of Mother Earth's creations, and does not apologize for his misdeeds. He has no regret, and therefore does not see the need to apologize. He has no compassion for those animals that have been pushed from their rightful place on Mother Earth. How could man regret his actions? How could he sympathize? How could he empathize? How could he show compassion? It is all a tower of cards. If you don't respect one creature, it cascades over to others. On the surface, it may seem like this is not me, since I did not directly kill or destroy the Lion's habitat. However, I was a silent observer, who in time became oblivious, and eventually arrogant. Am I any different from other men?

If a man steals from another, we quickly name him a thief. He is a petty thief who makes his living through stealing. There are a thousand books written about this morality and the punishments awaiting. How come the rape of Mother Earth has gone by without any justice? Is it that a petty thief is a nobody compared to someone who is sitting on a high chair and raping and pillaging behind the dazzling screens? Oh, he gives jobs? Is that what it is? Or am I too comfortable in my existence to question this rape happening right in front of our eyes in broad day light? I realized the observer is as guilty as the perpetrator. In this story, I am both an observer and perpetrator.

The Lion had spoken, and I heard him loud and clear. It is *our* legacy— not theirs, not mine—that needs saving. The legacy of paradise needs saving. The legacy of Mother Earth, the wise mother, filled with wisdom needs saving. She has instilled wisdom in all her children, but man has become lost in the teachings of his parents. These teachings must change. When I woke up from my dream, I looked in the mirror and saw a rapist, a thief, a perpetrator—they were all in me, the observer. I saw the Lion and the man in me, too. It was clear, I am responsible for it all. I cannot ignore this anymore or continue to be an observer. I am here to carry through the legacy of the Lion, the man, Mother Earth and all creations as one. There is only one legacy that needs saving: the legacy of oneness. This legacy is the only legacy worth saving, worth mentioning or worth discussing, for the legend lives in the oneness.

Faithfully,
Your Oneness

CHAPTER 3: ADMISSION

I must admit. I must. I must. I must. The life I live is a mystery to me. The life I planned is different than the one I live. My plans were aligned with my longings, my pleasures, my dreams and my mandates. The life I envisioned and the life I live are in contrast—a contrast I did not expect, for I could not have planned this. A life lived through planning, what a joke. Had I known that my life would not turn out to be the way I had envisioned, I wouldn't have sweated the planning. In spite of my new wisdom, I still plan. Why? It is in my blood. It is all I have known. I have to control every step of the way, so that I or those around me are not disappointed. Is this a joke? Living a life, planning a life, just for the sake of not being disappointed? Guess what, when I tried to live a life free of disappointment, I found it in every corner. I invited disappointment into my life by planning to evade its presence. It was like an uninvited guest. I didn't want it, and there it was.

And, so, my life is filled with disappointment. Had I known better, I would not have planned to evade disappointment. You may think, "Oh, I am not like that. I don't *always* evade disappointment. Maybe sometimes I do, for I am only human." Think hard. Have you not? If you say no, you are lying to yourself. Is this a life worth living? Hiding our disappointment? Evading disappointment? Lying about our disappointments?

Acting as though we are not disappointed? Wearing a smile, as if life is good? Even when you say you are blessed do you feel a slight twinge?

Or have you suppressed that twinge, so that lying comes easily? What is it? Only you will know. If you really want to know, you have to be open enough to know the truth, the truth that comes from your wisdom—no, not your father's truth, no, not your mother's truth, and not the truth your family and friends talk about either. It is another kind of truth. It is *your* truth. It is the kind of truth that pierces your being. It is the kind of truth that you cannot evade. It is the kind of truth that bugs you, when you are aware of its presence. How long do we lie? How long do we accept the lie? Which one are you seeking: the lie or the truth, the truth in the form of a lie, or the lie in the form of truth? Which one? You decide.

Look around. Have you ever questioned anything? If you haven't, you have denied your own truth, the truth that you have not cared to hear. Are you someone who does not care about the truth or someone who doesn't want to know the truth? Are you someone who is oblivious to the fact that there is a truth, a bigger truth? Admit it, dear one, admit it.

In this admission, you will seek the truth. What truth, you ask? Well, your truth. Ask the question first. Do you dare to ask, or do you think this is stupid? If you think this is stupid, there is all the more reason to ask the question. Admit it, you don't know what it is to live a life in truth. You may say, "I never lie." Don't you, dear one, don't you lie? I don't want to call you a liar, for that is an accusation. Who wants to be accused of lying? No one, yet there is some lie we all live in. You may take this personally, and this is okay. You will never guess the lie that you live in because it comes in a different package, and you cannot distinguish the truth from the lie. You are so used to being lied to, that it has become your mantra. If I tell you all the lies, you will either get angry or you may call me a liar, or you may be surprised by the lie you live in. Why do you think I know your lies? I know because I have lived the same lie as you—living in the status quo and getting through the day with not one iota of care for anyone but myself.

You may say, "Yes, I have cared about others, too." Yes, you may have, but that is not what I am talking about, dear one. You care, of course you do. You care about your family, your friends and you help them when in need. But, dear one, that is not what I am talking about.

See, it is taking me all this time to just make you see the lie. Do you know why? You are so inundated in the lies that you are unable to see them. That is okay, dear one. If you seek to learn the truth, just say so and it will be shown to you. When I speak of the truth, you may not like it. When you find out the truth for yourself, it will be far more gratifying.

Let me ask you a question, dear one, have you ever bought something out of fear, out of fear that if you did not have it, you may need it or one day or you will be in trouble. You see, dear one, that is a lie. If you closely examine it, you will see a thousand lies, and all those lies were based on perpetrated fear. You may want to justify the purchase. You may, dear one, but here is the truth: it was based on a lie—a lie that is not worth your life, yet you valued it. You spoke to an expert who presented all the facts to you about why you should buy something. I think I am getting somewhere with you, since I sense a slight admission.

When you make a list of all the things you have bought or done out of fear, my dear one, then you will understand the lie I am talking about. But it does not matter what I say; I am curious as to what you have to say. I am aware that I am making a lot of assumptions based on my life. There is one thing I know, though. We all have a set of things in our lives that are based in fear.

Did you or do you know of anyone who got married just because they were getting old or because they may not get to have a child if they waited too long? There you go, dear one. Yes, they were lied to, but you may say, "Is it not true that aging causes decline in producing an heir?" Is it true? You may say, "There is scientific evidence to prove it." You are right, but how do you really know, dear one? Doesn't science contradict itself sometimes? Wasn't it a proven fact that the earth was flat at some point in history? I am not saying science is wrong, merely pointing out an example. Please don't get carried away with this example.

Back to our truth, your truth. Have you pondered your truth? I know I am being a little demanding in making you admit this. But I am merely trying to make a point about the mirage of your life. It is up to you dear one, if you want the truth or not. If you are interested in the truth, read further. If you don't want to know the truth, I still encourage you to read further, but the choice is yours.

I may be annoying to you at this point. Let us bring back the Lion. Let us ask him some questions since he is the one interested in showing us our destructiveness that will cost his life and his pride. Let me step aside and take you into my dream, so I can introduce you to him.

Here he is. He is beautiful. I absolutely love him. Please imagine touching this powerful, majestic being. Can you feel the softness of his coat? Can you smell the forest on him? Look behind him, can you see his pride—the pride he will lose and the loss he will suffer from our hands? His family, joyful and playful, is enjoying the fruits of the forest. Can you hear his roar? That is his roar when he is enjoying his family, his pride. Bear with me, dear reader. I am going to make myself the authority and ask the Lion some questions, and if you have some questions, you can ask away, too.

Dear Lion, I pondered on what you told me yesterday. You asked me to save your legacy, and here I am. I thought I would bring a friend to talk to you. I'm sorry, I know one friend may not be enough, but I think it is a start. For I have to start somewhere to save your legacy, our legacy. Why am I defending myself while you have not even said anything? Pardon me, my dear Lion, it is a habit. I live in a world where I have to constantly justify my actions, and it has become a bad habit. Anyway, speaking of your legacy, can you please delve into it more, so that my friend and I can understand a little deeper how to save your legacy?

The Lion roared and nodded. First of all, he was happy to see us. I love this beautiful creature. I request you, my dear one, to sit quietly in the stillness. You will hear the Lion, as I do in my stillness.

"I heard you talking about the lies," the Lion said. "Let me tell you one of the many lies that have been perpetrated about us. It is a lie that separated us, man and lion. This lie was perpetrated to hide man's lies. The lie that was perpetrated was that we attacked you. You may see a lot of evidence of that in your world, but I am going to rectify it for you. Hopefully, this will open some doors for your view on humanity. Before I go on, I am here to tell you this in order to bring us together, not to separate us again, for we have suffered from the separation. We are aware of the lie, but you are not. The lie that we have attacked humans and need to be separated was perpetrated by man to hide all the hideous things he had done when he lost his connection to his wisdom. Losing his wisdom was the worst suffering man has ever endured. In losing this wisdom, man was exposed to greed, lies and suffering. It is fine that he endured this, but it cannot continue. In losing his wisdom, man drowned into oblivion. This oblivion made him forget all the world's creatures and isolated him. He has fallen into despair and a deep depression. This isolation, despair and depression have caused him to overindulge in things that may not be the best for him, or for humanity and all the creatures of this planet. It is almost like getting addicted to a habit. Man has immersed himself in this lie and it has become his truth.

In his oblivion, the creations and creatures of Mother Earth disappear to support his addiction, and he is numb to it. In losing his wisdom and gaining the oblivion, he needs to be dictated how to live his life. He has come to believe the lies that are perpetrated through many. He is so lost in these lies that he cannot perceive the truth any longer. He is confused and isolated. This isolation has cost him severely, the severity of which has been lost on him. He is so oblivious that he does not understand the cost of his oblivion. The biggest cost is love—love for himself and love for others. In his loss of love for himself, he lost his love for humanity. He created war, rape and pillaging. He lost respect for the creations and creatures on Mother Earth.

There is one thing about laws of nature: lies cannot go on forever. A lie cannot sustain itself, as you have to tell several lies to cover a lie, and in it the original lies are lost.

In here lies the Lion's wisdom. Do you, dear one, see the lie? Can you commit for one second to be still and ask yourself if you live a lie? Can you? Do you have the audacity to ask the question? Or do you prefer to be oblivious? Don't worry what others will think, not everyone needs to understand your admission, for everyone has to come to their own conclusion on the path to truth.

The Lion roared again. I was mesmerized by his roar. In my trips to Africa, while camping, I have heard the roars. They always sounded ominous. They sounded like death was around the corner, but I was protected by the experts around me. I stayed still, since I had a question to ask the Lion.

"So based on what you say, is it true that you won't attack me if I go into the forest?"

The Lion roared. My wisdom said he was laughing at me. I listened to him through my wisdom. He told me that in the current state of oblivion, which caused disconnection between man and forest—and also due to the lies perpetrated and the harm done to him and his cohabitants by man—yes, he would attack. For instilled in his memory are all the deeds done to him. However, in the dream, from where he was, he would not attack.

The Lion then asked me a meaningful question. "When you eat chicken for dinner, are you attacking the chicken?"

"No of course not," I replied. "I am eating."

"Do you always attack a chicken when you see one?"

"No, of course, not," I said again.

"Then why do you ask me this stupid question?"

I had to laugh. He had a point. In the current separation, the Lion continued, it is not easy to explain the way of life from his time. It is something to be lived, learned and experienced.

"Can you explain childbirth from a woman's perspective?" The Lion asked.

"No." I shook my head. "I would have to experience it to be able to explain it."

"There you go. You have your answer. To understand the truth," the Lion continued, "one must be still. It is from the stillness that answers and wisdom arise. If you are constantly chasing something—be it money or wealth or power—you do not have the patience or the time to sit still and ponder the wisdom. Stillness is underrated in your culture. It is the best, divine gift. Wisdom arises from stillness, and from wisdom arises answers that you experience. Don't wait for someone to come and spoon feed you. Pick up your slack and ask questions yourself. When you ask, answers may arise in different forms. Be aware of those. Be present when the answer arises. This is the only way to learn the truth. The universe answers to questions in different forms until you pay attention. Think about your current situation: you were made aware of my legacy, our legacy, through your dream. Who thought answers could arise in dreams? But they do! If you expect answers in one form only, then you may not receive answers to the fullest. You could miss answers that are being shown to you. Be open to many methods, and when in doubt, ask your wisdom."

"Let me illuminate upon wisdom. You have been taught that only through learning from outside, you gain knowledge. It isn't true. Your guidance, your wisdom, does teach and help you reach out for things that will enhance the knowing, the knowledge. This wisdom has been curbed. You believed that only through external sources you can gain knowledge and worse, you believe that only a few are gifted. Let me tell you something, the idea that only a few are gifted is also a lie that has been perpetrated. This is the first and foremost lie."

The Lion continued, "You are innately wise, and your wisdom constantly gives you answers, but your oblivion has covered that wisdom with perpetrated lies. Look up from your oblivion and look around. Pay, pay, pay, pay attention. Look at the piles of garbage. Look at the children playing. Look at the cars driving and be still. There are a thousand and one messages just in these. But you have to be patient while coming out of your oblivion. The oblivion has dulled your senses. The oblivion has a purpose. The purpose is to numb you so much that you are addicted to things that don't serve you."

"Let us talk about addiction. If you think you are *not* an addict, I invite you to reconsider. You may be defensive, but I promise there is truth in it. If you don't want to trust me, then trust your wisdom. You are addicted to several things, and those things have a cost—a cost that is heavy not just for you, but for your family, society, and above all your cohabitants and me. You thought you were not that important; trust me, you are. When I say you are important, it is not in a good light. Your addictions cost Mother Nature severely."

"Look into your closet. Look into your drawer. Look into your purse. Look around you. You will find your addictions. What can you give up? I know it is a hard question for you, as you have lived with all these things that you consider necessities. Are they or have you been *told* that they are necessities? Don't be blinded by the shiny advertisements. Follow your actions from dawn to dusk and take it further. List the number of things you use, the number of things that are mandatory for your existence. Step back and see if you can fathom the impact and cost to my legacy. Are you shocked? Don't be shocked, it's the truth. I would rather you do something about it than be shocked. Oh well, you cannot not afford to be shocked, can you? If you only knew all that I have to give up for the things you have in your daily life, even the simplest of things, you would be surprised. That is the truth that my dear friend has been trying to explain. He left it to me because he wanted you to hear from the horse's mouth, or in this case, the Lion's."

"I digress. Let's get back to your wisdom. You are hardened by your oblivion; hence you may not hear the wisdom. It will take patience, time, stillness, but please don't give up. I request this only because there is a legacy to be saved, and it is ours, and it is dependent on you and me to save this legacy."

"Do you think it is worth saving, this legacy? Please don't answer yet. I am not looking for a quick fix. I am seeking a deeper commitment—a lasting commitment, and that takes time. I encourage you to take a harder look and a harder stance and listen to your wisdom consistently."

"Is it wise of me to ask this? Sit still and ask your wisdom. I am not seeking your sympathy, for it is useless to me. I am asking for your commitment for the sake of yourself, all of humanity and Mother Nature's creations. Is it worth sacrificing everything you have to save this legacy? Is it?"

"First and foremost, you must admit that you live a lie. That is a journey all by itself. Get started on that journey, if what I spoke of struck a chord. If it didn't, thank you anyways for hearing my wisdom, my truth. It gives me immense pleasure to share it with you. Now I have to leave. My pride is waiting for me. Nice seeing you again in your dream. If you would like to listen to my wisdom, call upon me. I will be by your side. By the way, bring your friend, too. The more the merrier."

Admittedly Yours,
The Lion

CHAPTER 4: CONCLUSION

*M*y dear ones, how do you feel about the legacy that has just been shared? Are you aligned with its message? Have you reached a conclusion on your legacy, the Lion's legacy, our legacy? Are you overwhelmed? So am I. This message from the Lion has hit me like a ton of bricks. I never expected this dream of mine to affect me. I did not realize that what I thought was merely a dream, was not. This dream that I thought I could get away with, saying whatever for the sake of it, no longer stays true. I must admit, I have to think about letting go of my ancestral legacy. The legacy that I considered very important does not resonate with me the way it used to. The legacy that my father and my mother worked hard for does not suit me anymore. I am just realizing that the dream was, in reality, a reality. Why have I not had such dreams before? Or have I not paid attention to the significance of my dreams? Am I missing many things in my life by merely ignoring their significance?

My life has been so filled with the chores of carrying my family's legacy that there has been room for nothing else. Even my children and my wife receive only a sliver of my time because I have been busy carrying on my family's legacy. I have lavished them with money and gifts. They have been silenced by these gifts to compensate for my long absences. My absence was equivalent to precious money. I equated minutes to money. I have been reduced to this thing, a piece of paper that has emphasized m value. In truth, I can be replaced by this piece of paper. When my children or my wife talk about my long absences, I dutifully remind them of my value and the luxury I provide to them. I am assuming that this justifies my absences.

Deep in my heart something has always stirred. But, you know, I always set aside the stir. When the stirrings became unbearable, I would do something to mask them. Diving deep into work or getting a drink has always helped. But lately, I am realizing I need more drinks or more work to suppress this stir that reminds me that something is not quite right. Still, I am unwilling to listen to it. Why do I resist listening to this stirring, this simple stirring within me? I have a feeling my wisdom knows that there is something bigger I need to address, and if I address my stirring, I will have to give up something...or worse, everything.

To be honest, even if I had more time, I am not sure whether I would want to go and enjoy my time with my family. It is almost like I have all this work and engagements just so that I could avoid going home. Don't get me wrong, I have a lot to do, but years of ignoring my family while I carried my family's legacy has cost me severely. Up until now, I enjoyed the male pride of being the one who provided for my family. Until now, it seemed okay. But talking to the Lion has stirred something more in me, something I can't ignore.

I saw the pride on the Lion's face when he saw his pride. He was happy to be with them. There was peacefulness and contentment in him that I wish I could say I had. Unfortunately, I have a lot to learn from him.

So, I went into my slumber and called upon my dreams. In my dream, I called upon the Lion. He roared. He was starting to feel like my guardian angel. I have never believed in guardian angels, but I realized I had a lot of questions for the Lion. He roared, announcing his presence. Every time I saw him, there was a love that flowed through me that I can't explain. I remember that feeling when I first met my wife and then when each of my children was born. It was pure unconditional love. That is what I am starting to feel for the Lion. I am awakened by this feeling that I have felt only rarely these last couple of years. The Lion licked my hands and sat down by me. As usual, I saw his pride, his cubs, and his lionesses hanging around in the background.

I started my usual ritual of sitting still right next to him. I had several questions for him. First and foremost, I want to ask him why I no longer feel a pull towards my family—the love and care I once felt. The Lion sat quietly. I wasn't hearing anything through my wisdom. He licked his lips and dropped his head to his paws and closed his eyes. I waited patiently. I knew something was coming and it was not good. I was a bit nervous.

The Lion raised his head, looked at me, and said that this was going to be a long chat. Well, I kind of knew this was coming.

"Man is never this way in my time," the Lion began. "One of the reasons I wanted to talk to you is for this very same reason. You see, this is the state of man in your time, due to your lack of respect for others and yourself. What you are experiencing is the future of man from where I am. Man has put in place many rules, many laws, many plans, all of them contrary to Mother Nature and her cohabitants. These laws man has put in place are to control others in the name of doing good for society."

"Man's true nature is unconditional love. It has never been otherwise. His true nature is to be one with Mother Nature and the inhabitants of Earth. This would lead to man's natural state of unconditional love. Man, in your time, has lost the art of unconditional love. What you give your wife and children is *conditional* love. You make money and make them happy, and then expect them to love you in your absence. Does that seem right to you?"

I never completely understood unconditional love, so I could not really answer the Lion. I have had spurts of unconditional love in my life, but I knew they would not last.

The Lion heard my thoughts and roared. "That is it. The biggest problem with humanity in your time is the loss of love and respect. Do you respect yourself?"

"Of course, I do," I answered, almost defensively.

"Are you sure?" Then he paused and asked me. "Why do you respect yourself?"

"For one," I said, "my parents taught me to respect others, and I know that included me." The moment it left my lips, it sounded so hollow to me.

He pressed me again. "So, is that it?"

"No, I have a good education. I make enough money. I am a good provider. I take care of my family and their legacy." I had a long list.

"So, this makes you respect yourself?" The Lion looked at my curiously.

Yes," I said hesitantly. Suddenly, I was not sure.

"Okay," he said, "if your parents did not teach you respect, would you not respect yourself?"

"I am not sure."

"Let us say your parents did really teach you respect, but you did not go to college. Would you respect yourself then?"

I paused, and said I was not sure.

"If you looked at another person who had not gone to college, would you respect them?"

I shrugged my shoulders. I was on shaky ground, and I knew it.

"Let us say, your parents taught you respect, and you did go to college, but you do not earn good money, would you still respect yourself?"

I knew I would not. "Probably not," I muttered.

"Do you ever lie to your wife and children?"

This was very uncomfortable. I said that I sometimes did, and lately more than I cared to admit.

"Do you respect yourself when you lie to your family?" the Lion asked.

"No, I don't. I really feel bad, but I can't help it."

"Where do you think respect comes from? This is an important aspect of the basic tenets of living on Mother Earth."

I said I was not sure.

The Lion paused and turned toward me. I saw sympathy in his eyes. It made me uncomfortable, his sympathy.

He asked me, "Do you respect a tree?"

I replied that I had never thought about it.

"Why not?" he followed up.

"Well, it had not occurred to me that I would have to respect a tree."

"Why not?" the Lion continued.

I was silent for a moment while I pondered my reply. "Well," I said, "I can't think of respect, but I could think of value. For example, if an apple tree bears fruit, then it provides more value than a tree that does not bear any fruit."

"Ah," the Lion said, "so you see value only when you get something?"

I hesitantly said yes. I knew that was not the answer the Lion wanted to hear, so he continued the line of questioning.

"So, a man who does not make money is no better than the tree that does not bear any fruits?"

I did not like this analogy, but I said, "Sort of," because I did not want to admit the truth.

I really could not imagine being the homeless man whom I had seen on the streets every day. He was always bundled up in a comforter, with food and cartons and a cart around him. I never stopped to say hello to him. I realized that I hadn't believed he deserved a hello from me, for I had too many important things to do. I also realized something else: I had blindly believed what my parents had told me. I also noticed that most of the homeless were from a certain ethnic group. I started to realize that I had to ponder what my parents had told me about hard work. I had a feeling there was more to it than what I was taught. I wanted to be angry at my parents but realized it would not serve a purpose. I had to go on this journey and find out for myself. Didn't I learn in the past couple of days that the best lesson was the lesson that was learned through my wisdom? I decided I may not know a lot about the homeless man, but I was ready to learn. I was ready to change my legacy. I also pondered the concept of respect. This subject was a difficult one, but I was going to play with it. I was going to try to look past the judgments and try to respect everything. I was going to try it as part of learning the path I was paving towards my new legacy.

The Lion came back. He roared, "Were you able to see the homeless man with respect?"

"No, but I have come up with a few things I want to try." I told him of my plans to look past the judgments and try to respect everything.

He roared again, and I knew this was a happy roar. He said he was glad to learn that I was taking the lessons into my own hands. "The student learns the best when he takes charge of his own education."

I have to admit, making the Lion happy secretly made me happy. "This thing about respect is tough," I said, "but I know where this is leading." I knew the lesson was tied to respect for all creations and creatures on Mother Earth without judgment or opinions. In my heart, I knew this was a key component of my new legacy— the one and only legacy worth saving, the legacy of Mother Earth. The legacy is that we belong to her without a doubt. Every weed, every animal, every worm, every bug, every rodent, every creature in the ocean deserves respect, regardless of what I thought, of what we thought. I also realized that some of the things we throw away and dismiss as mere weeds are as important as the apple trees. I was grateful for all this information, but I really did not know how to put it to use.

I thanked the Lion and bid him goodbye. He roared with pride. Until next time.

Respectfully yours,
Man

CHAPTER 5: SHAME

Shame, it is the current that flows through man in his current form. It is the current that constantly buzzes through him. The buzzing that never stops is a melody he has known most of his life. The buzz he hears is the fear that accompanies his shame. Fear and Shame gave birth to an ugly child named Guilt. This inseparable family has thrived through millennia. This unhappy family thrives together.

Why do you think I try to carry my family's legacy? I carry it because I will be shamed and made to feel guilty if I don't. I will be an outcast and then I will have nowhere to go. Fear, my constant companion, always whispers in my ears that I can't make it in this world by myself. Fear wears a cloak of wisdom. My family whispers it too. What will you do if you are not part of this legacy? Who will you be? What will your identity be? I fall for the trap every day. I am ashamed that I have these thoughts of leaving, and I feel guilty that I am not there for my family. Fear is thumping through me trying to remind me that I will be alone in this world if I don't adhere to the rules of my family. The rule of my family is to carry our legacy.

What is our legacy? Our legacy is to make more and more and protect the more and more through various venues. We do charity, since it is expected of us, and it is a duty we maintain because of our legacy—a laughable legacy, a legacy that has no place for humanity, no place for compassion, no room for creativity. It is a gaping hole that sucks your life out to replace it with legacy. I would be a fool to leave this legacy, for it gives me certainty, luxury and comfort. Could I release all these holdings?

Who would I be if I did? How would I be taken care of? What would my family do? Who would take care of my wife and children? What would my life look like? Would I respect myself?

I have a lot of questions and I would like to seek answers to those questions. I will have to reach out to the Lion and continue our conversation. But before that, I have to be clear about this respect thing he discussed with me. I am sure there is a lot that has been concealed from me. I cared nothing for poverty or not having enough. I always thought that those who did not have enough didn't work as hard as my parents. I thought that my family, my parents had figured out an equation that worked, and the rest of the populace had not figured it out. Little did I realize the absurdity of my thinking.

I have gone to places of worship. I have prayed. However, I have always prayed for my family and our legacy, nothing beyond that. I have never thought of doing anything beyond my comfort zone. I have never done anything purposefully that has had a positive impact on humanity. Bad impact, yes, but nothing good.

Talking with the Lion, I am realizing there is so much more that I need to understand about the planet I inhabit, that we all inhabit. I am realizing that Mother Earth is a living and breathing creature that is wise beyond what my mind can fathom. I am realizing my larger role in the legacy of Mother Earth, who until now I never cared about, let alone considered a living entity. I had always thought of Mother Earth as just a globe with a bunch of things. I have heard and read about global warming, blah, blah, blah. In our firm, we always talked about going green and being green. We did it only because we had to pretend like we cared about

Mother Earth. How could we really care, given our history of plundering Mother Earth? It was a farce, a far and worse lie I ever admitted to myself, let alone others. It was like running a brothel and supporting women's rights and human trafficking simultaneously. But we have been able to conceal ourselves pretty well.

Now the initiatives to combat global warming that I thought were supremely overrated are striking a chord in me. I understand for the first time the term greed in a true sense, and I am realizing that greed is part of my family's legacy. The legacy I am trying to sustain will cost Mother Earth, the Supreme Mother. The Supreme Mother has been plundered, pillaged and raped by hard working families such as ours, to maintain our obnoxious legacy. This legacy, that my family expects me to continue by holding our legacy torch, will burn and destroy Mother Earth, our Supreme Mother, our Wise Mother.

That destruction will impact my children, other's children, everyone's children. While here I am, ashamed for not wanting to be part of this destruction, guilt-ridden for not being good enough, oiled with the fear that consistently feeds the fire of greed. I am going to come clean. I will be honest, I wasn't trying to hide things before, but I just did not know the impact of what our legacy was doing to our Supreme Mother. No, I am not coming clean for just the sake of our Supreme Mother. I am sure she appreciates it, but I am doing it to carry the legacy of the Lion, who has lost his pride. You know, I just realized that he never talked about himself. He talked about all creations and creatures. He was concerned about the wellness of all living beings. I, for one, never in my life have thought about all living creatures. That was not a value that my family instilled in me. Making profits through many means was one of the main goals of our family.

We have bought lands for building factories all over the world. We have dug deep into Mother Earth to exhaust her resources for personal gain. We have usurped lands where animals roamed freely and curbed their habitat. At that time, none of it seemed like a big deal to me. We toasted with champagne and celebrated with expensive dinners at expensive restaurants. Money flowed at these dinners. Nothing was spared since we were so accomplished. We gave speeches on our growth and acquisitions with pretty charts. We were applauded and praised by many.

At the moment, this pricks my conscience. If plundering and pillaging is what is carrying my legacy, then is it worth my life to be part of this legacy? I am ashamed to call it a legacy. I feel guilty about what my family has done. I fear for the future.

No matter what, this trinity—shame, guilt and fear—follows me. It has become part of my legacy. This is the force that drives me to grow our family legacy. But I forgot one more addition to that trinity. Well then, it is no longer a trinity, is it? Call it whatever you want, it is the ego—the ego that wants more and more. Nothing is ever enough. When we made our first million, I remember my dad coming home and celebrating with us. I remember I was barely five years old. I remember sitting down at our dinner table for our celebration and my dad telling me, "Remember kid, this is not enough. Nothing is ever enough or good enough for my family. I will buy and own half the planet if need be, just for my family." At that time, I was in awe of him, at what he said. He was my hero.

See, that was the ego, that never-enough that keeps going, that pushes me to save my family's legacy. Never- enough is disguised as hard work. Don't get me wrong, my father did put hours-on-end into his business, but he was rarely around. This is the legacy I carry with me. I am never around for my family and I put hours-on-end into the same business that has multiplied hundredfold since my father ran it. Is this the legacy that I plan on handing over to my sons? I am depressed by this thought.

I wanted to talk to the Lion. I closed my eyes and I was taken over by the peace and quiet. I was still and quiet and reached over to my wisdom. The Lion came. He stood and looked at me. He didn't sit or lick my hand. I wasn't sure what he was waiting for. He roared. I listened.

"Did you come prepared about respect?" the Lion asked.

"I have come up with some revelations that may be tied to the respect."

"Okay." The Lion sat down. He looked disinterested.

"Is something on your mind?" I asked.

"No," he said, "but I don't want to waste my time if you aren't prepared. Don't get me wrong, I would love to hang out, but I would rather hang out with my pride, if you are not prepared."

"Relax. I have made some headway, but I'm not sure if it is aligned with what you have in mind."

"Alright, as long as you know that you have made headway, it is good enough. Given that you have called on me so many times, it seems you have been thinking a lot."

"Yes," I replied, "I have been thinking about a lot of things and I have some questions for you." But I also wanted to talk about respect, so I said to the Lion, "I still don't understand how to respect someone with nothing. I realize respect, the way it is, is a farce. I have had no connection to the common man, due to my privileged upbringing. I have been respected wherever I go, due to my family status and name. I realize that all of this respect was related to the money and wealth we had accumulated. No one respected me as a person, only for my money. That is the only kind of respect I have known in my life."

He nodded, and I could see the pride in his face. "Bingo!" he said. "You are a faster learner than I thought."

"The disconnection I have endured with common men has made me unaware of the life led by billions on this planet. Hence, it makes me a minority. If I was told by my parents that through hard work I can achieve anything, then I am being told that the rest of the seven billion or so people are not hard working and do not have solid values or discipline. That makes my family exceptionally good. I subconsciously thought that those who served us were beneath us. I thought they should feel privileged to work for someone like us. I remember giving speeches at our companies about what a wonderful place it was to work. My pride is tied to all these things that are nothing but a farce—a farce for it has cost me dearly as well as my Lions and Mother Earth, our Supreme Mother. Based on what I was taught, seven billion people did not deserve respect and did not make it in my world. Not only that, but our family's legacy has taken a fair share of resources from these seven billion people. Where is the respect in that? I am realizing that one's mere existence on Mother Earth deserves respect. I thought respect had to look a certain way, and I realize that it was my way, my family's way. I now realize that all creatures deserve respect since they were created on Mother Earth. Whether I thought that they deserved respect or not is immaterial. They are respected. It is just what is."

The Lion roared. I knew he was getting ready for a speech. "Well done my man! Well done! You have learned this lesson much better than I expected. This comes from your wisdom—not your mother, not your father, not your family. Your wisdom and yours alone, and that is very powerful, believe it or not. Now, this lesson you learned will stay with you, since it is who you are. A man deserves respect, regardless of who he is and what he is. Now, let me ask you again: can you respect that homeless man you saw by your home?"

This time, I did not hesitate to say yes. I told the Lion that the man's mere presence on Earth deserves respect. The Lion roared.

"Lion, I have some more questions for you."

The Lion nodded. "Go on."

"I understand this respect thing now and I am very happy about this knowledge. However, I keep constantly bumping into shame, guilt and fear. No matter what I do, good or bad."

"Take a breath," the Lion suggested. "It is okay, one at a time. Just realizing the meaning of true respect is going to open doors for you in every direction. Realize that shame, guilt and fear are built into your education. As always, I am going to ask you a bunch of questions. Here we go. Where do you think shame, fear and guilt came from? Can you remember?"

"No, I can't." I slumped. "They have become such a part of me that it feels like I was born with them."

"When you were born, you were already respected by Mother Earth and the creatures and the creations around you. You did not feel shame. You inherently knew your worth. You knew you deserved to be born and thrive. Let me ask you again: do you think you acquired shame right off the bat?"

I said that I was sure I did not. "Okay," the Lion continued, "now that you are clear, do you realize that you were not born with these burdens."

"Yes, I know I was not born with them."

"Listen," the Lion added, "I am not trying to make your family wrong. They were as much a part of a society that dictates things to them as you. I don't want you to think I am bashing your family. Your father did what he did, your mother did what she did, based on what they knew. So, I want you to be open in your thoughts when I share some things."

"Okay, but I am feeling anger towards my family and my parents. I might as well add that to the list of things I want to understand."

"Great! This is a good dialogue." The Lion looked encouraged. "Can you remember the first time you felt shame?"

I had to pause and ponder. "I believe I was in third grade."

"What happened?"

"Someone hit me and called me names."

"Then what happened?"

"I cried and ran away."

"And then?"

"I was called a wuss and told that I cry like a girl." I was not enjoying these memories.

The Lion urged me on in my story. "And then what?"

"I went home and told my parents."

"Please go on."

"My mother hugged and comforted me, and my father said I needed to learn to be a man."

The Lion asked, "What did you learn from this interaction with your parents?"

"Well, I was happy that my mother hugged me, but ashamed that I was not being a man. I felt guilty for not standing up to the bullies. I know I was scared to stand up to them."

"So, tell me something, what does it mean to be a man?"

"It means to be strong, to provide, to take care of your family," I told the Lion.

"What is wrong with crying?"

I told the Lion that real men don't cry.

"Really, so what do you do when you want to cry?"

"I just man up like my father taught me. I don't share my emotions. In fact, I do not know how to cry anymore."

"So how is that going for you?" the Lion asked.

"Fine, so far, I guess."

"So, you think if you cry that you are like a woman, and that it is shameful? Am I correct?"

"Yes."

"So, if you are like your mother or your wife or your sister then it is shameful?"

"Aren't I a man, who needs to behave like one?" I asked the Lion. "Isn't crying only for women?"

The Lion roared loudly. "This is the irony of your society, telling how a man and woman should behave. When was the last time you cried?"

I had to think. I could not even remember.

"Okay, no worries if you can't remember. Let me ask you this, when was the last time you felt compassion?"

"Well, I think I feel compassion with my kids."

"What about your wife?"

"Well, sometimes, yes, I do feel compassion for her."

"Does your wife cry?"

"Yes, she does cry," I said, "I can't stand it when she cries."

"Why not?"

"It is uncomfortable, and I don't know what to do."

The Lion continued to push the subject. "Do you think it a sign of weakness that she cries?"

"Yes, I do think it is weakness."

"Do you think women are weak?"

I shrugged. I did not want to answer this question.

"Listen," the Lion continued, "don't be afraid to answer this question. In being true to yourself, you will be liberated from the falsehoods imposed on you by society. This is not who you inherently are. This is all taught behavior."

I was embarrassed, but knew I had to answer. "I am ashamed to admit that I secretly do think crying is a sign of weakness." I tried to justify my thinking. "However, I see very strong qualities in the women in my life— in my mother, my wife, my sister. In fact, I think my mother is very strong and helps with the firm, and so does my sister."

"Do you think your wife could run your firm?"

"With proper training, yes, I think she could."

"Do you think she is capable of running it without any training?"

"No, I don't think so."

"You don't think so, because she is a woman or because she needs training?"

I wanted to dig a hole and disappear. "It is a combination of both," I replied.

"How would you feel about one of your sons running the company?"

"I will be glad when they take over."

"Okay, let's go back to shame. So, you think a man crying is a shameful act?"

"Yes, it is."

"Do your son's cry?" the Lion probed.

"Yes, but they are younger."

"Do you have a daughter?"

I told the Lion that I did not.

"Imagine you have a daughter then," he continued. "Would you be okay, if your daughter cried?"

I nodded yes.

"So, you are okay with your son's crying since they are young?"

I nodded yes again. I knew the next question.

"But if they grow up and feel like crying, you want them to hold it together for your sake, correct?"

"Yes," I replied. "Society will think I did not teach them to be strong men, which is my job as a father."

"Okay, fair enough. Let me ask you this: when you were born, if you did not cry as a baby, it meant death, right?"

I nodded. I could see the hint of wisdom.

"Mother Nature wants you to cry. It is a sign of life. By stopping the crying, what have you done to yourself?"

"I have taken the life out of me."

"Good. By taking the life out of you, what has happened?"

I paused, I had to think about this one. "I have stopped feeling things."

"Like when your wife is sad and cries?"

I wanted to defend myself, but I thought better of it. "Yes. I hate it when she cries."

"Why do you hate it when she cries?"

"For one, I do not know how to handle it. Two, I feel less of a man when she cries, since mostly it is tied to me. I feel I have disappointed her."

"So, if you cry, you are not a man...and if your wife cries, you are not a man. Wow! That is pretty messed up." The Lion seemed a bit exasperated but pushed on with the conversation. "This is a lot of work, undoing what man has done to himself. The ancient man of my time is vulnerable and close to his own wisdom. He lives an easier life. I cannot imagine why man has traded his life for the life you lead in your time. By not allowing this most basic emotion—one that Mother Nature bestowed upon you when you were born—you have thrown away her gift, just like that. Do you understand that by not crying, you have numbed yourself to other emotions?"

I explained that I only had a vague understanding about what he was saying.

"I hate to say this to you," the Lion continued, "but you are half dead."

"What do you mean?"

"Let's save this conversation for another day."

I persisted. "How did we go from shame, guilt and fear to crying?"

The Lion looked at me for a long moment. "You don't realize that this is all tied together, do you?"

I shook my head. I did not have a clue that they were all tied together. I let out a big sigh. I knew I had a lot more homework to do.

"I really hope you save our legacy for all the work that I am putting into this." The Lion looked tired. "I love you, but this is too much. I am realizing the greater extent to which you have veered away from Mother Nature's path. This has caused you so much pain and grief. You are numbed by that pain, which could teach you so much. Let me tell you something that I want you to ponder. This is going to be radical for you. Think about feeling those emotions just for one day. Whatever comes out, even crying, let it out and see what happens. If you have forgotten how to cry, at least see what happens if you feel sad or angry. Just let it out. It is okay. I am telling you that it is okay. And if your wife cries, even better, sit beside her and be there for her. Try to listen to her. Set aside guilt, while you do this."

The great Lion roared. I told him that I had absolutely no clue how to do what he was asking me to do. He told me not to worry, and just give it a try to see how far I could go.

"Remember, by denying Mother Nature's basic emotion you have numbed yourself. Feel the numbness, and it will be a start to open your emotions. You are smart. You will figure it out and learn what is right for you."

Your Lion,
Exhausted talking to Man

CHAPTER 6: VICTORY

*V*ictory at all costs is how we play the game of business in my family—and we play it well. My father started this game. He was a ruthless negotiator. Nothing escaped his vision, mind and thoughts. He was like an eagle, able to spot things and people who could help save and continue his legacy. He got whatever he went after. This victorious torch that he played with has been handed over to us. We were proud to take on this torch, which carries our legacy. The flames may have burned our hands, but we wore these wounds with pride, since they allowed us to carry on our legacy.

"Nothing comes easy, does it?" my father would ask rhetorically as my mother nodded. "Hard work is what is necessary to be victorious." This was our family motto. There were hiccups and setbacks, but as my father grew the family business, it was considered a privilege to be involved with him. In his later years, my father did not even have to negotiate; people and businesses just came to him. He was at the pinnacle of his success when he passed away. People murmured at his funeral about whether our family could sustain his legacy. We wondered the same. Even on his death bed, my father kept insisting on the values and the victory torch that we must carry.

Now, here I am so many years later. My hands are callused from holding this torch. It has become heavier and heavier over the years. I have felt like I have stooped lower and lower carrying this vicious torch. Its flames are greed and it cares for no one—not even the planet. We own a significant amount of property and wealth. You can't even count it all! Our wealth was built with dirt, blood and sweat on our hands. It is an admitted fact in my family that you have to be ruthless to grow. This is not considered immoral. My parents, who preached morality, decided to ignore many of the immoral dealings our family had. It was just the way of life, they would say. Thinking of which, I do not even know if my parents had a good relationship. I know my father wore the pants, and that was it. You did not question him. He worked hard for the family and future generations, so he was not to be questioned. I know he had several women in his life, and my mother turned a blind eye. After all, she would say, he was a man. She was comfortable in her role. I am not sure if she ever felt hurt. She had to keep it all together while my father worked.

Which brings me to me. There is a problem with my parents' story, it sounds very similar to mine. My legacy is identical to my father's. But is this the family legacy I want to carry? When my wife tries to reason with me, I shut her up. I have to deal with work and then come home and deal with her. I am working for the family, what does she want me to do? That is how I have always justified my behavior. In my family, we don't divorce; we have affairs. My wife has stuck it out with me all these years. I always take the easy way out, which is to blame her, rather than look at myself. You see, ours is a victorious family and we don't need to answer to anyone—that includes my wife. That is the arrogance and obnoxiousness I carry as part of my family legacy. It is something I have been proud of, until now. My unfaithful lifestyle is an accepted fact in my circles. How else can a man relax and live a little? He needs to do what he has to do. This is the justification that we live by.

My initial guilt and shame eventually wore off. The more I lied about my affairs, the more I covered up, the more I was arrogant, the easier it became. Eventually, my wife stopped complaining, and it was easy for me. At some point, we became strangers in the same house. However, we kept up appearances for the sake of our legacy—a victory torch that burns your heart, burns your soul, burns your being. It destroys families and humanity in order to sustain greed. This torch, which has been my family legacy, no longer serves me. I think I would be happier being a monk, at this point—though I know that is not the right path for me. I want to be there for my wife, my kids and for the planet. I have wasted a hell of a lot of time, carrying on this worthless legacy that could destroy the future of the planet. My wisdom—which has never spoken to me or to which I have never listened—is getting clearer. I never even knew we had wisdom, until my dear Lion pointed it out to me. He is wise and intelligent. He is imparting his wisdom to me, and this is the legacy I would like to carry from here on out. Speaking of which, I did my homework. Let me tell you what I learned.

You already know that I can't really cry, at least not yet. However, I am able to feel things, to feel them in my heart. I have been actually spending an awful lot of time feeling—feeling things when I lied, when I was listening to my wife and children, when I was weighed down by the burdens of my legacy. I feel these things in my heart. I feel the separation between me and my wife. She has become a zombie around me. She goes around as if I don't exist, and this hurts me. Her ignoring me is now starting to hurt me, unlike in the past when I was relieved. When I met my wife, she was vivacious, cheerful and full of life. She comes from humble beginnings. She did not care about my wealth. We just fell in love. My parents did not support our marriage. I married her in spite of their opposition. Within a couple of years of marrying me, she lost her luster, her joy. The burdens of the lies we were living were already starting to cost her. She seemed well taken care of, but trust me, this was for appearances. I know she is one of those people who would give up everything for the sake of love. I am not saying this just to convince you. It's actually one of the reasons I married her. And, yet, this relationship that mattered most to me, I gave up. I pretended that there were more pressing matters—more pressing than my family, my love. Since we have grown apart, I have stopped feeling things for her. It is easier this way, but is it worth it? I have not had the audacity to talk to her about these changes. Believe it or not, talking to her about this scares me more than my business dealings. I can do a lot of things but talking to my wife is the most difficult of all.

I had to talk to the Lion. I called upon him. He sneaked up on me, and I was caught off guard. He quietly stood by my chair. I asked him to sit.

"Okay," he replied, "but please know that talking to you is exhausting. I am sleeping more than I usually do. When my cubs wake up to play, I don't have the energy. I am here to pass on my legacy, our legacy, but it seems like you are imparting some of your habits to me. Anyway, a pact is a pact, and I am here to help you. What did it feel like to feel?"

"Tough," I said.

"What do you mean?"

"It is easier not to feel anything," I explained. "That way, I don't have to address the situations and life in general. I can continue to live my life as is. I don't have to work so hard on my life. This work is harder than my job. Is it meant to be this way?"

"When you have not felt anything for a long time—and you begin to feel something—you feel uncomfortable during the transition. It's just what is. Feeling the real you, the you that you have masked behind your addictions and power, is a new experience. You may feel like it's a new you. However, the masked self, the one that doesn't feel, is an illusion and never really existed. I realize I am jumping to a new conversation, but did you talk to your wife?"

"No, I did not have the courage to talk to her. Now that we have grown apart so much, and I have to own up to so much. It doesn't feel good. I am unsure how it will end. In fact, I will be honest. I am really scared."

"Fair enough. It is quite normal to feel those things," the Lion said. "Have you thought about what you will say to your wife?"

"I have an idea, but I don't know where to start."

"What is at the top of your list?"

"Not having been faithful to her."

"Do you think she doesn't know?"

"I am not sure. Maybe."

"You underestimate her," the Lion admonished. "Consider that she knows. Does that make it easier?"

"No, not really. Actually, that makes it worse," I said. "Knowing that she has put up with my charades for so long and stayed with me in spite of knowing all this..." I stopped my thought. It was painful.

"Why do you think she stayed?"

I shrugged sadly.

"I do not understand your life fully. However, my wisdom has shown me things in your time and how they came to be. Do you remember that we talked about laws and rules in your time?"

I nodded, vaguely remembering.

"How does your society view marriage?"

I paused to think. "Mostly you are expected to live with the one you married. You work things out. You stay with one person all your life, unless something drastic happens. What about in your world?"

"The laws and rules that you have in your time do not apply to us. We view love very differently than you do. Your love is conditional. I am here as part of your wisdom to show you unconditional love. I don't think humanity has experienced unconditional love to the fullest in your time. Humanity has lost its core wisdom that imparts the knowledge of unconditional love. Your wife is as much a part of that societal conditioning as you are. You can feel shame and guilt as much as you'd like, but part of your masked self is the shame and guilt. It's a by-product of your every action, there is no room for self-love or unconditional love. Have you ever loved yourself?"

"Yes, I think so," I said, "a long time ago."

"How did it feel?"

"I did whatever I wanted. I laughed. I went on trips. I enjoyed my life. It felt good."

"So, do you think you loved yourself unconditionally back then?"

"Yes, I do."

"Did you respect yourself then?"

"To be honest, I don't think I respected myself in the truest sense."

"In that case, consider you have not experienced unconditional love to the fullest. Unconditional love and respect go hand in hand. Do you respect yourself now?"

"Well, at least now, I am aware that the mere fact that I was born on Mother Earth makes me deserving of respect. However, I carry shame and guilt about all the things that have happened in my life, my legacy, and my family's legacy."

"Do you know how to forgive?" '

I paused. "Yeah...I think so."

"Really? So, what is forgiveness?"

"When someone does something you did not like or hurts you, you let it go and accept what they did and who they are."

"Hmmm." The Lion pondered my reply. "This is not forgiveness. Can you forgive yourself for everything that you have done to your wife…all the lies, all the affairs, the negligence?"

"No, I cannot forgive myself."

"Come on, what would it look like," the Lion nudged, "if you forgave yourself?"

Honestly, I have no clue. My fear is that If I forgave myself, I would keep doing the things I do."

"You haven't forgiven yourself now, but you continue to do the things you do anyway. What's the difference? Can you forgive the boy who was teased at school, who couldn't stand up to the kids who bullied him, who was called a girl for crying?"

"Yes, I can."

"Listen, it looks easy on the surface, but it is not what you think. Forgiveness is not a simple act; it is a profound act. It is a humane act. It is a courageous and bold act. It is the act of God, an act of kindness and compassion. It is a worthy act. It is worthy of you and you are worthy of it. It is an act of love, unconditional love. It is a humble act. True forgiveness doesn't allow you to reason about why you should forgive. If you are looking to find reasons to forgive, that is not true forgiveness. This is still reasoning based on conditions. Let me ask you this: why were you quick to forgive yourself as a boy as opposed to your current self?"

"It is simple," I replied. "As a young boy, I was innocent, but as an adult, I am not."

"What is the point of forgiving someone who you think is already innocent? If someone bullied you now and you did not stand up for yourself, would you forgive yourself?"

"No."

"Why?"

"Because I am a grown man and should have learned by now how to defend myself."

"See you are reasoning forgiveness. So, let me ask you, should I, the Lion—if I lived in your time—forgive you?"

"No, because of what has been done to you by man."

"You keep going back to reasoning why or why not to forgive. Forgiveness, just like respect, is always there for humanity. There is nothing that cannot be forgiven—literally no thing. It is a privilege to be forgiven. That privilege does not come with rules and laws. It is what is so, just like respect. Remember, you are respected just for being born and inhabiting Mother Earth. Similarly, forgiveness is an inherent quality. It can't be masked by shame or guilt. Your forgiveness of yourself will heal you. It will heal your family. It will heal your legacy and give rise to a new one that will make your heart sing with palpitations you have not felt in years. Would you not want that for yourself?"

I nodded enthusiastically. It intrigued me that I could be forgiven for just being human and inhabiting Mother Earth. I am gaining a new level of respect for Mother Earth. I asked the Lion what would happen if I continued to behave as always in spite of forgiving myself.

"You would continue to forgive, for in true forgiveness there is healing. It cannot be otherwise."

I felt relieved. Here I was thinking that forgiveness was a one-time thing. It gave me a lot of relief knowing it was a continuous act. "This is great. I am so relieved. However, I would also like my wife to forgive me. I think it will give me even greater relief."

"That is her choice," the Lion roared, "to forgive or not. Waiting for her forgiveness is not your path to healing. Her forgiveness is her path to healing. See, here is where humanity is confused in your time. You think by someone else forgiving you that everything is set. When another person truly forgives you, it does heal the situation. However, you have to go on your own path of forgiveness as well. You can't ride the wave of another's forgiveness. It is deeper than that. If you are trying to ride on another's forgiveness, you are missing the point. No one can heal you but you. Forgiveness should be part of everyday life for yourself and others."

"So, if I forgive myself, is there a chance my wife and I will get back together, back to how we were?"

He roared again. "That is a misconception. Healing comes in several forms, and no one can predict the outcome. Your job is to stay in a state of forgiveness. In that state, your wisdom will know how to handle the outcome. If you become attached to an outcome in your forgiveness journey, you will be sorely disappointed, for this is not true forgiveness. Anything attached to an outcome or result is your ego dictating your actions. Your job is to know how to distinguish your ego from your wisdom. This is something you have to learn by being more aware of who you are. Remember how we talked about being numb and not being able to cry? You will start to feel things, as part of true forgiveness. You might cry. You might laugh. You might be sad. Forgiveness brings out true emotions from your inner self. You are worthy of these emotions and you are releasing years of pent-up fears and judgments. The reason you have this issue about forgiveness is that you are judging yourself. You are like a movie trailer that runs the scenes over and over to justify why you cannot forgive. Change the movie trailer and see your life shift."

"Of all the things you have taught me so far, this is the best. I never thought I could forgive myself." I could see that the Lion was happy, since his wisdom had finally hit home with me. I felt a lot lighter than before. I was relieved beyond measure, but I still had one more question. "Lion, how do I keep shame and guilt at bay?"

"You have lived with it for a long time and this is all you know," the Lion replied. "Imparted forgiveness, respect, wisdom will help, and it will be a song and dance—just like a child learning to walk. Would you ever chide a child for not knowing how to walk? Don't beat yourself up when you feel shame and guilt, just recognize it. Don't beat yourself up when you don't forgive yourself or another, just be with it. Letting things be part of your awareness elevates your learning, for you have come to learn. Learn the wonderful things that Mother Earth imparts as part of her wisdom. You know that is the best part about living on Mother Earth. She is very forgiving."

"So, she would forgive us for all that we have done to her as part of my family legacy?"

"Yes, she would, for is this not where healing lies? Why would she do or be otherwise? It is her privilege to take care of her children. She knows her children fall and bruise; she can't punish them for that. Think about this: here you were going along carrying your family legacy and I come in your dream and talk to you about the most pressing matters of your times. I have not even lived in your time. Isn't that a miracle?"

I paused. I had not thought about the miraculousness of my learning from the Lion.

"Mother Earth knows how to communicate her thoughts and feelings to her children," the Lion continued. "She knows the right way to teach them and impart her wisdom. Your job is to be open, to receive her wisdom. She talks to everyone on the planet. No one is left out and no one is special. She talks to them in the same voice, the same tone, only the venues differ."

As we finished our conversation, I felt a lot better. I felt calm and collected. The arrogance of my past was waning away. Humility was beginning to take its place. It was a new feeling for me, being humble.

The Lion roared, bidding me goodbye.

For the first time, I felt truly victorious with nothing but the knowledge of forgiveness. I had struggled with my shame and guilt for so long that it seemed my life was impossible. The knowledge of forgiveness had renewed my strength. I decided to give it a try, this forgiveness. I knew I would have a long and winding road ahead, but at least I was committed to taking the journey. I would not be here were it not for my Mother, my Mother Earth, my Supreme Mother.

Lovingly Yours,
Forgiven Man

CHAPTER 7: LOVE

"*L*ove, in the truest sense, is an emotion forgotten by many. When you numb yourself to your God-given abilities to have emotions like love, you impact everything. When you conceal any single emotion, it cascades into inhibiting other emotions—love is one such victim. If you have lost your ability to be compassionate, you have lost your ability to love as well. It is not one or the other. Love—a wonderful flow of energy that comes from your heart, from your soul, from your being—permeates the air, the water and reigns Mother Earth. Yet, love is misunderstood by humanity at this juncture. Don't get me wrong, I have not lived in your time, but wisdom tells me such is the calamity at the given moment."

"What is love you ask? You are asking a Lion about human love. Well, who cares who you ask or who could explain the wisdom, as it comes from one source—the same source that serves every being in the Universe. It is always present and waiting to be tapped. If you cry that you have not felt love, consider that you have not allowed yourself to love yourself. Humanity has come to believe that the love people want to experience is out there somewhere, and that you only need to wait for it to appear while you go about your chores. I want to ask you, how is that working? How is that going? How is it really going, my dear Man? Please tell me. I would love to hear."

"I got a glimpse through our conversation on forgiveness yesterday. See, that is what I mean, these things are all tied together. Your forgiveness of yourself and others is tied to unconditional love. Your respect for yourself is tied to unconditional love. It is an ever-flowing pure energy that is untainted. No one can ever taint love. It can be misunderstood, but never tainted. For its source is a higher divine power that surpasses everything in the Universe. It is an uninterrupted divine flow of energy—the energy that soothes, heals and blossoms all forms of creations on earth. A plant is loved by Mother Earth. She ensures that all nutrients and climatic conditions necessary for the plant are provided—that is love, unconditional love. There is not one being on this planet, not one creation on this planet, that has not experienced love, the unconditional love of our Supreme Mother."

"Dear Man, do you understand what I am saying?"

"Yes. Thank you for your presence in my dream. I look forward to your presence and without it, life seems empty and meaningless."

"In reality," the Lion roared, "your life is an illusion. Did you know?"

"No, I did not. But isn't love real?"

"Yes," The Lion answered, "it is."

"If love is real, how can life be an illusion?"

"Life is an illusion," the Lion replied, "but the expression of love through your life is real."

"If my life doesn't exist," I rationalized, "then love cannot exist, because there is nobody to love."

"What do you think happens after you die?" the Lion asked.

"I don't know. I have heard there is a heaven and there is a hell and I will go to one or the other. Given what I have done so far, I doubt there is a place for me in heaven… unless I do something good before I die."

The Lion roared heartily. "Is that it?" the Lion asked through his laughter. "That is what life is to you? You are born, you do good or bad, and then you die and go to heaven or hell?"

"Based on my knowledge of Earth so far," I responded, "Yes, I believe that is it."

"Ok, do you believe in a soul?"

"I have heard about this concept, but never understood it…nor have I cared to."

"Fair enough, but would you like to understand it?"

"So far, what you have said has made more sense than anything else I have learned in my life, so I am very open to hearing what you have to say."

"Okay, then let me go back to love. What if I told you, whether you were born in a human form or not, you could still experience love."

"How could that be?" I asked. "Love is an emotion that I experience through my body. If I didn't have a body, how could I experience it?"

"Do you think the air experiences love?"

"I don't think so. Air doesn't have a body," I said, perplexed by the Lion's question.

"Air doesn't have a body, but water does. So, does water experience love?"

"But it does not have flesh and blood." I was confused.

"A caterpillar has body and flesh. Does a caterpillar experience love?"

I said, I did not know.

"But you said that having flesh and blood supports the feeling love. Doesn't the caterpillar have flesh and blood?"

"To be honest," I shrugged, "I do not know."

The Lion tried again. "Let me ask you this. Does a caterpillar have a mother?"

"Yes," I answered, "but she lays eggs and leaves her offspring, doesn't she?"

"Yes, but do you think there is only one mother for every child or creation born?"

"Based on my upbringing, yes, that's what I believe... unless you are adopted."

"That makes sense based on what you have learned," the Lion said. "So, you think there is one and only one mother for every child or creation born?"

To sound intelligent, I responded, "Well, at least only one mother births it."

"Are you sure?" he asked me.

"Yes," I replied confidently. "There was only one mother who bore me."

"Okay, but if Mother Earth were not here, would you have come into existence on this planet?"

"Are you trying to say that Mother Earth is also my mother?"

"Yes, that's what I am saying."

"Until now, I have not thought about it in this way. I can't touch, feel or talk to her."

"Really? You have never talked to Mother Earth? You might not have consciously talked to her, but that is another conversation. What do you do, when you feel thirsty? How do you know that you need to drink water?"

"My mom taught me to drink water when I felt thirst."

"If she did not teach you, would you not know to drink water when you are thirsty?"

"I probably would not...although, I am not sure."

"Did your mom teach you to breath?"

"Of course not."

"Your mother did not teach you to breath, but she taught you to drink water? When you were born, there were certain things you already knew.

Mother Nature implanted this knowledge within your being, along with your wisdom. She does not exclude any of her creations from this knowledge. You were not destined to be protected from Mother Earth in a room, swaddled in a big bundle, crying. You were supposed to be exposed to Mother Earth when you were born. Your society has forgotten this wisdom and goes to great lengths to protect you from Mother Earth when you are born. This may be too drastic and radical for you to understand right now, but I want you to at least hear this information. Let me ask you, does an animal in a forest give birth in the open?"

"Yes, I think so," I replied, "but it is too radical for me to think about not having doctors and nurses present for the birth of a child."

"But every one of my cubs were born in the wilderness and they are all happy and healthy. Sometimes things happen. That is just part of life. Do you think if there is a problem my lioness will go to a hospital and find a doctor to help her with the birth?"

"No, but why would she?"

"Why wouldn't she? Is it because me or my mates cannot think intelligently? Is it because we are inferior to you, and that is why we haven't developed the necessary amenities?"

I wanted to say yes but held my tongue. I did not want to arouse the wrath of the Lion. So far, his wisdom had reigned. I decided to just listen and process what he was saying.

"Listen, man is different than animals—no doubt about it. However, what man has done with his intelligence is not what it was intended for. Let us talk about bombs and missiles and nuclear weapons. Is it a kind and compassionate act to create things to destroy Mother Earth? Would you ever plan to murder your own mother?"

"No." I suddenly felt ashamed. I would never kill my mother.

"There are people in your society who have gone to prison for killing their mothers. How come they go to jail, while those—mostly in your governments—who make these weapons are not arrested?"

"We don't use these weapons," I replied. "We keep them only to protect ourselves, in case someone attacks us."

"Why would someone attack you?"

"Because they don't like us."

"Oh, really? So, when someone doesn't like you, they attack you?"

"Well, there is more to it than that," I stammered, "but to keep it simple, I would say yes."

"So, you don't think I would understand this concept without simplification?"

"Well…" I was becoming uncomfortable with the conversation. I searched for the right words. "Well…I have never talked to a Lion about war."

"You have never talked to a lion about respect, compassion, love and wisdom either, until now. So, what is the problem? How do you know that the people or countries or whatever want to attack you?"

"We have been told by our governments and media that they want to attack us."

"Aren't these same people who have also lied and told you that we lions want to attack you?"

"Yes, but you did tell me that in current times you do attack us."

"It is true. Have you ever thought about why we might attack you now and not in the past? Did we just wake up one day and decide to attack you? Do you think we are so cruel that we just attack for no reason? Did we sit and plan on our attack just like your governments, with no cause or because you are more intelligent than us? Believe what you want, but don't believe blindly. You have to question why someone says an animal would attack or a country would attack. There is more to it than what meets the eye." The great Lion had been pacing as he questioned me. Suddenly, he stopped and looked me in the eye. "For the most part, you have believed everything your family taught you, until we began talking. Based on our conversations, what do you think about those teachings now?"

I dropped my head to avert his gaze. "Not all of them are true."

"Expand that knowledge. Not everything you hear is true. Take your time to understand what you are being told. If you want to save our legacy, then you have to get more in tune with your intuition and wisdom.

Every lie that is perpetrated eventually becomes the truth. The true cause of what happened is then concealed and masked with more lies. These lies separate humanity from love. Making you hate your neighbors is a wonderful way to keep you separate from the unconditional love that flows naturally through you. It never stops flowing, but by listening to the lies of others, you have veered away from that flow. Why do you think I showed up to talk about love today?"

"I don't know," I said honestly.

"Love, true unconditional love—love of humanity, love of self, love for the planet, love for your neighbors, love for your brothers and sisters, love for animals, plants and Mother Earth—is the only force that will save your legacy and the legacy of this planet. If you really want to contribute and be part of this journey, you better buckle up and start learning to answer your own questions. Man, in his current form, is a zombie. He follows lies from dawn to dusk. He does not even understand or know that he is being played. As a result, he has lost all conviction for love and life. The life he lives and the lies he lives have been acquired along the way. It is time to shred those lies and see the truth, which will liberate humanity and unite all living creatures, no exceptions."

The Lion took a deep breath before continuing. "You see, it is a privilege for me to talk to you. It is a privilege for me to be part of your life. It is a privilege to be part of your dream. It is a dream to be part of my future legacy, our legacy, the one and only legacy that is worth saving. Here is a list of things that I would tell you were fabricated:

- that there is danger
- that you need to be fearful at all times
- that you need to build a castle, a wall, a boundary to keep away your brothers and sisters
- that you must steal their resources, if they are poor, and perpetrate lies about them and make believe they are true.

This is your life. Standing from where I am, it is not the best future that I see. There is nowhere else I want to be at this moment but here with you, working to heal the future of the planet. Mistrust, fear, doubt, and danger are easy tools to stir up the human population, for you have been fed these lies for millennia. You don't know anything better and are easy targets for these lies. But there is a different way. You can create love."

"How do I do that?"

"Feel the love that is already there. Reach out to your heart more than your mind. You are used to learning everything through your mind. Learn from your heart. Your heart is the most important organ in your body. It sends feelings of love when needed. It sends feelings of compassion when they are most needed. You see, that is where the Supreme lives. Start listening to your Supreme, your wisdom. It will never fail you. It will never teach you not to trust another. It will never teach you not to love another. It offers the deepest relationship you can have with yourself. The deeper you understand your heart's desires and directions, the more apt you are to follow your soul's path. Your heart will never mislead you. You may not always understand the path it offers, but lessons and wisdom will be revealed along the way. At times, you will want to quit. You have a choice to quit, but guess what? You will be brought back to the same path. The path has already been laid, it is waiting for you to step in. The Universe works very differently than you think. You think you control everything in your day-to-day life. Consider there are far more working elements that dictate and direct your life. When you have something in abundance, give and share it with others. It starts with this simple act of opening your eyes and sharing with the world. No boundaries are needed. This is a lie that has been perpetrated over and over again. Ammunition has been developed, wars have been waged, human lives have been lost, and Mother Nature's resources have been sacrificed to protect those boundaries and borders, which are all based on lies. Is it all worth it?"

I continued to listen intently, for there was nothing for me to add. I did have a question, though. "How do I know what unconditional love is?"

"Unconditional love is a love that does not discriminate between your neighbor and your family. It is the uninhibited divine flow of energy that flows through your heart chakra into your every cell and atom in your body. It does not define who you are; it *is* who you are, love. You are love. I am love. The air is love. Rocks are love. Mountains are love. The ocean is love. The Earth is love. Everything is love, nothing is not love."

I was mesmerized and hesitant to interrupt the beauty of what he was saying...but I had another question. "What is a chakra?"

"It is an energy source. You have several energy sources and your heart is one of them."

"This love that you just taught me, I would like to feel it. What should I do?"

"Let go of the numbness and control of your emotions and you will start to feel the flow of love. Spend time with yourself to feel the divine you—you in reality, not the man who has to bear it all. Above all, be vulnerable. It is okay to be vulnerable. You don't have to carry the weight of Man. Let go of it and create a new you. The you that serves you. The you that loves you. The you that is joy and bliss and allows the flow of love. When you are love, you permeate an odor, a scent that is unique to love. It is not a scent in the real sense, but something that draws people and creations together. When you permeate love, you can hear the air, you can hear the water, you can hear the trees and you can hear the birds calling to you. You will begin to feel a oneness with all things. You were born to experience this oneness. You were not born to run around and tire yourself and feel shame and guilt for not being perfect in all areas of life. You are here to sense the separation and close the gap. You are a divine creation of the Supreme. The supreme that does not distinguish between man and woman. The supreme created two equals. You are an energy, not a form. Man is an energy and woman is an energy. Love does not define who you are; it is who you are. Love knows no borders, no gender, no boundaries, no inhibitions. It is a constant supply of energy that can never be exhausted. It is the only resource that you can keep digging. The more you dig, the better it gets. When you are stripped of all these rules and laws, you are a dazzling creation that is one with creation itself. You are one with the Supreme; you are one with the Supreme Mother. It is your natural state of being to care for yourself and all others, no exceptions."

"I love this love conversation." It felt as if my whole body was smiling.

"Have you talked to your wife?" the Lion asked.

"Not yet."

"Nothing wrong with that. Your wisdom will tug at you until you are ready. Just listen to it." With that the Lion bid me goodbye.

The next morning, I woke up groggy and tired. I felt like I had tossed and turned all night. I could still feel the Lion's presence. I looked around the room which was empty. My wife and I do not share a room anymore. For the first time in years, I missed her presence in my bed. I knew it was time to talk to her. I made a mental note to find some time to talk to her that evening.

Lovingly Yours,
Man longing for his wife

CHAPTER 8: MIRACLES

I went to work as usual, my mind full of anticipation. Today was the day. I was going to talk to my wife. I called her from work and asked her to join me for dinner. She was surprised and asked if everything was okay. "Yes, things are fine with me," I replied happily.

"But you have not asked me to dinner in ages." I could hear the concern in her voice. "We have not been on a date for such a long time. What has changed?"

"I have a lot to tell you, and I miss you."

She laughed. "Remember we live in the same house. How can you miss someone who lives in the same house?"

I told her that I'd had an epiphany and wanted to talk to her in person. We arranged a time and place to meet and I went back to work.

The day moved slowly, yet too quickly. I was really dreading this conversation with her. I was unable to concentrate on my work. My thoughts kept going back to all the things the Lion had shared. He knew more about love and family than I had ever learned. I thought about the wisdom that is inherent in all of us. I realized the Lion was right. It is much better to lead a life guided by wisdom, rather than opinions, judgments, laws and rules. Looking at the current state of the Earth, it felt like humanity had messed up a lot of things by taking advantage of the wise. The Lion is wise, and we took advantage of him and many others—humans, animals, plants and more.

I am open to change, but it also scares me. Today's conversation with my wife would undoubtedly bring about many changes, and I had no idea what they would be. I am willing to try this forgiveness thing, but shame and guilt keep popping up. I am struggling with this new concept. Can I ever forgive myself fully and completely? Having heard what I have heard about forgiveness, I know it is the path to healing, and I really want to heal. I have lived so long by masking my emotions, but to be honest, I am a bit overwhelmed. There is so much knowledge and wisdom that has been shared with me in the past week that I don't know where to start. However, I must admit life has become a little clearer than before— actually, a lot clearer than before. I imagined what would happen if I never learned any of this. What would my future life look like? I imagined it would not be much different than my father's.

I am ready to step down from my duties, from our family legacy, but I couldn't think about it now. I needed to talk to my wife first. For the first time in years, something was stirring in me. I would say it was feelings of love. I realized my love for my wife had never died. I just got distracted with other things. This destroyed our closeness, and slowly we became strangers in the same house.

How could I face her? What would I tell her? I rehearsed everything a million times. I practiced what I would say to her, but each time the conversation looked different. I decided I was going to call on my wisdom while talking to her. Figuring out what to say was too much to handle on my own. I was going to live in the moment, be completely honest with her, be completely present for once in my life…just for the sake of being. It might not look pretty, but this was how I was going to deal with it. I had avoided this conversation for such a long time, as if it didn't matter. And, yet, my wife mattered the most in my life. How come I had never admitted this fact in the past? I had not known the significance of this revelation until now.

I stepped away from my office to get some fresh air. I sat outside. The sun shined on my face and the air was cool. It was a bright, beautiful day. I had never enjoyed a moment like this in the middle of my work day. It was a pleasure to be here, enjoying the gift of Mother Earth. To be honest, the moment was a bit funny for me. Usually, I would be crunching numbers or trying to close a deal in the middle of the day. I never sat outside in the daylight, enjoying the breeze and thanking Mother Earth. This was a miracle, I thought, an unexpected miracle that had been dropped on my lap with no effort on my part. I wondered how many other daily miracles I had ignored. I realized respect was a miracle. It was a miracle that I would have never guessed. I had never thought of respect as a miracle. Who thinks of respect as a miracle? I am starting to understand the nuances of life; the nuances that every day prior, I had ignored through my oblivion. I spent about half an hour outside until I was called back to work. It was my brother who needed to talk to me about a business deal. I was on the call but was only half listening.

My brother stopped in the middle of his sentence. "Is everything ok?"

"Yes, of course," I snapped back into the conversation. "Why do you ask?"

"You seem different."

"Really? In what way?"

"You seem very distracted," my brother said, studying my expression.

"Oh, I don't know," I lied. I was not ready to share this part of my life with anyone yet. In fact, I wasn't even sure if I was going to share it with my wife. How was I going to tell her, "Oh, by the way, this lion in my dreams has been teaching me things about life"? Should I call it spiritual growth when I tell her? I don't know. What will she say, if I tell her? Will she believe me? Will she accept me? Will she laugh in my face and tell me I'm crazy?

I tried to tune back into my brother, who had continued throughout my internal conversation. "No, you definitely sound different. You're not your usual self."

I shrugged, trying to seem casual. "I have a lot on my mind."

"Anything I can help with?"

"No, thanks, nothing big."

He and I talked about work and other important things related to our empire. He said he needed my help, which was good, since it occupied most of my afternoon and took the edge off my nervousness. It was almost three when I thought about my wife again. I pushed through the rest of the day, finished early, and took off to meet my wife. This date could be the beginning of either a whole new life, or the end of everything. I had no idea.

I decided to stay away from blame and guilt during our conversation. I got to the restaurant and got seated. She was already at the table, waiting. She looked flushed, and I realized that she might be nervous, too. We smiled politely, and I gave her a peck on her cheek. I felt something with the touch. She felt like a stranger, as if this was our first date.

We ordered some drinks and eased into conversation. I called upon the Lion to help me. I actually heard a roar. I looked around and everyone in the restaurant was continuing as if nothing had happened. Oh good, I thought, no one else heard the roar. Then I had a doubt. Am I crazy? Is my wisdom the Lion? Are my wisdom and the Lion the same?

"Great job dude," the Lion said to me, "waking me up from my slumber. You should be paying me a zebra every time you wake me up. You know I have a life too, right? You know my life doesn't revolve around you?" I sent him thoughts of gratitude.

"I am sorry," I said without moving my lips. "I need your help to hold up this conversation."

"Don't use me as a crutch. Go deep inside your heart and speak from your heart. It is full of wisdom and it will speak the truth."

"But I don't have the time," I pleaded silently. "If you could just whisper in my ear what I should tell her, it will be easier."

"Absolutely not," the Lion roared in my skull. "This is your training. Use all the wisdom you have gained. Trust yourself. Trust your wisdom and you will be fine. By the way, she looks lovely. How did she fall for you?" the Lion chuckled softly. "Anyway, got to go. Good luck. We will talk later. Call upon me in your dreams." With that he vanished from my thoughts.

My wife looked at me as if nothing unusual had transpired. "What is it you want to talk to me about? Why all of a sudden?"

"I have a lot to share with you. It may take an entire evening or more, but this will give us a start. I have been going through some changes. I am no longer enjoying my work. It feels more like a burden now. I lack the gumption I felt in the past. I am realizing that this life I've created through my father's legacy is not my own."

She looked at me puzzled. "Are you looking to leave your firm and business?"

"At this point, I'm not sure. I'm starting to look at life differently. I may prefer a simpler life, a life that is more aligned with my true heart's desires."

She laughed. Such a lovely laugh, I thought. "When did you start thinking about your heart's desires?" she asked. "I thought you had lost your heart a while ago." She smiled in a knowing, straightforward way, with no malice. "The heart I once knew, I can no longer hear it or feel it. Have you been reading some books or what?"

"Believe it or not, I think I am changing. I am changing into me, the real me." She put down her fork and looked straight at me. How could I have ignored those beautiful eyes for so long?

"First of all," she said, "I am happy for you. I am happy you are seeing beyond what your family expects of you. But I think there is more to this than you are sharing."

I nodded. "Yes, but please let me finish. With this new feeling, I am not sure what is next or how my family will take it. I am not going to quit yet, but this thought has crossed my mind more times than I can count. But this is not what I want to talk to you about tonight. I am here to talk about you and me. I still love you. I have ignored you and your existence for a long time. You have been good and kind to me. You are the only woman I have ever loved. I know I may not have shown that over the past few years, and we have grown apart, but I have never stopped loving you. I replaced you with other things, as if they mattered more. I was hung up on things that are not important to the heart. I have continued to hurt you and cover up my own lies. You have tried talking to me several times about all this, but I have shut you down. I have been arrogant and obnoxious, and I am sorry."

"Thank you," she stammered. I could see tears filling her eyes. "Never in my wildest imagination did I think I would hear this from you. This is a miracle. But I know there is more than that. What happened to you? What brought about this change?"

"Yes, there is more." I was quiet for a moment, as I gathered my courage. I did not know how to discuss my affairs with her, even though she may already know about them. I did not know how to share this burden that I had been carrying around. I excused myself and took a bathroom break. I looked at myself in the mirror. I was shaking. Worried and nervous, I splashed some water on my face before heading back to the table.

I took a deep breath as I sat down, and then launched right in, my eyes lowered. "I have been unfaithful to you. I have not cared about your feelings or your commitment to me and our family and our marriage. I have taken you for granted. I have been avoiding you to conceal my lies. I have realized that I cannot continue my life like this. I want to live an honest life. I am not sure, where this will lead."

When I looked up, there were more tears in her eyes. I did not speak. Instead, I tried to be with her in her emotions. I could feel my heart in my throat. It was thumping louder than ever before. My silence and her tears made it feel like we were the only two people in the whole place. I did not care what people thought or if they were looking at us. What did it matter? It's a messed-up world anyway. Doesn't every family have secret that they try to conceal? Well, now, mine was finally out in the open. The lie had festered and stunk for years while we both pretended like it did not exist. We knew, both of us knew, but we didn't acknowledge it. Actually, If I'm being completely honest, I did not acknowledge it. She tried talking to me several times. In my lies, I always pushed her away, thinking why do women have to talk about everything? Her requests to talk exhausted and irritated me.

As she continued crying, she excused herself and stepped away to the bathroom. I had a moment to ponder things but saw a future life that was unclear. Not knowing was not something I had ever been comfortable with. I heard a tremendous roar in my head.

"What are you doing back here?" I asked.

"You woke me up and I couldn't fall back to sleep, so I decided to stay and watch the exchange. First of all, good job coming clean. That took a lot of courage and strength."

I nodded quickly, but I was worried.

"Don't worry," the Lion continued, "it will all turn out for the better. It is your life and you make it anyway you choose."

"But she may not be part of it." I was beginning not to feel well.

"That is true. Give her a chance to process everything. She is very vulnerable right now. Just be there for her. You have an opportunity to make the wrongs right. She needs your support more than anything."

"But what if she doesn't want me around after all this?"

"That is a possibility. If that ends up being the case, you will have time to contemplate other things that are about to be brought forth in your life."

I told the Lion that I did not want to know more. I felt completely overwhelmed. The room, filled with people laughing and enjoying their meals all around, seemed to be spinning.

"Yes, it can be overwhelming," the Lion affirmed, "but as you lead a life that is true to your heart, you will seek more lessons. This is just the nature of life."

"What if I chose to stop this conversation with my wife and just continue my life as is?"

"It is your choice, but eventually you will be brought back to this path again."

"When?"

"I don't know. That is up to you and your soul."

"Right. We were starting to talk about the soul yesterday."

"What do you think a soul is?"

"I have no idea. So far, it's not something I've had to deal with."

"Can you live without your heart?" the Lion asked me.

"No, of course not."

"You cannot live without a soul either."

"But I can't see my soul."

"That is the beauty of it. You humans seem to need to see everything in order to believe it. You need someone to scientifically prove the existence of things, otherwise you don't believe in them." The Lion sighed. "Why do you think you have the parents you have?"

"I don't know," I said, "since I did not choose them."

"Do you think they chose you?"

I told the Lion I had not thought about parents in this way or understood that I had a say in the matter. I thought two people came together, had sex, and voila, I was born.

"Really? You think that is all that happened?" The Lion shook his head.

"To my knowledge up until this point, yes," I said, "that is all I thought happened."

"Consider your soul, that you cannot see, plays a vital role in everything about your life."

"Okay, I can consider that."

"Your soul," the Lion continued, "is like a book that tells the entire story of your life now and before."

"What do you mean by 'before?'" I queried.

"Before you were born into this life," the Lion answered.

"You mean to say that I may have had more than one life?"

"Yes, you have had more than one life."

"I don't believe that."

"That's okay. We're not having a competition about who is right or wrong here. Let's table the more-than-one-life idea for the moment. It is too much right now. I understand. Could you at least comprehend the idea of soul within your body?"

"Yes, I can imagine that."

"Do I really believe it?"

"Not entirely at this point, but I can try to imagine it."

"Fair enough, that is a good start."

"Wait a minute," I said suddenly. "It has been a while since my wife went to the restroom. Let me check on her. Hold on to that thought."

I went looking for my wife, but she was nowhere to be seen. I realized she had left the restaurant. Who could blame her, right? I tried calling her. Luckily, she picked up the phone. "Please find a place to stay tonight," she said between sobs and gasps, and hung up. I could tell that she was having difficulty breathing.

I sat for a while and pondered. I felt horrible for having hurt her so deeply. I wanted to hold her and cry, but I couldn't; she was gone. I needed solace. With a heavy heart I paid the bill and found the nearest hotel to stay the night. I went to my room quickly to be away from people, to be with my emotions and continue my conversation with the Lion. I felt very vulnerable and craved his companionship and wisdom. Now more than ever, I was hungry for information from the Lion. I wanted to know everything to save my relationship with my wife. I had created a mess. What a mess! I ached to be with my wife. I had a big lump in my throat. I wanted to cry. All I felt was sadness, sadness for the loss of my wife. Sadness for what she endured with me and my family. As if he knew, the Lion manifested in my room.

He looked at me with compassion. "Would you like a moment to be alone?"

I shook my head no. "I would rather talk to you now. I am eager to learn about my relationship with my wife."

The Lion nodded and continued our conversation about the soul.

"Now can you imagine a soul within your body?"

"Yes, I can."

"Do you know why your wife was your wife over any other woman?" the Lion spoke softly.

"No," I replied, but he had my attention. This was a perfect conversation for tonight. I had never thought about this. Now here, on the worst night of my life, the question was posed by the Lion, so that I could understand. I paid extra attention to what he was saying.

"Consider that it was part of your soul's journey to meet her."

"Okay, I can do that."

"You are successful and rich, but you found a woman of whom your family did not approve. You fought with your family in order to marry her. You, who had abided by the rules of your family throughout your life, chose to marry her of all the people. I know she is beautiful, but I am sure there were other beautiful women in your circles before you met her."

"Yes, there were plenty."

"So why her?" The Lion tilted his head as he asked the question.

"She was beautiful, kind, compassionate and smart," I blurted.

"Is that why you married her?"

"Yes, absolutely."

"So, don't you find it odd that a rich kid who's last thought was compassion found a woman who was kind and compassionate?" The Lion was watching my expression as he spoke. "Do you think it was an accident that you met her? Let me tell you, she was placed at the exact place and time for you to meet her. It was not an accident."

As the Lion continued to watch my face, I pondered the many things in my life that I had thought had been accidents.

"And your kids," he continued, "your kids chose you and your wife as parents.

I stayed quiet for a moment trying to process this information. Then, I asked, "So, I chose my parents too?"

"Yes, you did," the Lion replied. "But not only your parents, you chose your friends, and your brother and sister, even before you were born."

"So, are you saying that nothing is an accident?" I was trying to wrap my head around this idea.

"That's right. Nothing is an accident. Nothing. People and circumstances are constantly brought into your life for you and your soul's growth."

I was dumbfounded. Though the Lion had shared a lot of radical ideas with me, this was way too much for me, especially tonight. I thought I controlled life, at least I always felt that I had. Now, I was learning from a Lion, no less, that I was totally not in control of anything! It was exactly the opposite of all my thoughts and beliefs before this moment.

"Part of the reason your wife is in your life is to help you learn the important life lessons you need to learn."

"Does this mean she will stay with me?"

"That means," he roared in frustration, "she will be part of your life one way or another until your lessons are complete."

"What if I don't finish my lessons with her?"

"Then you will continue to learn them after you leave this life."

"What does that mean? How will I continue to learn after this life?"

The great Lion hesitated. "You may not be ready for what I have to share in that regard."

"True, I may not be ready, but I want to know."

"As I was trying to say before, this is not the only life you and the people you know have lived together."

"What do you mean?" Maybe the Lion was right. Maybe I didn't want any more wisdom tonight. I felt perspiration across my brow.

"Do you ever get the feeling that you have met a person before, although it is the first time you are meeting them?"

"Yes, occasionally. That's how I felt the first time I met my wife. I even told her that I felt like I'd seen her before somewhere. She thought I was trying to flirt with her and laughed it off."

"Did the conversation flow very easily with your wife when you first met her?"

"Yes," I smiled sadly as I remembered, "but how did you know that?"

"I just took a guess. Why do you think the conversation flowed easily?"

"Because we were compatible?" I knew this was not the right answer.

"How is it that there are more than seven billion people on Mother Earth, but you felt that the conversation flowed easily with this one woman? You had met other women before her, hadn't you? Why is it that the conversation did not flow as easily with them?"

"I don't know," I said. "I never really thought about it."

"She is your soulmate," the Lion said matter-of-factly. "That's why."

I'd heard this term before in the movies, but it had new meaning now. It gave me hope. "Does it mean I will get back with her?"

The Lion roared again, this time it was a roar of laughter, perhaps because of my persistence.

"Laugh at me," I said, rolling my eyes, "that's fine. My life is laughable at this point anyways. I, who had longed to get away from my wife for years, now wants to throw myself at her feet and beg her to let me back into her life. I get it, plenty of irony there to enjoy. Laugh away."

"Listen, my friend, life does not come with a perfect roadmap."

"I understand, but you're telling me that things are laid out for us. Then can't you see the future and tell me if we will be together?" I could tell from the Lion's expression that he knew I was getting desperate at this point.

"No, your life is a puzzle, a mystery that only you can solve." I felt a warm pressure on my shoulder, as if he had put his great paw there to comfort me. "It does not mean you win or lose. There is no winning or losing in life, only lessons to be learned. If you pay attention to the puzzles and mysteries, the lessons will be learned. You will not always know why you are on a path or what lesson is at stake. Sometimes only time will reveal the lesson. You will have to be patient. The only things that are destined are the lessons you must learn. The in-between path will constantly change. You see, there are several players in this puzzle, not just you. If it were only up to you, your wife would be back in your arms tonight. But she is also part of this puzzle. You both have different lessons to learn and until those lessons are learned by both of you, you will continue to be part of the puzzle with her."

"I have never thought about life like this. It's an interesting concept." I was feeling a bit more hopeful, because both my wife and I had lessons to learn.

"It is not a concept, it's the truth. Would you want your wife in your arms without her free will?"

"Free will? What do you mean?" My head was spinning with all these new terms.

"Don't you want her to choose if she wants to be part of your life or not?"

"At the moment," I said with a weak, half grin, "it would be so much easier if she did not have a choice."

The Lion smiled. "But really, have you ever done anything that was not your choice?"

I thought for a moment. "Yes, I have."

"What was it?" The Lion leaned forward.

"When I was young, I did not want to learn to play the piano. I did, only because my parents did not give me a choice. I hated going to piano class. I hated learning the piano. I hated all of it."

"Well, that is how it would be if your wife could not choose. You will be worse off than now, if she did not choose willingly to be with you. It would be a miserable existence. Think about this, she has been living with you the past couple of years as though she did not have a choice to live without you. She has been miserable in this process. You have been miserable as well."

"Are you saying we both are victims?"

"No, both of you have chosen to act as though you are victims. You are not victims, but you act like you don't have a choice."

"But don't choices have repercussions?"

"Of course, they do. But every minute of your life is a choice. You could kill yourself or choose to live. That is a choice. Do both choices have repercussions, yes? But that is life. You live every second, every micro-second and every nanosecond of your life through choices. You just don't realize it."

I let out a huge sigh. *Have I missed my own life? I have failed to pay attention to the details*, I thought.

"Don't worry, you are certainly not the only one on this Earth that is oblivious to those things. Most of humanity needs healing. Consider yourself lucky to have had these revelations."

"Are you telling me that this conversation I am having with you now has always been on my path, part of my soul's journey?"

"Yes," the Lion said enthusiastically. "The time is ripe for your growth. Today, you have a choice to either not choose this path or to choose it. Either way is fine."

"But if I don't choose it today, I will simply be brought back to this path again in the future, right?"

"Yes, that is how lessons are. They will be brought to you over and over until you realize the lesson."

"If that is the case, I might as well choose this path today. My choice will have a lot of repercussions, won't it?"

"Yes, it will," the Lion said, looking more serious. "That is part of the journey—learning about those repercussions is part of the journey as well. There are always lessons inside the lessons."

"Are all lessons this gloomy?" I asked, planting my face firmly in the palms of my hands.

"No," he roared with a comforting laugh. "There are always several miracles found in the lessons. They are the best part. You experience new miracles and begin to pay attention to the existing miracles around you. Given what I have said, don't you think meeting your wife was a miracle? We are all supposed to live a life filled with miracles. That is Mother Earth's intention. Miracles abound in life, but you have placed value on things that have masked those miracles. You will realize your very existence is a miracle. On your path, you will start to realize your unique beauty. You will begin to see yourself as a miracle, for nothing in life can be a miracle without you, without your presence, without your existence. You were chosen by Mother Earth to exist on this planet at this very juncture. She decided to board you, to feed you and to provide you with abundance, not the abundance of wealth you and your family have created, but rather the abundance which is a miracle by itself. Mother Earth, who has chosen all beings and creations, brought them forth knowing full well that they would be fed and sheltered."

"Then how is there poverty in the world?"

"You must be tired," the Lion said. "Let's leave that discussion for another day, as it would require a long discussion."

He bid me goodbye. I thanked him for being with me when I needed him the most.

I sat on the bed, alone, wanting to reach into the fridge and drink an entire bottle of wine. Perhaps alcohol would ease my pain. I didn't want to feel the pain in my heart, but I resisted the alcohol. I knew alcohol would not take the pain away, so instead I chose to feel the pain. I stretched my tired body across the bed and thought about my life, my life with my wife. Tears filled my eyes. I missed her. I missed her dearly. It was now past midnight. I knew she would be in bed by now, but still I called her. She did not pick up, so I left a voicemail. I was crying like a baby when I left the message. I told her about the pain in my heart that would not go away. Yes, I did. I waited for a while, hoping she might call me back. I made sure my phone was charged and on. I did not fall asleep until early in the morning. Finally, exhausted, I dozed off.

I woke to my phone ringing loudly. I grabbed the phone. Perhaps it was my wife. Disappointed, I saw my brother's name on the screen.

"Hello," I grumbled, half asleep.

"What the hell is going on?" He was clearly irritated. "You missed the meeting."

"Listen, I am in a hotel."

"By yourself?"

"Yes, by myself."

"Did she kick you out?"

"Not exactly ...well, sort of."

"What did you do this time?" I could hear the irritation in my brother's voice.

"The usual," I said. "The usual things our family does." My brother went quiet.

"Hey, do you mind covering for me today? I'm just not up for it. I have some soul searching to do."

"Soul searching? Um, okay. Call me if you need anything." The phone clicked off.

I took the day to be with myself and, yes, to do some soul searching.

Feeling sorry for myself,
Man

CHAPTER 9: "SOULD"

My dear Lion, full of wisdom, has opened my eyes. Until yesterday, I was not privy to my soul. I thought I could do whatever I wanted in this lifetime. Yes, I knew there would be consequences, but they were contained to this life…and being rich, I have been able to buy my way out of any mishaps. It was so easy to do what I did with that false knowing of no soul. Had I understood my soul, I think it would have directed me. Maybe it did direct me, but I was simply oblivious. Now, I am realizing that life and death are not what I had imagined them to be. My soul had lessons for me.

Through my conversation yesterday with the Lion, I realized that I had so far sold my soul. I had sold my soul for many purposes, some for others and some for myself. Let me share with you how I sold my soul.

I "SoulD" my soul. I "SoulD" my soul for reasons that were motivated by my ego, that blown-up doll that feeds my greed and more. My ego will sell itself out for anything that makes it feel big. In reality, my ego is puny. It has to do things to make itself feel bigger than it is. Until recently, I never realized I had a soul; all I knew was my ego. I fed my ego all kinds of things to keep it happy—the more, the better. No matter how much I fed my ego, though, it was never enough. It was never fully satisfied. There were glimpses of satisfaction, but this was always short lived. My ego was bound by the rules of society, my family and my own need to feel better.

You may ask, "You grew up rich, why would you have to be bound by the rules of society?" Well, let me tell you, many of the wealthy have their own rules. It is worse than what you have. We don't play by your rules. We play by our own rules. Our rules are way worse than yours. The fact is, most of your rules and laws were made by us, so that we could be wealthy. In other words, our laws and rules supersede yours. We are all about making sure you, the masses, are convinced at all times to buy whatever we are selling. We find reasons to justify why you should buy what we are selling. We have information spewed out everywhere in every form, so that you are constantly reminded of the things that you think you need. We encourage consumerism, constant consumerism, blatant consumerism, and it is an addiction. You don't even know you are being played by us. You assume you need a whole bunch of these things and services that we offer.

Many of us seek to be the puppeteers where you are the puppets. You think you are making a conscious decision when you buy. You are not. You are our puppets. Funny thing is, we have created this lie, this mirage. See, a lie can stay a lie from a distance. When you get closer, you quickly figure out it is all a lie, that you have been played. Still, don't be too quick to defend yourself. I come from the upper echelons, and I know what we have done. You think we care about you from the upper echelons? We don't. We make sure you live in fear and that fear may seem like you care about yourself. That fear that you think is caring for self makes you buy stuff and things. Our formula works, completely and fully, never disappointing me, never disappointing us. We may have to tweak it a bit here and there, but that's it. Our lies always work. For the lies are imbued with perpetrated fear, an easy and fun tool we play with. We create an illusion through this fear, an illusion that you need something—this is the commodity we sell.

Making you buy whatever we make is our motto. And we will figure out a way to justify the usefulness of what we make. We will come up with anything that needs justifying, to make you believe. You don't even know the number of channels we use to constantly remind you to buy things that in reality you don't need. We have created this false need for you to own things. It is propaganda filled with lies and fear. I am not talking about advertisements. That is an easy one. No, we have crept into areas of your life where you don't even know that things are being sold to you. You think it is information—good information that will save humanity, packaged brilliantly with sophisticated lies. These messages come in a great many forms, from well-wishers in society. These well-wishers are paid by us to dictate what we want them to say, like parrots. You think it is their idea or their profession. We know that if the message comes from them, you will receive the lie better. In fact, you will believe the lie, and we want you to believe it. You see, not only are we selling it to you this way, sometimes the things that are in direct contradiction to those things are also sold by us. Isn't that funny? Not really, it is sad, but there is a satirical humor in this. Don't you agree?

Never mind, I don't want to make you feel bad, but this is reality. I am not that old, but in my lifetime I have seen, negotiated, sold and bought things that would make you cringe. I am a master manipulator. I can manipulate anything I want. You see, that is how I "SoulD" out my soul.

I get an image of a house having a "SOLD" sign in the yard. That is what happened to me. As part of my family legacy, I sold my soul. I think my entire family has sold its soul. I picture myself walking around with a plaque on my chest that says, "SOUL SOLD." In the upper echelons, we wear it with pride. We don't carry any shame or guilt about this. Instead, we get a nod, and sometimes a pat on the back.

We pillage and plunder Mother Nature's resources to do everything that we do. In the upper echelons, which is an exclusive club, we wear these like a badge of honor. We know not to step on each other's toes to ensure that we are all plundering the wealth we want. We don't even use the word money in our circles. Instead, we call it "wealth." Everything you use from dawn to dusk is made and dictated by us. Yes, you are our puppet to play with and be used.

By selling our souls, we also tricked you into selling yours. It is a trade of souls. Yes, aptly put, it is a trade of souls. In the current trade of souls, you don't even know your soul is being "SoulD" by someone else. Even if you knew it, you'd think you were doing it for your own good and for the good of your family.

See, we are good! We have cunningly made you give up your soul. You will want to blame us but take a second to think about this. Based on what the Lion, my buddy, stated, you had a choice in the matter. You chose to believe the lies, and fell into the trade, which stripped you of your wisdom, your respect, your love—the unconditional love that is life's true miracle. Until recently, I believed miracles were few and far between. That is a lie, too. I am confused about leaving the upper echelon to join you the puppets, but would that solve the problem? I am a puppet, too. Don't get me wrong, I am a puppet that controls other puppets. What has happened to us? When we traded our souls, we became robots, zombies. It feels so real and so important—what you do, what I do—but we are puppets controlled by a regime that is so much in the shadows you don't even know it's happening. We have created a zombie apocalypse for you.

Do you want to know something ironic? While doing all this soul trade, we would come up with causes to support to show our commitment to society and humanity. A sliver of my time, of our time, was dedicated to doing good. We would give speeches about anything that made us look like we were contributing to society. We would contribute to foundations to mask our uncaring behavior towards humanity and Mother Earth. The joke is on you. The money we pretended to contribute to these foundations, has now been claimed back. We had means laid out to do that. Ha, see, how clever we are? We sold our souls, while pretending like we actually had souls.

Seeing is believing, right? If I don't see my soul, it doesn't exist. Then, I don't have to think about it, right? I do have a heart, but I don't get to see it out in the open. And even if it were out in the open, I would have looked at it as an organ that keeps me alive, and nothing more. So not only have I sold my soul, I have also forgotten about my heart, other than its functional purpose. What a simpleton I am to think that the heart is just to keep me alive. I took care of my heart. I saw the doctor and got checkups routinely. We had a family doctor who came at our every whim. I ate right. Of course, I drank a lot…but somehow, I have managed to keep myself healthy. I am still young, so no harm done, at least not yet. Here is the funny thing: we who spend billions on physical maintenance of our hearts don't spend a dime on matters of spiritual maintenance of our hearts. Why would we? Then, we would have to look at our souls. The souls we so conveniently sold.

A man who has "SoulD" is talking about the soul he has sold. Not only did he sell his own soul, but he SoulD humanity's soul as well. I imagine myself as part of an auction where human souls are bought for cheap, requiring only a small material investment—that is it. Souls are easy to buy at the auction. We are able to buy one and get one free…or an entire family for free. Yes, souls are that easy to buy.

Can you believe it? Yes, that is our trade, the soul trade. We get better at it every day, every minute, every second. Don't ever come back to us to reclaim your soul. You SoulD it to us, but you can't come back to reclaim it from us. Isn't that ironic? Please don't be angry with me; I am merely the messenger. I am not trying to be arrogant. I am actually seeing the irony in all of this. Yes, the complete and total irony. You could acquire all the wealth in the world to try and retrieve your soul, but you cannot buy it back. Here is the bigger problem, if you have acquired excess wealth, you are already part of the soul trade. You cannot buy back your soul, but you get to be part of the soul trade. Once you start trading souls, you get addicted. Your ego cannot be satisfied. You need more and more and more. It is like a demon who drinks blood. You don't believe me? That's fine. Just ask yourself if you live a soul-driven life. I am not talking about being a holy person. I am talking about you being a real human, living a human life led by your soul. I know I am not one of these people, but I can spot one when I see one. I see the SoulD people all around me, and once in a while, I get a glimpse of someone who has a spark. But until recently, I knew nothing about souls, so I couldn't tell for sure what I was seeing.

Having SoulD your soul, what do you do? To be honest, I have no idea. I am only a soul usurper, not a soul retriever. You'll have to figure that out on your own. We can do it together, if you want, but based on my Lion's wisdom, we may not always stay on the same path. There should be a better way to retrieve our souls, right? Hmmm…. I know the best person to ask. Let me first check if he is available. He doesn't like being disturbed.

I saw the Lion. He was standing over a big rock, looking out, like the way lions do in the movies. Maybe I should make a movie about him. It would sell well. Sheesh! See how my SoulD ego works? I went to the Lion and stood by him on the rock. It was a wonderful view from where he stood. I admired it. I was envious of him and his paradise. What a world! I wish I could stay here forever. I have to talk to him about that possibility.

That would solve all my problems. Maybe I will find my soul here. Or, having been a soul trader, I might be tempted to usurp souls from this paradise. I don't know yet. Anyways, I asked the Lion if he had some time for me.

He laughed. "You know time is an illusion, right?"

"Why do you always have to have an opinion for everything?" I asked.

"I am sorry," he replied earnestly. "My intention was not to judge what you are asking, merely to point out that time is an illusion, since I have come to show you a few things."

"Never mind," I replied. "Sorry, I'm a bit testy today."

"No worries," the Lion replied. "It's all in good humor."

I like his chill, nonchalant manner. He really exudes confidence like it is nobody's business. "Hey," I ask, "do you have a soul?"

"Yes, I do. By the way, thanks for intruding my space. I truly appreciate it."

I appreciated his sarcasm, too. Always on point. "Listen," I continued. "I'm really sorry for intruding, but I really need your help."

"What's new?" he replied dryly.

"Oh, come on. Don't be like that."

"Like what?"

"You know," I retorted, "giving me the cold shoulder."

"Giving you what?"

"The cold shoulder," I replied. "Oh, never mind. I mean you are being standoffish."

"Dude, you come into my area, you disturb my peace, and you think I'm giving a hot or cold shoulder? What is wrong with you?" It was clear the Lion was becoming a bit irritated.

"Please don't bust my balls. I am already hurt."

"Fine, fine, I will talk to you," the Lion said. "Did you ask me if I have a soul?"

"Yes, I did."

"What a moron you are to ask me this question after talking to me for almost ten straight days?"

"Sorry," I said. "I guess the answer is 'Yes'? What I meant to ask is do animals have a soul? Never mind, I got it."

"Wow! You are smart." The Lion was now pacing around, as if he were trapped in a cage.

"Enough with the sarcasm, okay?" I was concerned. The Lion did not seem like himself today. He was not the calm and composed creature that I had come to know. "What is going on? You are so moody!"

"I am concerned about my future, the forest's future, the future of man, the future of Mother Earth." The Lion paced as he spoke. "I am concerned about our legacy. Every day I spend talking with you, I gain a deeper understanding of the havoc humanity is causing to our beloved Earth and its creations. I am worried and sad. Sorry to take this out on you, but standing here, looking at this paradise, well, I know that one day it will all be gone. I will be pushed away or locked up in a cage. Do you know what a horrible existence that is? Don't answer that. I will tell you. For someone like me, who has roamed the expansive Mother Earth and cared nothing for borders and boundaries, the thought of being locked up in a small cage, where all I can do is pace back and forth, is unbearable. You know the worst of it all? My friends from the forest will be locked up, too. Do you have something called zoos?"

"Yes," I said quietly. It was difficult to look at him as I admitted this.

"Wow! My wisdom showed this to me last night, and I have been pretty disturbed since then. To be honest, I have a piece of mind to attack you. Do you see my point?" He growled, giving me a clear view of his large, ferocious teeth.

"Please don't attack me." I felt afraid for a moment but knew the Lion would not attack me.

"Shut up," the Lion snarled. "Don't play that card, as if you are helpless. You see those animals in those cages over there? They are helpless, not you."

"Listen," I said. "We may be able to stop that. I am here now, and fully committed to helping us both—you and me. Please help me retrieve my soul, so I can help you."

"Retrieve your soul? What? Do you think I have it?"

"No," I said, "Of course, I don't think you have my soul. I have realized that the reason humanity is the way it is in my time, is because humanity has lost its soul."

"So, you think it is lost?" The Lion looked perplexed.

"Maybe. I don't know, but I want it back."

The Lion let out a huge sigh. "You really exhaust me. Okay, let's go and sit in the shade."

I followed him to a beautiful tree. It felt so cool under the tree's lush branches. Now I understood why the Lion enjoyed his slumbers. Who wouldn't in this paradise of abundance filled with birds chirping as a constant reminder of Mother Nature's music? I have always loved the chirping of the birds. During my travels to Africa, I tented under the trees and woke up to the chirping in the morning. It was such a beautiful feeling. Here it was even better. I saw birds of all colors, shapes and forms. They had beautiful plumes and came in different sizes. I could see myself living here, in this paradise. I turned to the Lion. "Okay, tell me, tell me how to get my soul back."

"What do you think it means to get your soul back?" he asked.

"It means that I will be more thoughtful and care more about Mother Earth."

"Listen, that is very nice and altruistic of you," the Lion said, "but just so you know, you don't get a medal for caring for Mother Earth, okay? Aligning with your soul means taking care of yourself. By taking true care of yourself, you abide by Mother Nature's wisdom. The rules dictated by her wisdom will far exceed your expectations. Also, she doesn't need saving. You need to save yourself. Let us be clear on that point."

"Is it not selfish to care for myself?" I asked. "Isn't that what me and my family do now?"

"It is not the same. When you take care of yourself through the guidance from your soul, your acts are aligned with Mother Natures' wisdom. By aligning with her wisdom, you create a system that is well balanced. Mother Nature is waiting for you to align with her wisdom. She is not waiting for you to save her."

"Could you elaborate on that?" I was truly perplexed.

"Let us talk about the soul, and you will get a better perspective. What do you think happened to your soul?"

"I didn't know I had lost my soul. Did I lose it through all my bad deeds?"

"You never lose your soul or your wisdom," the Lion instructed. "It is inherently part of you, and that is who you are. When you come into your body, your soul gets seated in your body. When you are done with this body with your lifetime, the soul departs for other purposes beyond what you can comprehend at the moment."

"So, my soul is still in my body?"

"Yes, it is. It is like your heart. You can't rip your heart out and walk away, can you?"

"No, I can't."

"The same with your soul. You can't separate your soul from your body. This body you inhabit in this lifetime is the body that the soul chose."

"The soul chose me?"

"No, the soul chose your body. You are not your body. You are more than this body."

"I am more than this body?" I was really confused now.

"Yes, you are more than this body."

"Could you please explain this with some examples?"

"Alright, right now, you are sitting with me in paradise—this is different from your timeline. You are doing this either through the dream or through your imagination, right?"

"Yes. I bring up your image when I want to talk to you outside of my dreams."

"Consider this as time travelling. You live in a different lifetime than I do, yet we communicate, right?"

"Yes, I understand. Does this mean I can talk to my father?"

"Absolutely. In fact, his soul is waiting for you to talk to him. He has his own wisdom, you know. He may not have done good things, but his own soul has been learning."

"So, once a soul comes into your body, it never leaves until you die?"

"Yes, that's God's plan," the Lion explained.

"I want to ask about God, but I will save it for later," I said. "This SoulD, how do I retrieve it? Pardon me for using this language, but I don't know the right word, other than 'retrieve.'"

"Let me offer you a word. Tell me if it suits you. The word is 'align.' You see, your soul is present, and it is always aligned with you, but you forgot that you were aligned with it. Your job is to train yourself to seek that alignment."

"This is very fascinating to me," I told the Lion. "I am excited about this alignment. Could you tell me how I can learn to align?"

"You already are doing it. The soul always gives you opportunities to align. It nudges you toward alignment. You either are unaware of this or ignore it, since other things have taken precedence in your life. It is as simple as that. At this juncture, your time is ripe and hence you are having this conversation with me. You have come for a purpose, and that purpose is to be in alignment with your soul. It is a divine purpose that surpasses all your needs. It is aching to be felt. Misalignment, just like lies, can't be concealed forever. They are intertwined, your misalignment and lies, that is. Once you let go of one or the other, they both dissolve. That is the beauty of it. For example, if you stay in forgiveness, unconditional love can be felt, compassion can be felt, beauty can be felt, truth can be felt, wisdom can be felt...and the list goes on and on. Take one thing a day and practice it. Take time to practice it in every aspect of your life, whatever you choose. That by itself is you reaching out to your soul for guidance. Your Soul will be aligned to its true nature. Yes, I heard you talk. I listened to your whole SoulD spiel and was very impressed. I think you are ready. But I want to know why you think you are ready?"

"I am not sure. This is an overwhelming amount of information. I am not sure what indicates that I am ready."

"Your mere intelligence to ask the questions, the right questions, puts you on the path to ascension. When you have the right questions, the right teacher will appear. Before I showed up in your dreams, you were starting to ponder about things and life in general. So, it was not an accident that I showed up. In your time, if you had a school for spirituality, you would be acing it. It would contradict all paths of spirituality this acing thing, but you get my point, don't you?"

I nodded. "So, you think I am on the right path?"

The Lion looked directly into my eyes. "What do you think?"

"I think I am ready."

"I am not going to be around for too long, so learn to lean on your own wisdom. It is a wonderful and amazing tool. The good thing about wisdom is, when you are truly aligned with it, everything is clear as a bell. You can't miss it. Your heart and soul will know. As a result, you will know. When your wisdom reigns, it will become one with your thoughts and you will never need another to confirm if you are doing the right thing. For example, you knew when you met your wife that one day you would be together. Didn't you?"

"Yes, but how did you know that?"

"Just a guess. But you see, that is your wisdom; that strong pull and knowing from your heart that you wanted to be with her and no one else. You convinced your family and married her. You did not need anyone to convince you or confirm it for you. That is the conviction that wisdom provides. Use this tool on your path to ascension."

"What is ascension?" I asked, having not heard the Lion say this word until today.

"Oh boy," the Lion wiped his face with his paw, preparing to explain what must be a complex idea. "When you align with your soul, it will raise you to a different level of living and from that place you will understand ascension. You talking to me in my lifetime is a piece of your ascension. That is the best way I can explain it from your current viewpoint. Think of it this way, when you are at the base of a mountain, the view looks different. You see things from your focal point at the bottom of the mountain.

As you ascend the mountain, the view changes. You see more, the view is broader as you move up the mountain. As you get higher, you see more than your eyes can handle. Does that make sense?"

"Yes, somewhat," I nodded. "Thanks for giving me a glimpse into my future. I like it." I said goodbye to the Lion and left paradise. It felt really different coming into his world. If this is what ascension feels like, I like it. I plan on ascending as often as possible."

"I am SoulD," I shouted out loud. "I am SoulD. I am SoulD on this path to ascension. I am SoulD on this path laid by my soul. I am SoulD."

Soulfully yours,
Man

CHAPTER 10: GIFT

I am a gift to my soul. My body that I am born with, is a gift to my soul. It is a home that my soul has come to embody. This body is not any body; it is mine. Its sole purpose is to house my soul and take good care of me, and I know it is a temple that I house my soul in. Your temple that houses your soul is a precious one.

You were given this body to nurture your soul and do things as per your soul's path. Please don't judge another for their body, as their path is different from yours. You see, your body houses only one soul, but your soul has housed many bodies, many characters. In this lifetime, your soul has come to embody this temple. Take care of it as a temple, yet don't get too attached. Your wisdom will teach you how to house your soul in this body. Your soul will tell you how to house it in this body. Your heart will tell you how to house it in this body. You have so many venues that will teach you to embody this precious soul. Your body has been given to you in perfection.

Your eyes are your soul's window. When you are misaligned with your soul, your vision is very contained. It can only see as much as the eyes are meant to see just through flesh and blood. Your eyes, as seen through your soul, are expansive. Your eyes are capable of looking deeper into another's soul, the connection that is felt past the reality in which you exist. Make sure to see everything through your soul's eye. Remember you are the only one through which your soul can see. Don't suppress it. If and when you suppress seeing through your soul, you will feel a lot more judgments laced with opinions. You are gifted with more than your physical eyes to see, to envision, to dream, to receive visions.

You are a gifted being. You are gifted with several gifts and one of them is your multidimensional vision. Visions, dreams, serendipitous experiences are all part of being able to witness through your gifts. When you understand your gifts, you see beyond the vision of the eyes. You are gifted with a third eye, which is the invisible eye that sits between your brows. This mind's eye takes you to a vision that walks you through things that you may need to know or envision. Your mind's eye is a vision that could transport you to another reality that is different from the one you see. Therefore, you can create a new reality other than the one you see. When you let go of fear and envision that which you want, you can create your life, and your life aligns with this new reality. For the new reality to align, one must understand that the reality that one creates is as real as the one that exists. When you are able to see through your third eye, you are able to envision your own gifts and understand the metaphysical and multidimensional world around you. You are able to see things beyond what you have known before. All preconceived notions are shattered by your third eye as you understand that you are beyond the experiences that you have encountered in your life. That is how I came to talk to the Lion. The interactions I have with him are clairvoyant by nature, as it involves visual encounters with him.

In order to enhance this vision, this gift, you will have to become aware of it. When you become aware of it, you will feel its presence. When you are aware of its presence, it becomes real. In this new reality, you are able to create new realities, new ventures and new visions that align with your gift. You cannot have a new reality unless you accept and witness your gifts. In order to do so, you have to release those things that hold you to your current reality. When you let go of your current reality, you are able to step into the gifts that have been bestowed upon you. Your vision is a powerful manifestation of your ideals—the ideals that you might think are unachievable. They are unachievable as long as you do not acknowledge your gifts. Your gifts are potent. They have a potency that cannot be explained. This potency makes you powerful. This power gains your wisdom. This power makes you who you truly are, which is the gifted being. When you acknowledge your gifts, they become real and you become the magic. Your gifts are not to be taken lightly or ignored. When you ignore your gifts, you are setting aside your God-given right to flourish.

When you align with your gifts, you will align with your soul. When you align with your soul, you become expansive. You are able to be who you are in your body and beyond your body. When you become someone who is expansive, you are able to acknowledge the gifts you are embodied with that are beyond the senses that you physically feel. Your physical senses become heightened. When your physical senses are heightened, you become attuned to your gifts. The sharpening of your physical senses becomes your gateway to the other-worldly gifts that you embody.

To be aligned to your gifts requires you to be physically present to your body. If you wish to experience expansiveness, you cannot ignore your body and its senses. Your physical sensations are the gateway to your gifts. One cannot exist without the other. When you ignore your physical body, you are unable to receive the gifts in their truest form. When you feel your body, you become aware of your body more fully. When you feel your body completely, your body will lead you to your gifts. It is pivotal to be one with your body before you embark on the journey of gifts. Ignoring the body does not cause awakening. Rather, it is in acknowledging your gifts through the body that the body becomes a vehicle to experience the gifts. This is what enables the awakening. When one understands that the body is the vehicle to experience the gifts, one awakens to the gifts. It is not one or the other, it is one and the same—your body and the gifts it brings.

Your third eye, your mind's eye is the invisible gift that sits in between your eyebrows. It was a gift from the Almighty to be who you are, a gift. It was seated there to transcend all the things that you see with your physical eyes. It was seated above your eyes so you could understand that your mind's eye, your invisible eye, is above your direct vision. Whatever you see in the physical world, you can transcend through the vision of your mind's eye. Anything you see, can be transcended to a vision that is true to who you are. Your eyes are pivotal to this higher vision. The issue is when there is a separation between the vision your physical eyes hold to that of the third eye. Your life is a combination of what your eyes see and what your third eye sees. The vision that the eyes hold can be enhanced by the vision that the third eye brings. I have experienced this myself through my interactions with the Lion. When I talk to the Lion, using both kinds of vision, I am clairaudient. We have come here to experience every gift that was bestowed upon us. We cannot see this temple beyond what one is taught. The more you align with your soul, the more you will come to feel the other invisible senses in your body. You will feel their presence strongly.

Imagine you were blindfolded all your life and you believed that you were blind. Through being present to the body, you would start to feel new sensations and feelings. When you start to sense things by being present to your body, you awaken your third eye. It is that simple. When you become present to your body and become aware of yourself fully in your physicality, your body's wisdom awakens. When your body's wisdom awakens, you awaken wisdom within. When you awaken the wisdom of your body and your consciousness, you are able to access those gifts that have never been used. When the wisdom starts to enliven its presence in your body, your blindfold starts to unravel. Then, one day, you are present to this gift with no doubt. Your wisdom addressed it on your behalf and all you needed to do was become present to your body, to embody. When your wisdom unravels your blindfold, you are no longer aligned with lies. You understand that you are gifted with a vision. This is your third eye.

Your third eye is one of the many gifts you bear. You bear it with ease. The heaviness and fogginess that you encounter initially will be released through your wisdom and the teachings of your wisdom. Use your body as your guru, watch it, feel it, sense it as if you are an observer. As you observe, you will continue to uncover your gifts.

I called upon the Lion to share my wisdom.

He roared. "What's up?"

"You sound quite cheerful," I replied. "What's new?"

"I just got enough sleep without any disturbance, thanks to you."

We shared a bit of chitchat, but I was eager to learn more from the Lion. "So, I am seeing you through my mind's eye, right?"

"Yes, through the sixth chakra," the Lion responded. "This is one of the energy points."

"What else and who else can I see, and how do I see them?" I asked the Lion.

"You can see anyone from other dimensions. Your vision is unlimited through the third eye. Your vision is expansive."

"Tell me about the other dimensions."

"This is not the only plane in which you exist. You exist in several planes. You are able to witness the plane you live in, because this is the only plane that seems real to you. As you expand your wisdom, you will come to the understanding that you are a multidimensional being. Your reality changes as you witness yourself as a multidimensional being."

"Am I meeting you in another plane?"

"Yes, you are talking to me in a different plane."

"I get that." At least I thought I did. "So, you are a being from another dimension, but you are also from the past, right?"

"Dimensions and the past can be synonymous, because you can access your past from the present. You can also experience your future in the present. There is no easy way to explain this in words. It is an experience to be multidimensional. Explaining and experiencing are not the same. But it is the simplest way to put it. When you allow yourself to experience yourself as a multidimensional being, you witness those things that you have not witnessed before. You live in a three-dimensional world and when you think of it as the only reality, you witness what you witness. Once you shift the perception of yourself as a multidimensional being, you are able to experience yourself beyond the three dimensions."

"Are there other beings in those other dimensions, and, if so, who are they and how do I see them?"

"Yes, there are other beings. There are beings of light, who work in the frequency of God's energy. Then there are also your forefathers, your ancestors whom you can witness, and there are many more. They come in many forms and when you are ready and finish your lessons, you will either be able to feel, see and hear them."

"Just like I am hearing and seeing you?"

"Yes, just like you see, hear and feel me."

"How do I see these beings of light?" This concept intrigued me.

"You just ask...say that you want to see them."

"That's it?" I was surprised.

"Yes, that is it. Once you have asked, you just have to wait for your request to be manifested. Once you ask, it will be given. This is the law of miracles."

"So pretty much whatever I want, I can ask for...and it will be manifested?"

"Yes, pretty much anything can be manifested. However, I recommend that you are conscious in your asking. When you are conscious and clear in your asking, your asking will be manifested. Realize you are accountable for these manifestations."

"What do you mean?" I asked.

"You are manifesting things every day without realizing or being conscious through your thoughts. Your mind is no different than your body. You become what you feed it. When you nourish your body with the right things, your body flourishes. Similarly, when you feed your mind good thoughts, good outcomes are meant to be."

"So, whatever I ask is what will be given?" I asked. "If I think good thoughts then the outcomes will be good, and vice versa?"

"Pretty much," the Lion smiled slightly. "At this juncture, you humans have arrived at a place in the ascension where you have been through a lot as humanity and you carry generations of suppression in several forms. You automatically carry those thought forms. Don't get me wrong, some of the things that come from previous generations may sound very good. For example, you say, 'no pain no gain.' It points to the fact, that you must endure pain to see good in life. That is not true."

This idea confused me. "Could you please expand on that?"

"For example, your father told you that if you work hard, you can achieve anything, right?"

"Yes, he did," I nodded. "But here's the thing, my father was successful, and I still believe he worked hard and hence became successful."

"No doubt your father worked hard, but how about a maid who cleans houses? Isn't she working hard? She may clean two to three houses every day to meet her needs. You mean to say she is not working hard? Do you think she should continue cleaning more houses? See this 'work hard' thing is messed up. You are given several gifts. Your mind's eye is one of them. You are a unique being in a unique body. In this unique body, you come with unique gifts. You are born to express and share those gifts. Those gifts go unnoticed or laughed at most likely because you are unable to make a living out of those gifts, except for the so called 'lucky few.' You have been taught and trained not to pursue your gifts. Even worse, you are taught to discard your gifts. 'Work hard' is a mantra for the masses. It was a created structure to earn money and keep a few people on Earth wealthy. Money, a worthless piece of paper, has been made a God. It is worshipped by humanity and every existence is tied to it. People forgo their gifts just to sustain life. Even then, a large segment of the population is not sustained by their earnings. It is a constant battle to bring home what you call 'the dough.' Some have money in excess, some work all their life to create that excess, and some struggle day in and day out just to meet their bare minimum needs. This is part of the imbalance that has been caused by man. There have been several lies perpetrated around money. None of them are pretty. In fact, they are ugly lies to hide ugly truths."

The great Lion's head shook back and forth with sadness and frustration. "The body you were born with has come here to experience your true self—your gifted self, the self that is self-sufficient in every way possible, the self that is living in a paradise of abundance. You are created to experience divinity here on Earth. You have come here to experience divinity in human form. Yes, you have God within you. You are an aspect of God, just like any other creation on Earth.

"You can see aspects of divinity in all things when you see through the soul's eye, the third eye. When you see through the soul, you are able to heal anything and everything around you. If you see something that is unfair, you can see through your mind's eye the perfect vision for healing the situation. You are a self-contained temple. Your heart connected to your soul houses memories that are beyond your recognition. It remembers many things that you may not know in your current form. Your heart is a beautiful violin, playing the tune that you like to hear. The better the tunes you play, the better your life's song will be. Your heart feeds your soul. Your soul aches to feel the whole you. It is so excited to be in your body. It doesn't want any other body except the one you inhabit because this is the body that it has chosen. It is like going to a store and customizing a body. That is what your soul did. Before it inhabited your body, it knew that this was the body it wanted. It couldn't wait to see through your eyes, listen through your ears, sing the tunes of your heart, feel the air on your skin, feel the touch of your loved ones, experience all the sensory nerves and have the experiences with which you have been gifted."

The Lion's head was no longer shaking. Articulating the soul's journey into its chosen body had shifted his mood. He seemed completely at peace again.

"If you ever look at your body and reprimand it, remember you are insulting yourself and your soul. If you ever ask, 'Why this body?' stop and think how cruel you are to yourself. If you ever look at yourself and wish for a different color of eyes, a different texture of hair, a different set of lips...stop and think, because you are insulting your soul. Nothing good comes out of insulting your soul. You are not you, you see, you are your soul and beyond. Your soul implanted itself in your body knowing fully well, this was the holy land it would inhabit. Yes, your body is a holy land, so do not insult it with ugly words, gestures or thoughts. If only you understood the impact these insults have had on your body and soul. You have been taught who and what it means to be beautiful. It is all a lie. It is a perpetrated lie. The categories of beauty are very limited through your human eyes. Do you think my lionesses compare themselves to each other to see who is more beautiful than the other? Do you think we lions compare ourselves to each other to see who has a better six pack?" The Lion chuckled at the thought.

"You may think we lions don't have the sense of beauty. Guess what? You are sorely wrong. We know beauty beyond your rules and regulations. You worship a few for their beauty. That is your limited view. Seeing through your misaligned soul, your view is limited. It is also mixed with judgments, opinions and lies. The lies you inherited from your society, a society that is limited in its viewpoint. I encourage you to stop seeing beauty through these lenses. They have not been cleaned for a long time and have been touched by many who do not or did not care for their own souls. When you see through your soul's eyes, you see the perfect beauty that your soul chose. Your soul's sole purpose in this lifetime is to embody this temple that is a holy land and enjoy its gifts and fruits. When you see your body through the soul, you are able to see yourself in all your perfection. When you are able to see yourself in your perfection, you become the reflection of the perfection that you see through your soul. What you see through this reflection is your *light* body."

Feeling as if he had completed his lesson, the Lion stopped to see how I was handling all this new information.

"This is all pretty wonderful," I said to the Lion. "However, we still need to be fed, clothed and sheltered. We need money for our existence."

"I hope you are not including yourself in that statement."

"No," I said, though I felt a bit unsure. "No, I am not including myself." I knew that's what the Lion wanted to hear, but I didn't know if I fully believed it myself.

"Well, were you able to pursue your true passions because you had a lot of money?"

"Well..." I stammered, "sometimes...but...not always."

"Then, money is not what stops you from enjoying your gifts, right?"

"Not always, I guess."

"So, you agree it is not just money that stops people from enjoying their divine gifts. Money is only one reason people don't pursue their passions. There are many other reasons, tied to man's suppression of his true self. We have talked about a few already."

I nodded in agreement.

"Yes, at this point in your society money is still important for survival. However, you can shift that and keep marching towards paradise. When you shift the reality you are in, what is to come will shift as well. See, you have lived too long believing that what you experience each day is life. You have not had the opportunity to have your life led through your soul's choices. When you live a life led through the choices of your soul, you release the current realities of your life. You will witness a new world, a new you, a new reality, and a new adventure. This adventure will be beyond your wildest dreams. It will be filled with the amazing gifts you came here to experience. You will come back to experience those gifts, lifetime after lifetime. You have had a lot of disappointments, but they need not march with you into the paradise. Part of your learning is to trust that you will be taken care of. You will be taken care of by the light, the beings of light, the wisdom of self, the wisdom of Mother Earth, and more. You are just here in this lifetime to experience this all over as in any other lifetime."

"How many lifetimes do you think I have had?" I asked, leaning in.

"Honestly, I have no idea. But consider that you are much more ancient than you think. See, I am living with you in my lifetime. Yet, you are the same man born into a different lifetime. We have known each other through many lifetimes, hence there is a sense of familiarity between us. Like I told you, our meeting is not an accident. You and I are meant to be part of this expansive plan. We are meeting now in two different lifetimes. Isn't it crazy?"

"Yes." I tried to wrap my mind around what the Lion was saying. "About this coming back lifetime after lifetime, why is that?"

"Good question. So, let's say you went to a paradise that was filled with so much beauty and vastness and you were told that you have 80 years to see it, but it will take 800 years to see everything? Since you need to see everything in this lifetime, is it fair to give such limited time to experience all the beauty?"

"No," I shook my head. "That does not seem fair."

"Consider that so far in all your lifetimes you have been unable to experience this paradise to the fullest. You still have things to see and lessons to learn, but you are banned from coming into this paradise again. You only received one lifetime and your lessons are not complete. To top it off, you have unfinished business. Is it fair to give you only one chance to finish this business? Is it fair to give only one chance to any being? Isn't it everyone's birth right to be given chances?"

"Yeah but giving our society too many chances is not necessarily a good thing."

"Isn't it funny that you, having come into this paradise many times and in many forms, have lost your compassion to give chances to others. By your words, you imply that some do not deserve a chance. You have determined that some deserve a chance and others do not. Do you see a pattern here? It starts from the self. If you don't see your own worth and beauty, you will not see others as worthy or beautiful. What I am talking about is inherent worth and beauty, not the one that society has fabricated. Each soul has a cycle, and it may differ from one soul to another. Until your soul cycle is complete, you will continue to be reborn. You will be reborn to fulfill your dreams and experience your gifts and lessons to the fullest. No one can stop this cycle. Even your own current beliefs cannot stop this process. It is a divine right to be born. It is your divine right to die. It is your divine right to incarnate in different bodies. You need not get attached to this body. Would you ever want to wear the same clothing again and again? Why would you want to come into the same body? You are born in many forms, many genders, many races and many religions. Do you see the absurdity of your current view?"

"Yes, I see it now," I nodded. "Could you tell me how it works if a person is born a murderer or as someone who has done harm to another?"

"Let us take this example: one is a murderer and the other the victim. If you are given only one lifetime, then you are just a murderer or a victim—that's it. You are not to be given another opportunity to be born and have another experience, so your soul is either a murderer or a victim. You are probably thinking, 'That's it? No, that is cruel!' You're right, that would be the cruelest thing you could do to any soul. Why should any soul be stuck with the title of murderer or victim?

"Remember, each person takes several body forms. In some bodies, you have been good; in others, you have been bad. You have done good deeds and ugly deeds. For instance, when you have harmed another, you may be born again to have the same experience that you caused another. You are both a murderer and a victim. I have made it sound simple in order for you to understand, but I want to reiterate that life is beyond what you can comprehend. You have come here to learn your truth, not another's truth—not your father's truth, not your mother's truth, not your neighbor's truth, not your society's truth. You have come here to learn your truth. Your truth is resonant through your wisdom, through your soul, through your heart, through your being. You…"

"But isn't there a universal truth?" I interrupted.

"There is, but you have to listen to your experiences, and those experiences come from lifetimes of choices and lessons, with more to come. No one but you will know your truth. Your DNA is encoded with your soul's choices."

I was hopeful. "So, do you think I can shift my DNA?"

"Yes, I do," the Lion nodded. "Another of several lies perpetrated among your society is that you are born with a certain trait or inadequacy or supremacy over others. That is absolutely not true. You can shift your DNA encodings through your wisdom, through good thoughts, good intentions, and good deeds."

"Can you shift genetic illnesses?" I wondered.

"Yes, you can. You have been lied to that you cannot be cured of certain illnesses. You are told that almost nothing is curable unless you take medicine that you become dependent on your whole life. In the future, this misconception, this perpetrated lie, will not stand. You are born to be healthy. You are destined to be healthy. You are supposed to be glowing, and have healthy skin, teeth and eyes. This is the gift that has been given to you every time you are born. You are this amazing creature in this amazing body in which your soul rejoices. You soul has come to enjoy this experience, and it cannot be otherwise. You can heighten your senses by being present in every moment and experience the joy, the challenges, the beauty that is in every lifetime. You have not come here to experience just good or bad. You have come here to experience both. In fact, there is no good or bad; there are only experiences and lessons. Mankind has given them titles of good and bad but try going a day where you do not categorize one or the other. Just for the sake of play, try it. It is pretty fun. See, everything is made up in your society. These things were made up as a result of misalignment. It does not have to stay this way. Life can be aligned to humanity's true path when led by the soul. The beauty of each individual soul is found as it converges and diverges with other souls along the path. It is a beautiful song and dance that is orchestrated through the merging of souls. You come together with another soul to learn. You diverge once the lessons have been learned. It is that simple. Thank everyone who has come upon your path. Their presence was crucial to your growth. You will continue to meet many other souls, new and old."

The great Lion stretched, for we had been talking for a long time. "Every soul and being have their own experiences. Some souls are new and some old. The old souls may seem wiser, but younger souls bring their inexperience to experience life through the body. Young souls are as valuable as old souls. It is just that they are here for a different purpose. Every soul has a different purpose and goal. So, one cannot compare the life choices and lessons with one another, as it would not be a fair comparison."

The Lion paused and looked me straight in the eyes. "Cherish your life, man, for it is a gift. Cherish your experiences for they are readily available for your soul's growth. Cherish your time upon this Earth. Allow yourself to experience every aspect of life, every aspect of creation. Dream. Dream little dreams, big dreams, dreams of all sizes. No dream is better or less than another. Do those things that make your soul happy. Do those things that make your heart sing. Smile upon others as if you have known them all your life. Give a shoulder to your neighbor who is not your family. You have known him or her before you were born. You have known your neighbor much longer than you realize. Knock on his door to see if he is okay. Give a hand to someone who has fallen and give a push to someone who wants to swing. Ask someone to push your swing and laugh with joy. Love with an open heart. Love *through* your heart—this is the love that heals your heart and others' hearts. Fall in love every day. Fall in love with yourself every day. Fall in love with your neighbors every day. Fall in love with every creation on Mother Earth every day. Wake up and be thankful for being born in this wonderful body that constantly supports your life. Talk to your body. Be kind to it and give it loving thoughts, healing thoughts, and a loving touch. Hug yourself, your body. It is a gift that has been bestowed upon you to host your soul. It is a temple. Your soul loves your body, so who cares what anybody else thinks? If you cannot see your own beauty, who else will? Why ask another about your body or beauty? Ask yourself, ask your soul, ask your wisdom. You will hear whispers of love from your wisdom, your soul. When your mind tells you otherwise, thank it for being on this journey and tell it you are handing the reins over to your wisdom, to your soul. Tell your mind that you have decided to listen to your soul instead. Train your mind to surrender to your wisdom and to your heart's desires. You mind has a role; it is not to be suppressed. However, your mind is going to have a new role to bow to your heart, where the light resides. The mind's job is to salute the heart, the sanctum of the temple in which your soul resides. Your heart has carefully placed your soul inside it, to feed, house and cherish it. How could you ever hate your body, knowing this? Your inner sanctum is the sacred place where your soul resides, vibrating in its fullness and seeking your love to nourish and grow it. Worship your body, for it is you. Worship your true beauty, your heart, your limbs, your eyes, your being—your being that has chosen to be born in this lifetime and has chosen to be here on Earth, for it is paradise at this moment. You play an inherent role in this paradise. Just by the virtue of being, your presence is acknowledged. You may not know why you are here, but you will be led to that understanding by loving hands.

"My wisdom, the Lion's wisdom, asks every human that is born to see their beauty, the beauty of their temple, the temple that the soul inhabits. Your body is a holy body; don't discard or obsess over it. Just be with your body and love it in its entirety. Love your faults and your gifts equally. You were born to give yourself plenty of opportunities to grow. Be wise about the opportunities that are given and be open to learning through these opportunities. Keep your heart and soul wide open to all possibilities through your gift—your body—the temple in which your soul resides. Trust your body. Trust your soul. Trust your heart. Trust your wisdom. You have an army of angels and light beings awaiting to help you."

With this, the great Lion extended his large paws to me. "Hold my paws. I am happy to lead you to the Lion's den. Don't be afraid. I don't bite." The Lion roared a hearty laugh because he saw the flash of fear in my eyes and knew what being led to the lion's den meant in my world. It would not end in a good outcome. His eyes, though, were full of warmth and joy. "Come and play with us, with my cubs," he continued. "They are adorable. I am not saying this because they are mine. You should see them to make up your own mind. If you stay over, you can cuddle with my cubs while you sleep. They are soft and cute. They are mine and my pride. Please help me save my cubs and my pride. This is all I have. This is what I came to experience, just as you. I would like to see my legacy continued, our legacy continued. I don't think I can do this by myself. I need your help. If you are scared to hold my paws, hold my cub's paws. You will feel the love I feel for them. My adorable little cubs are here waiting to hold the legacy of our paradise. If I am lost, you will lose a sliver of this paradise. You may think, what is a sliver? But trust me, in the grand scheme of things, every sliver lost has an impact. You don't want that, do you? Hold my cubs in your vision along with other visions you have. I request you to do this on my behalf, on your behalf, and on our behalf. Help us save this legacy that is at risk of being lost. Let's take the paw of the cub and save its future, save our future. Remember you are not doing me a favor, you are assisting in restoring our future together. There is enough for all of us to share. The growth of my population will not impact yours negatively. Yes, the future is just going to look different, which may be beyond your comprehension at the moment. But it is going to look better. Come and join us."

Lovingly yours, inviting you to hold the tender paws of my cubs, inviting you to cuddle my cubs and feel the love, the love of humanity, the love of all.

I am signing off for the day to enjoy watching the cubs play. Unfortunately, we don't serve hot dogs and beer here in this paradise. I hope that won't stop you from witnessing this beauty. Who could resist watching the cubs play even without a beer?

Joyfully watching the cubs play,
Man

CHAPTER 11: BEAUTY

"I love this paradise—this paradise created by my mother, Mother Earth, the Supreme Mother. She is a humble Goddess who embodies beauty and divinity. I have played here as a cub and my cubs play here. My legacy is here. It is only here, nowhere but here. Oh, how I enjoy this beauty, which is all I have known in my life. The vast lands I see in front of my eyes, created in fullness, in perfection, in beauty, may all be gone one day. I have the freedom to roam the earth now. In the future, my neighbors and friends won't have the same freedom. It will be usurped by the usurper of souls who SoulD the planet.

"I am sad. Why was I given this information? I was happy not knowing it. Ignorance was a blessing that I enjoyed. Why did my bliss have to be ruined? One day, my land, my mother land, my father land, all that I have known, may be gone."

The Lion's head drooped as he slowly paced across the soft dirt path of his homeland.

"I see my cubs and lionesses playing and enjoying this garden, this paradise. They are oblivious to the information I have been given. I cannot imagine my cubs not being able to have this life here in this beautiful land that has been created with such care and thoughtfulness. All Mother Earth has done is care for her children, who will one day produce careless children, who at one point in the future will have SoulD out. How am I going to stop this? It feels like a huge burden to me. I enjoy my time with my family, but every time I look at them these days, it reminds me of the ominous days that are to come. I know it is a long time from now, yet it will come. That thought is unbearable to me. How could man hoard, plunder and pillage in such a way, so blindly, so uncaringly. Does he not understand that his own legacy will be affected by his actions?

"Why was I chosen to share this wisdom with man? Why wasn't an elephant, a giraffe, a zebra, a rhino or any of my other friends chosen? Why have I been asked to bear this burden—a burden I can't even share? Why me? Why me? Why me? Oh God, I sound like a man now. I sound like a victim. This is bad. I sound like the future man. Okay, I guess that is the showstopper of my pity party. But you do understand what I am talking about, right? I know you cannot see this paradise, so let me walk you through it so you will understand.

Maybe it will change your mind. This paradise that I see in front of me is a paradise such as you have never witnessed. It is a paradise that is never ending and everlasting in its beauty. This beauty was made for us to walk on, play on, feed on, sleep on...and on and on. This everlasting beauty is breathtaking. I am able to appreciate it even more now that I have seen the future, which is a dry, barren land with only patches of lush green. As if the patches were left out as tiny painful reminders of the past.

"You have to see what I see. Words can't describe it, but I will try my best. There are animals everywhere. You, too, are part of the animal kingdom. If you think you are not an animal, please save it. You are only different from us, like a zebra is to me, a lion. You can call yourselves whatever you want, but you are still part of the animal kingdom. Everywhere I see, there are lush trees filled with flowers and fruits of all kinds. The breeze is filled with the smells and scents of the fruits, the flowers, the soil, the water, the manure, the flesh, and everything. This is what we are used to in paradise. Every one of us has a duty. It is not a checklist we follow every morning. It is a duty that is encoded in our DNA, and in our wisdom. Our wisdom flows from our DNA, which has all the information needed to maintain this paradise. See, we are our Mother Earth's keepers. She has been very trusting in surrendering this paradise to us with no doubt in her mind that it will be taken care of, this paradise that she so dutifully and wonderfully created. See, I only told you about the animals that you know of. There are a lot of animals, amphibians, birds, bugs and more that you have not ever seen in your lifetime, or for generations before you. We are all beings and creations that take care of the cleanliness of this paradise. We are not careless as you are in your time. You eat and throw away, and then assume someone will clean up the mess you've made. In my time, we are not so careless. We cannot afford to be careless, since we are the keepers of this paradise that is my home. Each being inherently keeps this paradise impeccable. We recycle everything. Everything that is taken for consumption is consumed in its entirety. The leftovers are eaten by someone else, and whatever is left over by that someone is eaten by someone else…and on, and on.

"The bugs, the wonderful bugs—the bees, beetles, worms, and spiders—all have their place, too. They are more detail-oriented than us, and their job is to clean deeper. No one cleans paradise like the bugs. They work hard, cleaning paradise, for all of us. No one here fights about who will clean up. We all do it, as keepers of Mother Earth. She is so amazing, our mother, our beloved mother. She has laid out detailed instructions for all of us, and the beauty is we don't have to work at it every day to understand our role. She doesn't have to come and pester us to clean up. Call her lazy or wise, whatever you want. She laid out all the information for us, and let us do our duty, never having to interfere. She is not an interfering mother—loving, for sure—but without interference. She is a laid-back mother who is diligent and thoughtful with her creations. Did I mention she is also beautiful and wise, compassionate, loving, creative, and kind? I can go on and on about her, because I love her beyond anything. She is my mother who provides unconditional love for all her beings and creations. You have heard a lot about Mother Earth. I can talk about her without tiring, for she has worked tirelessly to create this paradise for us."

I had been listening quietly to the Lion in my dream, listening to this great creature express his love for his Mother Earth. Though I was attentive, the Lion seemed to be talking more to himself, than to me. Finally, he addressed me directly, "Do you know the one thing that I most missed when I came to your time? I know you are in your dream listening to this. I missed the colors. Your time is so lackluster. Yes, you have big expansive cities and tall buildings and so on that look great. But trust me, it is no comparison to the paradise that we live in. Yours was created by you, and I admire your creativity, but paradise was lost in your creations. In your creation, not everyone gets taken care of. It is an unbalanced creation. See, we know we can be creative in paradise without destroying Mother Earth. If only I told you what was lost to build the things you have built, you wouldn't believe me, or maybe you would ignore me. Here is the thing, you have a choice: you can listen to my stories of my paradise, our paradise, or you can ignore them. The choice is yours. If you don't listen, you will lose out big time—not just on paradise, but on yourself as well. You are sorely missed being part of this co-creative world and as part of the animal kingdom in this paradise. You have put yourself higher than the animal kingdom, even though you are part of it. The problem is, you think you are better than us. That is where your problem started. At least that is what my wisdom is telling me, and my wisdom is never wrong."

It was painful to hear what the Lion was saying. How could we have sunk so far and veered so far off course?

"How could man shift this beautiful reality so dramatically?" I asked the Lion.

"During your day, take time to focus on paradise through my eyes," the Lion replied in almost a whisper. "By being in paradise, you can recreate it."

I nodded in agreement. "Do you think I should do this every day? I do have moments of doubts though if this will help. Sometimes I feel it isn't real this envisioning."

"Yes," the Lion said patiently. "Remember, everything around you is an illusion anyway. If it is an illusion, you may as well create your own reality."

"If it is all an illusion, why bother at all?" I asked, still perplexed.

"Because consciousness is real, love is real." The Lion looked at me directly to see if I understood.

I let this idea sink in. "So, you are saying, even though I as a person I am an illusion, the love I create is real?"

"Yes," he smiled, "the unconditional love you create is real. That is the life force that creates the universe. When Mother Earth created you and me, she did not map us out as one better than the other. That is not how unconditional love works. Her unconditional love, which means respect for all, is what sustains paradise. This unconditional love is what creates beauty. This beauty that you see in front of your eyes was created through Mother Earth's unconditional love. Anything and everything can be created and destroyed because creation and destruction are Mother Nature's natural cycle."

I was beginning to understand, but I still had questions. "If creation and destruction are part of Mother Nature's natural cycle, then why is it wrong for man to have destroyed paradise?"

"That is where you are wrong," the Lion explained. The destruction I am talking about is part of Mother Nature's cycle of life. You are born at one point and die at one point. You can't keep inhabiting Mother Earth forever, there are other souls eager to be born. You pave the way for this new birth through your death. You make room for new life to come in, an action that is part of unconditional love, the love of Mother Earth. The destruction man has caused is not the same. Man pushed every creature and every creation away in order to keep all the resources for himself. You see, not only did you destroy most of the creations that were born through this unconditional love, but you also pushed your own kind to keep more for the few that would be wealthy themselves. This destruction comes from greed."

I nodded. I now fully understood what he was saying.

"You took wonderful concepts given to you by Mother Earth, and used them for destruction of the planet, the animals, the ocean life, the rodents, the bugs, the birds. What's funny, is you created a recycling system that is far inferior to Mother Nature's version…and then you wonder why it is not working. You put this broken system in place and then tried to put bandages on it to fix its many problems. When that didn't work, you placed more bandages on top of the original bandages. The places that fester with wounds, stench and flies, those are the ones you left for the people who can't afford anything better. Those flies that you think are bad are actually working hard to clean up everything for you because it is their job. Even worse, you wiped out creations that could have helped with the cleanup of the rotting things around you. This gave rise to a new kind of population, since you had killed the original population that had kept this population under control. As an example, take rats, who do the clean-up work. You keep killing the rats because you think they are dirty.

This creates a never-ending problem because you have veered away from a plan that was working beautifully. In your short-sightedness, you cut short the supply of the food systems for those bugs and rodents who eat human garbage and do the cleanup. You then blame those bugs and rodents, saying they are the ones causing illnesses. You destroy your natural food cycle, and then drag us into this inferior food cycle that you have created. You have destroyed our habitat to create a false kingdom for yourself. Now, you are unhappy in your kingdom and you wonder why. To mask your unhappiness, you take happy pills, which suppress your emotions. To make those happy pills, you further destroy the environment. I hope you understand why you exhaust me. In fact, you have exhausted me of every available resource that was at my feet. Then, you ask me innocently why my species attacks you. Through my wisdom, I see what you did to my future generations, my cubs, my brothers and sisters. We will feel the pain you have inflicted upon us for many generations—all for your own greed, your own pride, you own ego. My beautiful pride was lost to save your false pride. I will have nothing left and even the little I will have left, you slowly try to usurp. Now, I wish you would ask me why my kind attacks you."

I shifted uncomfortably in my bed, as I knew the Lion was right.

"The violence you have inflicted on us is unbearable. The violence you have inflicted on yourself is unfathomable. Yet, you have the audacity to ask me if I will attack you. If we do attack you, we do so out of fear, to protect this paradise that is lost. You have left us only with the lackluster cities you have created with the shining resources that you plundered carelessly from Mother Earth, never thinking about the future of the planet, the future of our legacy, the future of our Mother's legacy. Who are you? Who bore you? You bear no resemblance to the man the Supreme Mother once bore.

"You have a lot of work to do—not just physical work, but conscious work, too. When I say conscious work, reach for your soul. Lead a life of truth and follow a path of wisdom, a path of awareness, a path of love, unconditional love for self. On this path, there will be healing for the planet. On this path, the dream of paradise still exists on the other side of the veil. The more you dream about paradise, the more it will come into existence. Yes, you are that powerful. It is the divine gift you lost, your own power, when you separated yourself from us. The power you lost is so self-reliant. It has no room for judgments, opinions or greed. I honestly believe that your greed led to the judgments and opinions from which you now suffer. You are man, part of the animal kingdom, full of life, just like any other being on Earth. Feel us—yes, you can feel us—as we are all part of the same creation. Mother Earth implanted a chip in you that contains benevolent thoughts and actions. This unconditional love is benevolent. Violence is an act of forgetting this love for all creation."

"I am recruiting you to join the army that can save this planet. You won't need a uniform, guns or ammunitions. You just have to bring your love for Mother Earth. You need not know how to save the planet, that is not the goal. The goal is to save our legacy. Let's hold paws, yes paws, your paws and my paws and the giraffe's hooves. Let's let a bug sit on your shoulder—don't kill it. It doesn't have a paw, but it is innocent and wants to join our army of peace. We will create new meaning for the word 'army.' We won't plot and kill. Instead, we will create new friends and families. We will be an army for good. As we grow, let us take up the task of erasing borders and boundaries. Let us topple any plans of building a wall that separates us. Let us not be scared of each other. Yes, we are different, but we are also alike. We all eat. We all poop. We all fart, don't we? If you don't, you should see a doctor—that is not good. We are born; we die. We all follow this cycle.

"You humans are so strange. Not only have you separated yourselves from us, you have even separated yourselves from each other. I heard you have something called race. Is that right? It is like saying, me, the Lion from Serengeti, is different from the lion in the Kalahari Desert. He looks a little different than me, but that does not make him different than me. He eats, poops and farts, too."

The Lion noticed my discomfort with this last topic but continued.

"What is this thing with you guys, that disgusts you about poop? If you scrunch your nose, you know our poop gets recycled by Mother Nature for better things, right? It turns into dust and eventually becomes part of the recycling system. It is the best fertilizer for the soil, and helps paradise flourish, yet you scrunch up your nose at it. You have a lot to learn, especially about poop, poop, poop, poop—the best manure found on Earth. I heard you control your farts. Are you serious? You know that it has to come out, right, as part of Mother Nature's recycling system. If you fart, it is a good thing. Do you understand? I know you are embarrassed about it, but it has a purpose. I bet you have medicine so you never have to fart, or you are sold something that will make your farts smell better. Do you realize it is unhealthy to curb bodily functions? We are going to keep you away from the animal kingdom, until you learn to fart, and fart freely. Farting is like the natural air freshener of paradise. If someone is not farting or pooping on a given day, we know something is wrong.

"What is wrong with you, man? You hold in your emotions. You don't cry. You don't fart. You are filled with shame and guilt. Everything Mother Nature instilled in you—your very existence—you suppress. When you fill your body with unshed tears, with gases that need to escape, with shame, guilt and judgment, how do you expect to heal, mentally or physically? You think I am making fun of your fart? No, not really—well, in some ways, yes. I love teasing you about your habits, but there is more to it. By holding in an emotion or bodily function, what do you think you are doing to yourself? It is an unloving act. You could destroy your physical body. You think I am exaggerating? Well, you are welcome to think that. Every small emotion and bodily function counts; by ignoring or suppressing it, you are not serving yourself.

"There are so many things I can make fun of that I keep getting distracted. Going back to race...seriously, you think my mate from Kalahari is different than me? You've got to be kidding me! What is wrong with you people? I have heard you use the phrase, 'Don't behave like an animal.' Maybe you *should* behave like an animal. Teasing you has become the best part of my life. It pulls me out of my moodiness about the future. Seriously, you guys are too funny. You think you can usurp everything and live a comfortable life. Don't even come near me, if you have thoughts of making a dime off of me. You will not see the end of that wrath. You are listening to me, right?"

I nodded vigorously. What a Lion! I thought. He is so teasingly amusing. I thought he was one of those who was imparting wisdom on more spiritual things, now he is going to have me thinking about poop and farts all day, instead of unconditional love, beauty and all the fancy words he talked to me about earlier.

"Seriously, you had to end our deep conversation with poop and farts?" I said dryly.

"Chill, it is ok," the Lion smiled. "We have had several days of serious talk. I just wanted to add some levity. Live a little, will you? Isn't that what your friends say? Let's laugh a little. But you do understand that you guys are funny, right? What do you call it? ROFL, right? You know, for us it would be .... Rolling on the Dirt Floor Laughing"

I have to admit, there was more levity today than any other day that I'd spent with the Lion. Still, he has given me a lot to think about. One thing gets clearer every day: paradise has to be saved. I want to listen to Mother Earth's guidance, not my birth mother's. I want to join the army to restore the beauty of the lost paradise that I am aching to be part of. This paradise is my Mother's lap—the lap that nourishes, boards and feeds me. This lap is filled with unconditional love—love of self and others. This paradise knows no boundaries, no borders, no race, no color, no greed. It is where every creation is respected for being part of paradise. I know the Lion was joking about somethings, but don't you think his assertion about race was true? We have completely made up what is beautiful, and what is not. If we made it up, can't we unmake it? Let's start unmaking it. We have been making up stuff that is harmful to the paradise and to all of us.

Talking about paradise, I am reminded about my own body. It always does its job and when I ignore it, it has ailments. These ailments come because I have veered away from the diet of Mother Earth, the rich diet concocted by her just for us. She made us all eat different things on the planet as a system of checks and balances. If all living things ate grass, it would be an imbalance and such a waste of nature. If we all ate animals, that would not serve the recycling system. She is a worthy mother who created worthy creatures who are entitled to live their true life.

I am joining the army, are you? I am here to recruit you. I come in peace. I come in love. I come in forgiveness. I come in kindness. I come in compassion. I come with the wisdom of my Mother Earth, which teaches unity in nature as well as in the animal and plant kingdoms. She is eagerly waiting for her children to come together and play. She is distressed by wounds that have festered in her children. She is ready to heal her children.

She is stepping forward and reaching out her hands to inspire others to join the army—the army of peace and love, the army of creation, the army of the animals, birds, trees, plants, bugs and rodents. All are welcome to join her army. If you have lost a limb, don't be worried, you have a place here, all you need is love. A lost limb can be replaced with love. I know you may be wounded, but this army is here to heal you. Your mere presence in the army will heal you and us. Your presence is highly recommended and appreciated. Don't worry, there is plenty to eat and drink. You will not starve in this army. There is only one army, and it belongs to us and our Mother Earth, our Divine Mother, our Supreme Mother.

My dear Lion, my brother from the same mother, I am holding your paws with love. I know no fear, and I request the same of you. Do not fear us. We are healing and you are healing. I envision paradise as you guided that is an army of creatures living and coexisting peacefully. I envision the one and only army that Mother Earth created to nourish her creations."

The Lion nodded in agreement, showing his pride in me, his student. He encouraged me to continue with a nod.

In this army, we come in love and peace. Join us! Our perk is unconditional love—for self and the planet. We love you and welcome you. We welcome you with open paws—paws that are soft as Mother Earth's loving lap. We are here to restore the beauty of paradise, and the love for which we ache. Our army serves the best food, clean water, abundant shade, clean air from the backyard of our Mother Earth. She offers an abundant kitchen flowing with nourishment for every creature. It is a well-kept and tidy kitchen, for we have a 24/7 staff that works on our behalf tirelessly.

Come and join us! We promise you won't be disappointed. In fact, you will love it here. I know you are hesitant to leave your shiny offices, but trust me, paradise is much better. Its open air smells the best. Ask our Lion, he will tell you. Come out and enjoy the fresh air. Feel it on your skin. While you are enjoying it, please consider joining our army. We come with no lies and no guns. Here, take my hands, and hold it. Join us on this wonderful journey to march towards the paradise that I see through the Lion's eyes. Come and enjoy the beauty. It is for all of us to share. I don't want to keep it to myself, for I have tried to hoard it. But through the Lion's mouth, I have learned the wisdom of sharing. We march, march, march, march with love. Join our march to paradise, a paradise created for us, by us, and the creatures and creations of Mother Earth.

Envisioning paradise through the Lion's eyes,
Man witnessing the beauty

CHAPTER 12: ESCAPE

I wish to escape. I am wise with the knowledge of paradise as it used to be. The Lion taught me that time is an illusion. But if time is an illusion and it doesn't exist, why can't I escape to paradise? It is as if I exist here and I exist there, too. I believe the man that I saw in my dream, in the Lion's time, is me. If he is me, and I am him, then I could escape into his reality. I could bury this life like it never existed in this time.

If only I had known all this before, I would have escaped. Could I have escaped before I was born? Does this even make sense, since I existed in that timeline anyway? How could I be in two places at once? Is this even possible? Well, I guess it is. The man I saw in my dream is me—the wiser me who has embraced ancient wisdom. Today, we think we are the most advanced in human history. I think we are wrong. I should say I 'learned' that we are wrong, rather than I 'think' that we are wrong. Civilization today is considered very advanced. Let us look at what it means to be advanced. I am not saying that there is no truth to our advancement; I am merely stating that what we think to be advancements are actually quite rude. We simply assume that everything and everyone who came before us didn't have the capability or capacity to create amazing things like we do. We think they were primitive. Science has proven they were primitive. Yet, the ancient wisdom that I have experienced is beyond measure. You may not believe me, and I don't plan to try to convince you, but ancient wisdom is extraordinary. I want you to think about how we define "advancement."

Life has gotten better in some areas, but worse in others. In our time, we don't kill with a sword. Rather, humanity is killed by things that are slower to kill—like poisons injected into our blood. These poisons that you can't see are fed to us generation after generation. But if you can't see it with your physical eyes, it doesn't exist, right? That's what we believe as humans. Out of sight, out of mind. Even worse, if it happens to others, we think it doesn't concern us or assume there is nothing we can do. Our parents have trained us to stay out of our neighbor's business. Still, there are rebels born among us. They stand up to everything and everyone. Sometimes their lives are made miserable and lies are perpetrated against them to try to silence them and cover up the lies of those who wish to silence them out of fear or ignorance.

We have gotten really good about covering up lies. We believe in lies and perpetuate them in many forms. You may not realize, but you belong to one or more of these categories, if you were born in this lifetime. We have been living in times of greed and hoarding. Anyone who is part of the Soul Trade, and claims they are part of a cause, is lying. It is like rocking the baby and pinching it, too. Everyone who looks at these people will think they are rocking a crying baby. It is an illusion, you see. Humanity is arriving at a juncture where truths are starting to be revealed. The mask is being peeled back slowly and steadily. Some wish to hold on to that mask and struggle to keep it, especially those who are part of the Soul Trade. Still, the lies perpetrated about humanity are slowly being revealed. The liars, who have been lying on a cushy mattress, are starting to feel uncomfortable on the very same mattress. It is starting to feel uncomfortable every day, as the mask is being peeled and the truth is being revealed.

Some, who have lost their soul to this Soul Trade, are in shock. They are unable to believe they have been lied to. The institutions humanity created to protect them are also a lie. The upper echelons, who are part of the elite, who consider themselves above all laws, are starting to become uncomfortable. They are not uncomfortable with their lies; they are uncomfortable about the peeling of the mask and the truth that is being revealed.

The decorative mask they wear is made out of their plundering, pillaging and raping of humanity—raping of Mother Earth, of her resources. As their mask is getting peeled back, your mask can't stay either. You can't wear a mask of victimization, ignorance and lies any longer. We are marching towards a just world where every creation is put back in its place in the ecosystem of Mother Earth. The days are now gone where you can be part of the Soul Trade and go back to your false kingdom, your false paradise. For those elites who are wearing this glittery mask, prepare for the mask to be peeled back to reveal the truth to humanity. The deep wisdom—clear as a sunny sky, deep as an ocean, pure as a raindrop— says that we are all one. This truth is coming to light. No one is different from the other. Since you are one, you are inherently rich with abundance. This abundance is more than what you can imagine. The mere gift that you are allowed to roam and live anywhere on Mother Earth and enjoy her inherent beauty is undeniable. Some of you who want to divide humanity are going to feel pretty uncomfortable, as well you should. Truth is uncomfortable when you have lived a lie for generations. The lies perpetrated against Mother Earth are now being revealed. We are marching towards the light. No longer will the peeling back of masks take place at the rate of a snail. Once the peeling has begun and humanity has started paying attention, the mask peels at a much faster rate. Forces beyond your comprehension are working to accelerate this change. You cannot see this through your naked eye. However, it's a lie to say that you are incapable of seeing these forces. These forces are gathering every creation on Mother Earth to join her peaceful army. This army comes in love, in forgiveness, in humbleness, in consciousness. These forces are ready to join you in providing the helping hand needed to uplift humanity. They are recruiting those who have lost their souls and those who are part of the Soul Trade. They will not ostracize those from the SoulD Trade. They are here to make us Soul'ed.

The divine forces come to you with this mantra: "I am SoulD. I am SoulD. I am SoulD." They are here with the mantra singing the melody, "We are SoulD. We are SoulD. We are SoulD." Unlike being Sould (soul sold), we are SoulD (Soul'ed). In claiming our soul through this melody, we can align our souls, our truth, our light. The light that glows within you can be realized. It does not matter whether you lost your soul to the Soul Trade or you were part of the Soul Trade. There is a light in your heart that is glowing like a candle in the dark. This candle may seem small in a big, dark room, but it is a flame that cannot be contained.

This flame will not burn your finger. Instead, it will soothe you, heal you, love you. It is the light that is glowing bright in your heart, in your soul, in your consciousness. It is a light that nothing can blow out. No matter how many souls you have traded in your life, the light seeks to make you stronger and stronger. The more you are not present, the stronger it seeks you. It seeks all souls equally. It is beautiful white light that is so powerful, so illuminant that you cannot keep ignoring it. Its strong presence compels you to join the army of peace and love. This light invites you to join the movement of peace, the movement of oneness with Mother Earth. It aligns you with her greater wisdom. In this wisdom, you can hear her laughter, her cries, her soft steps, her whispers. If you allow yourself to embrace this gift, you can even see her. You can see her in the eyes of every creation. You can feel her in the touch of every creature.

Her gentle presence cannot be ignored. The more you seek wisdom, the louder her melody can be heard. Her beautiful songs can be heard through the mountains, through the water, through the air. The echo of her songs can be heard for thousands of miles. Her soft penetrating voice echoes in the universe, a constant reminder of her place in the kingdom. She is a humble Goddess, who is here to serve us. She melts away in the light to reach every soul. She dissolves in the air to feel the beautiful skin of all people. She becomes one with the molecules of the water to touch every river bed. She is one with everything, everyone, and every creation. She has been eagerly waiting for you to march with all her children, for she misses the children who have forgotten her paradise. She is calling upon us all to join her—to join hands, hold paws, hold trunks, beaks, tails, and noses, to call upon the butterfly to sit upon your shoulder. Take this march with her wonderful army.

This army will be the most powerful army on Earth. It will be unconquerable. This army, which seeks out every creation in every nook and corner of the Earth, is gentle, kind and loving. It is an army that only knows peace. Any baggage you carry can be left behind, any wounds inflicted from your previous wars can be healed, any lies perpetrated can be dissolved when you are in this army, which comes with support beyond your comprehension. It is a new kind of army. It does not have a leader. It does not have ranks. It does not know borders. In fact, every border that this army finds will be erased and every race that has been separated will be invited to join together. There will be no perks to join this army, only love—the love of the creator, the love of Mother Earth, the love of humanity, the love of light, the love of creation, the love of the universe, the never ending expansive, unconditional love of one's self. This love you are being asked to step into is not dangerous. It does not explode or kill. It is a love that strengthens truth, rebuilds lost bonds, uncovers lost wisdom, gives life, reclaims the lost garden of paradise. Its only motto is to restore paradise, as the true kingdom, where everyone wears a crown, a dazzling crown that does not contain diamonds plundered with bloodied hands. This crown glows with a perfect light that can be witnessed far from our galaxy. This light that can be spotted from anywhere in the universe. In fact, Mother Earth will look like a ball of light from far above, since every creature wears this crown—from the ants to the rats to the beetles to the spiders to the grasshoppers to the lions to man. Everyone belongs to this kingdom, to the paradise. This crown that you wear will shine with your beauty and the beauty of others. This is an army worth joining. It comes in light and love. It is the best army in which anyone could serve. You think I am trying to recruit you? In fact, quite the opposite. I am merely sharing the joy I feel. If you come near this army, you will feel a tug in your heart. If you are hesitant, you will hear a buzz, a roar, as all of paradise's creations speak to you. See if you can resist. If you can resist, you are still caught in the illusion of the Soul Trade. I am only going to tell you once, then you can make up your mind: the Soul Trade is built upon a false illusion. It doesn't exist. In our army, we dream to create a different reality, because we can.

Every day we dream. We dream of the lost paradise. We really believe that paradise can be recreated through our dreams. We know that paradise is being recreated through our dreams. Through those dreams, we march towards paradise every day. While we are awake, we are cleaning up Mother Earth—blessing her rivers, mountains, and dirt roads. We join hands with the supreme forces of healing. You can hear squeals of laughter as our masks peel off. All of Mother Earth's resources help us with this process of peeling. The gentle breeze touches our skin and helps with the peeling. When we step into Mother Earth's clear water the paint on our mask dissolves. The dirt brushes our skin to give a new tone to our being. Remarkably, we start to resemble Mother Earth. Are you asking if I have seen her? Yes, I have. She is quite present in her paradise, which we are recreating. You can't miss her. She is everywhere, in everything. Once you join this army, you can't miss her. She is with us all day and she visits our dreams, too. I can feel her in the thumping of my heart, in the whisper of my breath, in my soul, and in the sound of my voice. You think it is me talking, but my voice is mingled with her message. Her love permeates the forest, the paradise, the garden...and me.

My glowing crown seeks her glory, her crowning glory. My glowing crown seeks glory for others as well. It is a never-ending, everlasting glory. This glory, that has not been sought, emanates from the light, her beautiful white light. This light surrounds me, glows in my heart, whispers to my soul. This light is worthy of everyone and everything. This light that glows in your soul—never extinguishing, ever glowing—is yours to keep. Keep it forever, whether you live in paradise or leave paradise. This soul, which is dazzling in the white light, is yours and yours only. It is yours to keep. It is yours to share. It is yours to shine.

Would you like to escape your Soul Trade to join our army of light? We would like to have you. You may think your paradise is better than ours, but trust me, seeing is believing, right? I will show you the beauty of our paradise. No, I don't want anything from you in return. All I need is your hand to hold—that's it. No, I won't push you or pull you. If you don't want a hand, I can give you a paw, a beetle, or a butterfly. If that doesn't satisfy, I can show you my soul—my soul that I thought I had lost. Also, if you are a Soul Trader, guess what, you did not usurp any souls. Everyone is aligning to the memory of their souls. We thought our souls were usurped and lost. That is not true. Whomever thought their soul was lost, conveniently forgot its existence through man's lies. By the way, you can stop lying; the lies are going to be shed through the wisdom gained by the army.

Our army contains troopers, real troopers. They will show you their path and can learn your path, too. If you don't want to join, no worries; we have enough in our army to march towards paradise. Listen, if you want to be left out, it is your choice and your choice only. Don't lie and say we left you behind. Remember, it will be your choice if you stay behind to keep up with the old lies. Honestly, those lies are getting stale. They should not have a hold on you any longer. If you ever want to escape the lies, you know where to find us. When you are ready, we will welcome you with open paws, spread wings, a raised trunk and gentle flaps. You don't need to fear us. In this army, we know no harm.

The Lion came out of his slumber. "Good job, buddy. I guess my job here is done. Don't worry, though, I am not leaving. Are you kidding? It is my paradise that I am welcoming you into. Why would I ever leave? High five!" The Lion raised his great paw. I slapped it with my small hand.

"I know you may think my lessons are done," I told the Lion, "but I have a lot more questions. What is this I am hearing from my wisdom about other light forces that are part of this army?"

"Hmm, have you heard of angels?" the Lion asked.

"Yes, I have heard of them," I nodded. "Are you telling me they are real and exist?"

The Lion roared in acknowledgement. "You couldn't ask your wisdom this question?"

"Yes, I could ask my wisdom," I responded, "but I like talking and hanging out with you. Is that a problem?"

"No, it is not a problem," the Lion smiled. "We can hang out. Let me ask you this: you saw Mother Earth through your wisdom, right?"

"Yeah, I did." "What is she like?"

"Very beautiful," I responded, "very earthy. She is a woman."

"Do you think that is how she seems to everyone else?" the Lion asked.

Confused by the question, I tilted my head. "I thought she looked the same to everyone."

"No, you can create anyone the way you want to see them."

"Are you saying that whomever I am seeing might be seen differently by others or even by me?"

"Yes," the Lion nodded.

"What do you mean? How does that work?"

"Through your wisdom, did you see the light?"

"I am not sure. I envisioned the paradise per your request"

"The paradise you saw...you saw it through light, right?"

"Yes, I think so, but what do you mean?" I asked.

"When you see someone or something through judgment and opinion, you see them as mere labels. When you see someone without judgments, you see them through light, you see their true nature without any mask."

"Ah, now I understand what you mean. I am seeing paradise or recreating it without the judgment of the current state of reality."

"Yes, indeed," the Lion nodded. "Anything you see without judgment is your vision of that which is in its purest, untainted beauty. It is a vision of light."

"So, when I envision something outside of what *is*, I am recreating it to the true nature of it. When I am seeing something as *is*, I am seeing it through my lenses and its lenses."

The Lion stood up, walked up towards me and shook my hand, "Absolutely correct."

"Can you give me an example," I asked the Lion, "for further clarity? I want to make sure I have this straight. It's important."

"When someone is sick, you view them as sick. That is the label, the mask, if you want to call it that. When you choose to see them outside of the sickness as the true, healthy, vibrant being they are you are seeing through light, through perfection."

I was able to fully understand the Lion's teaching and was in awe of his wisdom. At this point, I was ready to give him anything—my life, his pride, his paradise, anything. "Thank you for showing me the depth of your wisdom. Could you expand a bit more about the mask?" I asked.

The mask you wear forces you to look at others through your projections of yourself and through the eyes of humanity in its current form." The Lion paused momentarily to see if I was comprehending. "Everything looks different when it is seen through light."

"Do you see me through light?" I asked.

"Yes, that is why I came to you in a dream. In the light, your mask is invisible. Underneath, without your mask, we are all God's children."

"I see."

"You are seeing me through the light, as well," the Lion said. "You just don't know that you are seeing me through light, but you are."

"How so?"

"You are seeing me, the Lion, not from your time or through the wounds you have inflicted upon my pride as a man. You are seeing me, the Lion, as I should be, without the mask or wounds or loss of my pride."

"I get it now. So, it is not really hard to see oneself or another through light...if you work at it, that is?"

"No, not at all. All it requires is willingness and allowing yourself to see another through light."

"Tell me about the angels, Lion. Are they beings of light? You said they are real."

"Angels work at the frequency of light. Therefore, they always see you without the mask as your true self. They have no idea that you could be anything other than light. When you are down, they still see you as light, without the mask. Therefore, they can lift you up through your own light and strength. They view you as strong, and vibrant no matter what your state. They are here to remind you of who you truly are. They never see you as weak. They lend you a hand to uplift you to your true potential. And, Of course, they are real. Also, have you heard about fairies?"

"Yes, I have heard about fairies. They are mythical creatures."

"What if they are real?" the Lion posed. "What if they exist, just like the angels?"

"So, angels *and* fairies are real?" It was hard to believe. "Is there anything or anyone else I need to know?"

"I will make this simple for you, so that you can have your own experiences through your wisdom. There are other beings that work with light. They are God's helpers. Their job is to help you, help me, help humanity. In fact, they have assisted you and I with this very conversation. Angels, fairies and other light beings all have a purpose. As you progress in your wisdom, you will be able to hear them more clearly. Remember, me talking to you right now is an illusion. It is an illusion that you are talking to a lion. In fact, it is the light beings who are talking to you in a Lion's form. If these beings had come and suddenly showed up in your dreams, you may or may not have been able to relate to them. That is why they come through channels and forms to which you can relate. Yes, I am an illusion, too, but the message I bring to you is true. We feel very real. At the same time, we are not real. I know that is a difficult concept to grasp. Yet, there is a lot of freedom in knowing this. Consider that what your parents taught you is an illusion. It is an illusion that paved the way for your current consciousness."

I remained silent. This was a bit too radical for me. Then again, everything the Lion had shared so far had been very radical. Yet, as I came to understand each concept he taught me, it became my wisdom. At this point, nothing he said surprised me.

"Listen, my friend, you can escape one illusion to another. You can always see a just world in an unjust world; that is the beauty of illusion. You can escape one reality for another. By shifting realities, you can create new realities. Aren't you confident about the new paradise?"

"Yes, I do think paradise will take shape, but I don't know whether I will be able to witness it in my lifetime." The thought of missing out on this transformation made me sad. Seeing my sorrow, the Lion comforted me.

"Just escape into a reality that will allow you to witness paradise in your lifetime. See, life is very simple. You have been made to believe that life is the way it is, and nothing can be done. It is a lie that has been perpetrated by Soul Traders such as you. In such a short time, you have changed your reality and have had several awakenings. Now, you have to go into your world. Go to your family and deal with all the things that are not aligned with your soul. You may be ousted as a misfit, but that might not be a bad thing. It may benefit you and your growth. When you are in dire need of help, call upon your angels, fairies and the light beings. They are always around you waiting to serve. If you allow them to serve you, they will help you with your problems."

"You mean they will solve my problems for me?" I was suddenly hopeful.

"No," the Lion said, sounding a bit frustrated. "They won't solve your problems for you, but they will provide you with the assistance you need to solve your own problems. They always offer you choices to help you decide how to solve your problems. They will never force you to solve the problem as they would. It has to come through your wisdom, and they will help with your choices. If you make a bad choice, they will be patient and nudge you in the right direction. Your job is to ask them for guidance."

"How will I know that they are present?"

"For one, by talking through me. They are always present near me. You will feel and see them in other forms, too. Just be patient. You will witness an abundance of miracles through them. Step forward, escape your current reality, and seek their help. Practice escapism. Don't try to escape from your problems. Rather, escape your current reality to seek and create new realities. The path may not always be easy. In fact, it may be very frustrating at times. That is okay. It is part of the journey you have chosen. "

I thanked him for his nuggets of wisdom today. We bid each other farewell.

"The Lion got up, yawned, looked at me over his shoulder, and bid me goodnight. "All right, time for my dinner, I will see you soon."

The Lion is my angel, my fairy, my light being. He has shown the light to me, so I can see it on my own. I retire for the day, to watch the moon—that bluish white disk in the sky that shines its light, without missing a beat, every perfect night.

Blissfully escaping into paradise,
Man

CHAPTER 13: WOUNDED PRIDE

My pride is wounded. Wounded it is through the lack of concern of man over matter. My pride was wounded through the uncaring thoughts of man. My pride that was wounded caused me to become ferocious. I became ferocious through my pride that was wounded. I was wounded, my pride was wounded. We were all wounded. Through the lack of care for his own well-being, man lost his pride, which cost my pride. The pride that was naturally within me has been stripped thin. Through the dialogue I am having with man, my intention is to restore my pride and his, thereby raising the pride of ALL creatures. The pride that was lost needs to be restored. In order to restore the pride, much work is to be done. Much work. Man and I are making strides. We are making much progress and it heals my wounded pride. It heals me as I heal him. It heals me in ways that restore my faith in my pride, humanity and overall existence itself. I cannot forego my pride that easily. If I have to, it will be met with wrath.

In defining my pride through the restoration of it, I am able to transcend the wounded pride through my own healing. My healing of my wounded pride is necessary to lift me and other creatures and creation. My wounded pride is not one to be taken lightly. Since I am one with *all,* my healing catapults others' healing. When man heals, he heals *all.* Hence it is crucial that he heals and therefore I am here talking to him and addressing his wounds which in turn heals my wounds. I need to restore the relationship that we once had. The relationship was a deep bond that tied all of us. This bond when severed caused the wound through the loss of my pride. My pride that was lost was lost through separation. The separation happened first within man. This separation caused him to be ruthless in his need and greed. His need and greed created separation within his own kind. When separation happened within man, he was able to discriminate between himself and his fellow humans. When this separation happened and he decided all humans were different, he descended into discrimination. When he discriminated his own kind and he was ruthless with his own kind, he wounded their pride through the discrimination. He couldn't help it. He couldn't help it, because it was the separation that caused the discrimination.

Through this discrimination, he created borders and walls that separated himself from himself. He created a border not just between his fellow humans but within himself. When he created this separation, he lost contact within himself, with his true self. When he created the separation, he could not view things through his true self. Who he truly was, oneness with all creatures, was lost. When he started being ruthless to his fellow humans, he descended upon us equally through this separation. He couldn't help it. The separation that he had created through his loss of sense of himself, caused a deep chasm between himself and others. When one is not true to oneself, one is in separation and this separation causes one to segregate and discriminate others through color, creed and race. This separation was a huge blow to humanity. Yet, it was disintegrating at a fast rate that humans did not know how to pause the descension and disintegration of their pride. When this pride disintegrated, they became ruthless to others. When one is ruthless to others, they do not realize that they are ruthless to themselves. They are ruthless to themselves by accepting the separation. This separation is an illusion, but they seldom understand that it is. It costs them severely, this illusion of separation. When this illusion happens, their pride swells up in ways that is illusory as well. True pride is inclusive. It lacks separation. It is about oneness. It is about treating everyone as One. It is about restoring faith in *all*. It is about understanding that we are all the same. However, when separation happens it is a new kind of pride. A pride that is wounded. This wounded pride wounds others.

This wounded pride separates others. It calls for discrimination and segregation. It calls for the destruction of what *it* thinks is in its way. You see, when one's pride is wounded, whatever is in its way to experience oneness it destroys. It destroys ruthlessly. What did you think wounded pride does? Destroy. It is singly motivated to destroy. The kind of destruction that is blind. That develops a sense of pride which is wounded. This wounded pride is not real, it is an illusion. When one who is wounded, wounds another, both sides get into a vicious cycle of destruction. When one destroys, the other picks up weapons with their festering wound to destroy the other and the cycle continues until one has no recollection of how, who and when the destruction was created. One has no idea, because it came from separation. When one is in separation, one can only be factual about what happened. When one is in Unity, one understands the nature of the destruction and what caused the separation. When one is not in Unity, it is a catapulting of destruction that furthers the destruction. This continuum of the destruction for one sake or another causes the destruction of the overall wellness of the self and others and Mother Earth itself. This destruction was due to the separation that was divisive.

Dividing is what one understands through lack of Unity. When one has lost their pride through wounds that were inflicted upon the self, that infliction continues wounding another and then another passing on the same wound. This is the continuum of energies that builds and builds when no one can understand what happened in the first place. At this juncture, this is where humanity is. No one knows where it all started. I don't think anyone can understand truly where it all started. But I can tell you one thing, it all started with separation of the self from the unity consciousness, the oneness consciousness. This lack of oneness, this destroyed unity, destroyed man. This destruction of the self also created extinction among several of the plant and animal species. It destroyed *all* that was oneness, which was in the way of man's new need to be in separation. Anything he came upon that would help him to revert back to Oneness, he couldn't understand, so he destroyed and I, the Lion, was one of them. I was a victim to the destruction, as much as he was a victim to the destruction.

Mother Nature is vast. In this vastness and Man's narrow mindedness, created due to his lack of unity, the destruction was inevitable. So, he destroyed and destroyed. Before this destruction, when he was in unity, he knew how to summon his needs. Once he lost his unity, he lost the will to summon his needs in a conscious way. When the consciousness was lost through his separation, he did not know how to exist without the destruction he was causing. This lack of consciousness lead to the destruction of *all*. We all were at Man's mercy and continue to be. Our lives were controlled by him. Our lifeline depended on him. Our population in numbers and geography depended on him. Our continuation or legacy depended on him. You see, I am not blaming him. I am simply pointing out that the separation that was caused by one, was felt by all and that is the Wounded Pride I am talking about. When one deeply goes to the other end of the spectrum that is not natural to oneself, one causes the deep chasm between *all*. Why him? Why is that him losing consciousness affected *all*? Why? If I was conscious and the rest of creation was conscious why is it that Man's illusion of separation affects *all*? Was it the lack of understanding? Was it systemic and went out of control? Was it because the rest of creation also found its way into separation? What was it that man's separation caused this drastic devolution of *all* creations? What happened?

Man was created to support and grow the consciousness further. He was here to elevate consciousness to the next level. By no means was he meant to do it all and be at the top of the pyramid. Not at all. He was equally one amongst us. During the time when consciousness was supposed to move further along, something happened. Something happened that distracted Man. He joined forces with the shadow. That is what happened. When he joined the shadow, he could not move along as One.

Before I move on, I think I need to explain what shadow is. When you are One with everything and you understand and feel that you are One with everything, you are a benevolent being. You are part of creation. When you are part of creation, you are part of *all*. When you are one with everything, you are supporting the light that is within you and you ignite the light within others. You are like a candle who can light multiple candles.

When you strike up a deal with the shadow, consciously or unconsciously, you are moved towards greed and separation. The Shadow plague had inflicted man. When this Shadow inflicted man, it spread like a forest fire. When man turned to greed, Man had to go all the way into it before he ricocheted back to the truth. When you are shadow, you cannot be infinite. You are limited and greed sustains this limitation. Greed works in the shadows and is limited in its view and its time. But it had to go all the way deep in the dark chasm. It had to fully reveal itself and show everyone who the master was, itself. However, because it is not *light*, it isn't eternal. It is limited in its life. It is a consciousness that has to dwindle in the presence of oneness, the *light*.

I call the *light* and oneness as synonyms. Why so? I do so only because, when you become One and you reveal yourself out of the shadow, you cannot be anything other than Unity. You cannot. It is not possible. When you come out of the shadow and you gradually discover who you are, there is no reverting back to shadow. Because you are being revealed to yourself as your expansive self. When you are revealed yourself to your own expansiveness, you begin to understand the limitations that you have lived by thus far. This limitation that gets revealed makes you understand what it did to you. You don't have to do a deep dive into your shadow, but it will behoove you to understand its true nature, which is that it is limited. When you understand that you are a vast being, you emerge into *light*. Once you have emerged into *light*, there is no turning back. You are becoming *light*. When you are becoming *light*, everything is clear as night and day about separation.

You get a laugh out of pretending that you were separate. Yes, it was a pretension. It is not *true*. This pretention was an illusion. When you hit the point of no return, you gradually experience expansiveness. So, when man went to the deep end of the shadow, man hit rock bottom with shadow. He is feeling the impacts following the shadow. He is becoming aware of the chasm he created for himself and others. The greedy self has been revealed as something that is other than One. It is not in the true nature of any being that was created. It was the wounded pride that took on greed. When pride is wounded, no amount of retaliation, no amount of rejection, no amount of anything is enough. That is how greed is born. It is born out of the wounded pride. It is born out of the shadows. It is anything but *you* and *me*. When man went to the far end of the spectrum I, the Lion, was impacted as well, because I shared a space with him and I had my own learning through experiencing this extreme and because I was one with him, I had to experience *all* of it along with him. Now, can I blame him for wounding my pride? I was part of the journey and experience. Now that I have stated it, I find a heavy burden lifted off my shoulders.

You see, this burden is carried by *all*, me, my pride and others. Laying this burden down releases the burden that every single one of my kind carries. Yes, every single one of them. That is how powerful it is to forgive. That is how powerful it is to not lay blame on another. I came here to have this experience and now I am here to impart wisdom. My time is coming closer to Man's. Our times are colliding and colluding. In this collusion we have become one. When we both transcend time, we are expansive and infinite and *light* is infinite. I am no longer the wounded pride but a thriving one.

When my pride is wounded, I am in the shadows. I need to emerge from the shadow. I cannot wait for Man to emerge and walk beside me with pride as One. If I have to awaken Man, I have a duty to myself to awaken first and foremost. I need to understand that I was dragged into this shadow as part of the contract I made with man. I was supposed to be here with him. As a result, I was impacted by his deeds. I am wise to forgive him, so that I can experience him as Himself. Not with greed, not in separation. I and Him are One. There is no separation between him and me. Now, when I declare it, everything around me has to shift. There are no, If's or But's. We are one. When we declare that we are one, the wounded pride, the false pride diminishes. It diminishes as it cannot withstand light. It cannot withstand light as false pride comes from separation. In light separation cannot exist. It is not in its nature.

When separation happened as part of the wounded pride, all creations and creatures were separated by borders and walls. The wounded pride that caused greed also caused grief. It caused grief through greed. When greed awakened from the slumbers of shadow, it was hungry. It was hungry as it had not been able to sustain in the consciousness of oneness. It had been starved by the abundance of light. Now that it had the sustenance of shadow, it was able to emerge from its slumber. When greed emerged. It had sharp claws that were never used before. It had a huge appetite and its pride was wounded. So, whatever it saw it took, whether it needed it or not. It clawed everything it could see. Whatever it saw it captured. It saw the abundance and it pillaged, plundered and raped. It took everything that was within its reach. It took animals, humans, resources and it saw no end as the forest was filled with things that seemed inexhaustible.

Greed took everything. It did not know that at the end it would deprive itself through this plunder. When it had destroyed and plundered that which was within its reach, it moved on to a different direction. Here is how we were divided. When greed moved to another place after it had destroyed one place, those who remained were left with nothing. Nothing. Their pride was wounded. They had lost everything that was close to them. The forest, the food, the water, the air, the animals and all of creations. They were destroyed. In that destruction, they were left without any resources to fend for themselves. They were left homeless and devoid of everything that was needed for their sustenance. When they were left with nothing and greed moved on to other directions, the ones who were plundered tried to move on to a different place. But oh no, they couldn't. Greed drew a border saying that they were beneath it and were paupers who were devoid of any honor and any strength to rebuild. It said what is on the other side is mine and I will not share this abundance.

Only greed could do that, it drew borders and separated those who were starving on the other side of the border. But then greed's nature is destruction. It destroyed whatever was in this new land it had moved towards. It did the same thing there and drew another border and boundary that no one could get in other than itself. And hence the beast kept moving. It created shadow everywhere it went. Those who were destroyed at its hands, lost the magic, the charm and everything that they had, the pride. They lost the pride. There were land locked and they couldn't move from one place to another. Even the ones who moved had to bribe greed and it took bribes from poor and rich equally. Greed had no compassion. It took whatever it could because it was in separation. It comes with a lack of compassion. Without compassion, without the Unity consciousness, greed was acting on its own. It had no empathy, sympathy or compassion. It just wanted to devour everything that was in its way. It kept devouring as long as was possible. And when it made a full circle back to the beginning, there was nothing left. Now greed was hungry, and it ate all that was left, eating people and creatures alive. It didn't care.

That is the story of the human race along with mine. I have been humbled by this experience. I have been humbled. In my humility I stepped forward to have this conversation with man, to awaken him. Because you see, nothing can be done to restore this paradise without his wakefulness. Nothing. He is part of me. I cannot leave him behind. That would be selfish and greedy. I am Him and He is Me. If we both are one, I cannot leave him behind and neither can he leave me behind. In light we are all part of it. I am nothing without him and he is nothing without me, lost pride.

In his awakenings, lies my awakening. In his wisdom, lies mine. Without him I will be a "wounded pride".

The greed that razed the forest, the supplies and the mother land, is devoid of things. You see, greed cannot become rich, it cannot become abundant. Abundance and Greed are a state of being. When you are abundant, you cannot be greedy, when you feel greedy, you cannot be abundant. They cannot co-exist. Abundance comes from light and light is unlimited, expansive and infinite. Abundance is a state of being that knows that it naturally has everything that it needs. There is no lack of anything in the presence of abundance. One cannot feel abundance and claim another in lack. Abundance is a miracle. Abundance inherently knows that it is infinite. Nothing is ever exhaustible. Food, water, resources, animals everything is in abundance. When greed steps in, it looks at water and it wants to claim water for itself, because it thinks that if another has the same water, greed will feel depleted. This is where abundance differs from greed. Abundance knows it will never be depleted. Abundance knows by standing in the space of allowing, abundance is naturally present. It is selfless as opposed to greed which is selfish. When abundance emerges, it knows it has no need to hoard. It knows everything is in full supply and it has everything that it needs in this moment. It is able to see through the eyes of light the naturally present supply of abundance. It is able to feel it, sense it and be it. Whereas, greed comes from fear and lack. It is scared that if it doesn't hoard it will lose it all. In the process of hoarding, greed has already lost it all. It has lost everything by the sheer notion that it is lacking. It cannot be satiated because it comes from fear of losing. When greed fears losing, it wants to win everything, it wants to be ahead of everything, it doesn't mind trampling another human, another animal or any other creation. It just goes running around with fear of being left out without anything.

This is the fear that cost Mother Earth her freedom. The inhibited freedom came in the form of lack. When lack emerged through greed and it inhibited freedom, it created lack in everyone around it, lack of being mindful, lack of consciousness. When one is in abundance, one is mindful. When one is mindful, one is in abundance. However, greed is not mindful. It is greed, so it lacks the necessary compassion to be mindful. For one to be mindful, one has to be compassionate. For compassion to flow, one has to feel the oneness, the light. When one does not feel compassion which sustains mindfulness, one cannot be without greed.

My pride is wounded and yet pride is emerging through the mind of man who is learning to be compassionate to all the things he wounded. He is awakening to his own deeds and his shadow self that was inhabited by greed. When one is light, one is in allowance of *all* that is *light*. *All* that is *light* is infinite. When greed inhabited Man, he pillaged, plundered and raped. He had no conscience of his deeds. He took things for granted just like greed takes it for granted. Greed takes everything for granted because it innately thinks that it owns everything. Whereas abundance knows it owns nothing, yet it knows it is naturally abundant. It knows that it owns everything yet nothing. Everything in this Mother Land belongs to it, yet it doesn't. Abundance is knowing that all beings own equally. All beings share equally. The light, the water, the air, the food are all equally shared and in spite of it everyone has enough. Greed however, has no concept of sharing. It has a sense of ownership. It has a sense of entitlement, whereas abundance knows nothing about entitlement or ownership.

Our brother, through his narration, has explained to us how he lived through entitlement. He assumed the things that he had came through his father's hard work. In abundance there is no hard work. One should never have to work hard to feed the children, one never has to work hard to sustain oneself. Hard work comes from greed. Those who are greedy needed others to work for them to support their greed and work to keep those things they pillaged and pillage more on their behalf. That is how greed works. Greed creates a structure. It thinks that those who had the gumption to pillage are on the top and those that are on the bottom support the ones on the top.

Whereas in abundance, there is no top nor bottom. It is a homogenous living. Greed cannot fathom it and it will fight all the way to justify that it is impossible to live through abundance. Greed, an illusion, thinks that abundance is an illusion. It lacks the ability to fathom that it caused the lack. When greed emerged from the shadow, it replaced abundance with lack as it suited it. However, since greed has reigned and knows of only lack, it is stubborn in its nature to believe in anything but lack. Even if it has a large supply of everything, it is very keenly aware of lack. While greed has much, it creates the illusion of lack so that others can depend upon it. It can give when it feels a little generous. When greed that has hoarded through lack gives a little, it feels generous. What about abundance, which is flowing in the infinite and never stops and never boasts of generosity when you take something from it? You see, there is nothing called generosity. There is nothing called generosity because everything is abundant. When everything was created equally and everything is equally available for everyone, no one will need to give to another or steal from another. Life for all is equally abundant. When you give, you are giving from the abundance, so it is not yours you see, that which you give. It belongs to abundance and when you share you are sharing the abundance that naturally exists.

Now, my dear readers, I am exhausted by greed. You are exhausted by greed. We both are equally affected by greed. We both are equally exhausted by greed. Let us move forward knowing that we live in an abundant land that was exhausted by greed. Now, the good news is that we are moving towards the light leaving behind our shadow. When we move towards light, greed cannot walk with us. It will be blinded by light and will thrash around to breathe. It will gasp from the abundance. It will die naturally as it cannot flourish in the presence of light.

Abundance restores lost pride. Abundance restores flow. Abundance allows *all*. It allows everyone, everything. In this *allowance*, you and I become One. The man, the lion and pride can all co-exist together. We do not need to kill and exhaust another to keep ourselves alive. We can move together towards the infinite leaving behind any semblance of greed. Let us step forward towards the abundance. This abundance replenishes that which was lost. You see, greed takes, abundance gives. Since abundance gives, it naturally will restore the peace of this mother land. It will restore all that was lost through your allowance of the abundance and light.

Light be with you. So be it, so it is.

Through a healed heart and pride,
The Lion

CHAPTER 14: UNTOUCHABLES

"My roar can be heard miles away. It is a roar that used to echo through the forest. Back then, I roared just for the pleasure of roaring. I enjoyed my roars. My cubs would ask me to roar, and I would just roar for the fun of it. My roar, which was filled with pride, is now laced with anger, frustration and sadness. My roar, that I had taken so much pride in, now sounds like a squeaky wheel to me. I hold my breath, wishing to die. I am sad. I am sad at the corruption that sees no end. They dig, they dig, and they dig. Digging, felling, demolishing seems to be their play. They have at it. They go at it, as if there is no moisture in their heart, and it has shriveled up. Isn't their heart pumping? Isn't their heart telling them? Isn't it speaking to them? Have they lost the ability to hear their own soul? They have sold their souls to the soul traders. They have to get a happy penny. They would do anything to feed their families. The jobs my friend mentioned—the jobs given to millions—is to destroy, disrupt, and disengage. If only they could feel my pain. They could, but would they allow themselves to feel it? They used to be so close to us. They used to respect us and be part of this wonderful paradise.

"I have seen what happened to them. They have been stripped naked. Can you believe one human stripping another? The ones being stripped have been reduced to dirt, as if their lives are not worthy. They have been stripped so thin that they don't even feel the pain and nakedness anymore. How did humanity come to this juncture? How can humanity strip a fellow being and pretend like it never happened? Worse, how can they pretend like it was the other person's own doing, as if they are so stupid they would do such a thing to themselves? How can that be? Are they not our brothers? Are they not our sisters? Oh, I see, the stripped ones don't look like the ones who stripped them. So, it is okay—is it? Is that it? As they were being stripped, they lost any volition to stop it. In their numbness, they SoulD and contracted to sell others' souls as well. The ones that joined the Soul Trade were raped and pillaged as well. Then they became numb to the pillage, the stripping, and raping. When they joined the trade, they did it with promises of a better, shinier future where they would help their fellow neighbors. That is what they promised, but they were hollow promises.

"Just because something is shiny doesn't make it better—but they didn't know that. Their paradise, filled with velvety leaves and flowers and abundance, was stripped. They were stripped of everything that was theirs. They were stripped, and then shiny watches were dangled in front of them. They were told that they were stupid for not wanting these shiny watches. Some of the wise ones from their tribes warned them. They told them. They were wise enough to understand that the shiny objects were only a distraction created so the soul traders could plunder and rape until no one could feel it anymore. See, they have lost their souls by the distraction of the shiny object. You may say it is their own fault. Maybe, but how simpleminded of you to state that of your brother—to just shrug it off like that.

"It doesn't have to be this way, does it? Or are you so comfortable in your shiny, cushy chair that you don't care? You have better things to do then think about us losers, who lost paradise, is that it? Here is the thing, that shiny object that you wear has a direct or indirect connection to those of us who were plundered and stripped. Have you ever even noticed? You stand in lines for hours to buy some new gadget. However, you don't have a second to think about your brothers and sisters, who have been raped and pillaged. You may just assume they are not capable of taking care of themselves or that they are inferior to you or are you oblivious to their existence? Just think about it. You may be about to deny it, but please don't justify it. If you are part of this charade, yes, you don't care. You don't care enough to look at yourself and your life. The shiny gadget you hold in your hand is tied to me losing my land and other humans losing their homes—all for you to have luxurious things. The irony is that I, the Lion, have to tell you this. Are you that blind? Or do you choose to be blind? Are you selectively blind? Which one are you?

"If you have been told that certain people are the way they are, I urge you to take a minute out of your busy life, playing with your gadgets, to think about this. Look at the gadget you are holding and ask yourselves how it got into your hands. Ask how many hands—tiny to medium-sized to big—that your gadget has passed through? You know those tiny hands were put to work due to man's pillaging, right? Those tiny hands are not meant to work. They are meant to play, but now they are working with tiny shovels or in dirt mines to get you this shining gadget. You may think this it is not true. Maybe you don't want to believe it is true. If you knew, then it would make you look like a bad person. You see, you have been divided and conquered. During this wonderful time of conquering, you were perpetuated with lies. It doesn't matter where you live, you were part of this charade—this dirty, filthy charade. I don't want to accuse you— after all, you just wanted the gadget. You didn't want to plunder. You didn't mean to support child labor. You did not want to take advantage of the poor. You believe that the company you buy from is known for its morals and ethics, right? This is what you believe, don't you? Some of the gadgets you have may be necessary, I get it, trust me, I do. Could you at least join the army to stop this rape—a rape where the ones being raped have lost their feeling? They have been raped for so long that they have become inanimate. You, who believe in freedom, are in fact tied to this oppression. I will bring it back to one thing that is funny and most crucial about you humans: when you don't see something right in front of your eyes, you assume it doesn't exist. Yet, you will believe the lies perpetrated against others, even though you haven't seen proof. Isn't that ironic? Just think about this.

"Do what you want but know that the time is ripe for all the lies to be revealed. When they are revealed, don't pretend like you didn't know. Your wisdom knows beyond your flesh and blood—that is its primary job. You have been trained to listen to others to validate the lies that are perpetrated over and over again. "Subconsciously you know. You also know subconsciously that if you admitted that you knew, you would have to take responsibility. That is a trait that you are losing slowly—your ignorance. Assuming you are accountable for some and not others is not a fair game, especially when you are tied to every single life on Mother Earth. It is easy to think another creature lives a certain life because they are not capable, or they are lazy or inferior. Thinking like this is easy, trust me. Why am I saying this with confidence? Because you are living like this now. Those who are comfortable are getting more comfortable every day. Things are easy to access—all you have to do is reach out for your gadget. As your life gets easier by the day, someone else's life gets more and more uncomfortable and unpredictable. While your thumb has easy access to your gadget, someone else's hands are being stripped of everything. Yes, you are that connected. If you are not aware; get aware. Don't tell me you didn't know. Now, you know. To create a false paradise, another's real paradise is usurped. When you strip another of their basic decency, basic livelihood, humanity has lost a civilized world. Don't even tell me you live in a "civilized" world. Your definition of civilized is very different from mine. My definition is that every creation and creature is respected for their existence. When you respect another, greed does not have a place. Even when it peeks in, you can decide what you value the most.

"Continue to value your gadgets and know that you are marching towards an unjust world—a world where not everyone is considered equal, a world that has been doused in lies and is unwilling to see the truth. You are so consumed by these lies, you cannot smell the blood and sweat. Don't let these lies consume you. Wake up and reach out for the truth. Don't ask others—that will only confuse you. Reach into yourself. Do your work. Do your homework.

"The elite—who run the government and are behind the Constitution—are no different from those who came to my forest, my paradise and plundered and pillaged. The elite know full well, for they are the ones keeping up appearances. They have a part in the charade, too. Even if they lie through their teeth that they have the best intentions for you, they don't. The ones who do care cannot exist with this elite. There is no place for a soul that is filled with wisdom among these elite. These elite are puppets to the shadow that plunders and pillages. They are a class of their own. They are human, but they are blood suckers. They don't know race, color or species while they suck the blood. Here, and only here, everyone is equal. They are equal opportunity blood suckers. You don't want to believe me? Let me have my brother, the man, narrate for you the deeds that he himself has done."

I was sitting there listening to the Lion describe me. This is me. I had to admit it. I had to admit to all the lies I had perpetrated, the cold lies. I could kill someone and be standing over their body and say, "I have never killed," and would not be questioned. I am above law. The Constitution.? I am above it. No one can touch me. I am untouchable. Not in a way of the real untouchables. Rather, me as untouchable, as in no one can touch me. That is how I am different from the other untouchables. I was part of the creation of the untouchables. They are considered worthless. Their lives don't matter, but mine does. I am untouchable. You see, two untouchables, but different rules. You want to hear another irony? I am part of a foundation for the betterment of the lives of these untouchables. You think this is funny? There is more irony that I can dig up, deeper than what I have dug to plunder.

I really haven't cared for the untouchables. I really haven't cared for the lives of anyone but myself. Had I not heard the Lion talk about the cycle of life, I would not even have engaged in this conversation. In my life, I have not given a fig about anyone else. That is who I was. It is beyond my mind's ability to even fathom that I could be forgiven. I can't tell you the number of horrors that I have committed. I am here speaking to you, to right the wrongs. Should I repent for my deeds? Yes, I agree I should. But I would rather heal, as healing would help us step into paradise. I would rather heal than repent. You may not agree with me, but you see, I want to heal and help in the healing of those who have been rendered helpless through my deeds and those who have been part of my soul trade. My wisdom has dictated the choice between repenting and forgiving. I choose forgiveness, which is my birthright, same as anyone else's. You may be disgusted. I may sound arrogant. But trust me, that is not what I mean. I am part of the army. I would like to extend my hands all around the world to join the cause. If you cannot be convinced, then let me narrate my story. A story that has never been heard, or let me clarify, hasn't been allowed to be heard outside our circles.

We make deals, deals with other puppeteers and we are ruthless in our negotiations. When I say ruthless, I mean we will make any and all threats to get what we want. I, myself, have threatened to take away the basic means of a population, if I am not given what I want. You wonder if I have that much power. I do. I have some establishment or another in each country and continent. The poorer the country or continent, the better for me. We have several things we have usurped from these lands, and now we have control over them. When anyone points out problems, I threaten to take away something, or worse, I threaten to do away with their families. Not me, why would I do such a thing? I have people that will do all this for me because I have bigger fish to fry. Why would I be part of such minuscule things? I am wealthy, you see. I can buy anything, anyone, including souls. Once in a while, a puppeteer will stand up for the rights of a population and we will squash his protest before he finishes his sentence.

We go to a place of wealth—not money, but Mother Nature's wealth—and force the population to move by making them many promises—promises, false promises we barely keep. The promises we do keep, we keep for appearances sake. We usually have a center where we are doing something good for our reputation's sake. We silence people who get too problematic. We call these protesters terrorists. That is an easy way to silence those impacted by this charade. It is a good masquerade to mask the truth.

When people rebel, we label them and tell the world they are the worst kind. You want to know what is even worse? At some point, if they really get to be a pain, we join them and provide them with shiny things so they can work for us and help us pillage, plunder and rape. Ah ha, you see, this is the cycle of life that I have been living. Do you want to know the number of humans, animals, plants and vegetation that have been destroyed? Well, I can't answer that, because there are far too many for me to count. This is my life, my comfortable life.

I have been too comfortable. You think I should be hanged. Listen, I invented crimes and I invented the punishment for those crimes. I know that it is now coming back to bite me. I guess I deserve your wrath. But here is the thing, let me be useful to you. Let me help erase the boundaries that I have created. I know of places and things where boundaries were laid, and why they were laid. I can be a useful tool. I know I don't deserve your forgiveness, but I choose to forgive myself. You see, I am a victim, too. Please don't look at me like that. It's true, I am a victim of my father's deeds. I know I am not going to gain your sympathy, nor am I asking for it. I was born into my life, my father's life, as part of my soul's journey. At least I am willing to change my path, my ways.

I will let you decide, if you want to work with me. Here is the request I have: even if you don't want to hold my hands, please hold the paws of the cubs. No, I am not using this as a tactic to get on your good side. To be honest, I don't think anything will help get me on your good side. However, through this awakening process, I have been led to join paradise. I am here to step into the conundrum. I really don't know what it will look like, but I have already joined the army. I request that you do, too. I am ready to plead guilty, but don't waste me on the perpetrator's stand. I am okay with being on the perpetrator's stand, but I would rather be with the Lion and all of you marching towards paradise. I will confess to all the crimes that I have been part of. I will confess to all the war crimes that I have instigated. No exceptions. I am not just saying this to confess, to get this off of my chest. I am willing to confess to cause an awakening—an awakening of the masses that have been lied to. You can shackle and drag me, but I request you do that once I have done my job. I am here to be fully and completely used for this peaceful war. I will serve any position you want me to serve, but I come in peace.

You may think this is a cop-out but trust me that is not what I am trying to do. I really want us to get back to paradise, the lost paradise. I love my brother, my Lion, who has taught me wisdom, who has been crucial in my spiritual awakening. I can't see him treated like he doesn't matter. He does matter, my brother does matter. You matter. I matter. We all matter. All of us matter. No one is beneath another. No one is untouchable in the cycle of life. No one is untouchable in the supreme light.

If the sun shines on all of us equally, with no discrimination, then we don't have the right to discriminate. Your soul and my soul are part of the same soul, the same source. Don't listen to the lies that have been perpetrated about the untouchables. No one is untouchable by the wisdom, no one is untouchable by the air, the water, the clear skies. If you are darker, lighter or even mauve pink, it does not matter. All creations matter. Please don't assume I am speaking just about humans. Even the bugs and worms that you assume don't matter, do matter. Don't misjudge someone by their size. Size doesn't matter. Color doesn't matter. Race doesn't matter. Remember, through the cycle of life, you have embodied several bodies and all bodies matter. Whatever your soul has chosen, your body matters. The other irony is the pretention that discrimination doesn't exist around you. If you believe that, please unplug your ears and sharpen your vision. I am not talking about just your eyes and ears, I am talking about your mind's eye and your heart, too. They both play a vital role in understanding. When your mind argues with you or tells you to disregard the clamor, reach out for your wisdom. This is how you got here, by ignoring the clamor.

Please join the army, the army of peace and love, the army that unites rather than divides, the army that conquers love, rather than land. Let's lift the tiny hands that work rather than play. I know these children are not part of your family, nevertheless lift them up. If you don't know how to lift them, but are interested in learning, please join the army, the army of love. There is a Goddess, Mother Earth eagerly awaits your arrival—the arrival of her children, which she is anticipating. She is an eager mother. She misses her children and their wisdom. Yes, you matter. You matter to her, for you are part of her family. Your family in paradise awaits your arrival.

The time has come to step out of our comfort zone. The time has come to join hands, paws, wings, noses, and tails. The time has come to lift the tiny hands that are worn out by the burdens laid upon them by the mafia. Yes, the mafia, I said it. Should I be worried about the mafia? No, of course not. I am the mafia. It is not the same one as you think. It is worse. It denies basic human decency and respect. The elite circle is an unknown mafia that lingers in the shadows. This shadow mafia—for that is what I have been part of—does not care for the tiny hands that scrub the floors. I certainly did not care for the tiny hands that carried this burden. I did not care for the tiny hands that begged. I did not care for the tiny hands that were beaten. I did not care for the tiny hands that bled. I did not care for the tiny hands that were hurt. I did not care, period. Yes, that was me. I do not say this with pride. I am speaking with humility, to divulge the lies that I have perpetrated.

I want you to understand that we do not just abuse the older, we also abuse the younger. The extent of our abuse is beyond my own understanding. When you have done it once, it is easy to do it twice, thrice, and more. I built a school at the place where I dug the hole. Right after the hole was drilled, I made sure a school was opened. I knew no one would actually go to that school, but I wanted everyone to know that there was a school. When tiny hands didn't show up at the school, I blamed the culture. It is easy to shift blame. I knew there were too many mouths to feed in every family, but I still decided to blame the culture. I made sure I plundered sufficiently, so they were at my mercy and I could get cheap labor, which I used to accumulate my wealth. I lied, saying I was creating jobs. It was easy to convince them with my lies. It is easy to blame others, those who have been pillaged. It is very easy. They don't have power like I do—the power of money, of governments, of the shadow mafia. I used to be proud of belonging to the shadow. That mask is wearing off. That pride, that false pride is wearing off. Let's lift tiny paws. Let's lift tiny hands. Let's soothe them with a kiss. Let's soothe them with love. Let's soothe them with their pride, for they are too young to lose their pride. Let us not destroy their pride.

If you want to hear more, I am here. Come and ask me. I will reveal the truth behind the lies. I will shed light on the shadow. Use me as your servant. Use me as your tool to dismantle the lies and pave the way to paradise. Are you with me? If you are still in disbelief, it is okay. Take time to process it all. I know it is a lot. Listen, I don't want to blame myself. It took time for me to own up to my own lies—lies that have been perpetrated by my circles and me for a very long time. I had become numb to them. Please use me to the fullest, to the best of your abilities. I have used people and even several countries for my own benefit, so now use me. It is time for me to be part of the cycle of life, to give back. I know it is not the same. You will want a life for a life, but I urge you to use me in a different way. No, I am not scared of death or being found out, I just want to help getting back to paradise. If we march together, there is strength in paving the way. Everyone counts, every paw counts, every tiny hand counts. Will you please hold our hands? If you are disgusted by my hand, hold a tiny one, hold a paw, hold a wing, your pick. Choose wisely. Use your wisdom. Call upon the light to lead you. Call upon the wind, which blows without judgment. There is a lot you can learn from the wind, as it flows freely towards all and allows itself to experience all.

Let us heal the prejudice. Let us heal the blame. Let us heal the judgments. Let us heal the wounds. Let us heal our path. Let us heal our hearts. Let us rejoice in our differences. Let's see the beauty in everyone and everything. Let us, let us, let us, let us just for the sake of it, just for the joy of it, just for love of it. Love is the one ammunition our new army uses unconditionally, even on me—on me, can you believe it? If I can be healed, certainly you can be healed. Every healing counts, everyone counts in this army. In this army, you can choose your gender. The gender that you relate to, not the one you are constrained by through the restrictions and the rules of gender. In fact, you don't have to play by your gender. If you want to, that is okay, too. What I mean is you have a choice, you have the freedom to choose. No one will take a righteous stance about your gender—no one. We just want you equally, no matter who you are. We need only to conquer in the name of love. You see, we conquer through love in paradise, the only thing worth conquering through. If you are interested, please join our army.

I want to leave you with something to chew on—just chew on it. How come certain counties, continents, countries and races are rich, and some are not? If you have a standard answer of how one is better than the other, step back and ask this question again. Ask again and again, until you find the truth, the real truth that resonates in your heart and soul, not your mind, not your statistical mind. These things that tally in your mind will not tally in your heart. This is how you distinguish between a lie and the truth. I am placing the signup sheets with love. I believe in you, and I trust in you to join and support our army.

Yours,

A new recruit

CHAPTER 15: MAGIC LAND

*L*et it come, let it come, let it come. Let the flood gates open. Let us not hold back. Let us not let fear hold us back. Let us not be fearful to tell the truth, to let the truth out. Let us not ignore the truth. Let us not live in oblivion. Let us not let the lies continue to be perpetrated. Let us stand up for our lives. Let us stand up for the truth. Let us stand up for one another. Let us be audacious in pointing out discrimination, even when it is not against us. Let us open the flood gates. There is no better way of doing this, let us not wait to be spoon fed. Let us be ready to be immersed and carried away by truth. It seems like it will swallow you up. Trust me, it won't swallow you. It just won't. If you are immersed in truth, it will take you to places. It will take you to places of self-discovery. It will take you to powerful places. It will work with you tirelessly. You will be drifted to the shore when needed, only for a moment, and then caught by more waves of truth—the unlimited supply of truth that you are part of. Yes, this is overwhelming, I understand. This is new to you, and it can be overwhelming. You have not witnessed this kind of truth before—this truth that resonates, a loud resonance that you cannot ignore. It is only the beginning, and I understand the overwhelming feeling, trust me, I understand. It will pass, so enjoy your mere presence on this journey. You chose to be part of this truth.

You are supposed to be the voice not just for yourself, but for the greater good. I understand your hesitation, your vulnerability, your doubts, your worry. I truly understand, trust me, I do. You question your power every day, every minute—wondering about the truth of your power. I get it. It is easier not to know your power. Knowing one's own power makes things different. You are challenged every step of the way, and your past creeps in to remind you that you are not that powerful, you are not that wise, you are not that aware. You hear whispers of your mind that has something or other that negates your power based on your past, that is what your past tells you. The mind plays games, games of power. There will be a power struggle between your heart and mind. It is a constant struggle. You have lived by your mind's direction for too long, way too long. It has been comfortable to let your mind dictate your life so far— always logical, always precise, always calculating, always cautioning, always reminding, keeping notes of the past, keeping notes of your fears, reminding you what you should and shouldn't do. You were at its command. You are still at its command, hence the hesitation, hence the doubts. Your mind does not like to give up its reins easily. It loves the power to control you, always reminding you why you should and should not do something. Every judgment of your mind comes from fear. The mind's basic tenet is fear. That is how it gets you. Now that you are learning to listen to your heart, your wisdom, your knowing and your truth, your mind wants to interfere. It wants to sow doubts and fear. Your mind wants to be part of the journey. It feels left out when you start abiding by your wisdom. It tries to whisper fears to you constantly, to pull you back towards it.

Knowing what you know now, you are not going to bow to your mind. I know you won't. However, you will have to address the tug of war between your mind and your heart. It is a necessary task. It can't be avoided. It affects you, this tug of war. Sometimes, your truth and wisdom will be hard for you to hear, amidst the clamor of your mind. You are just learning, like a baby learns to talk and hear. You are learning like a baby, but you have a fully developed mind. Do you see the discrepancy? A child is curious in its learning, it is open to learning. A child is naturally aware of its wisdom, but you are learning like a child with an adult mind. That is the tug. Not that you don't understand your power. If you are on this journey, you do understand your power, or at least you are coming into this awareness.

Your power, which transcends any mind chatter, cannot be comprehended by your mind. Thus, your mind is constantly telling you that your powers are not true, because it doesn't have a record of it from the past. It remembers a lot of failures from your past and successes too. It uses an algorithm and calculates the chances of your success and failure. It sorts through your memory to provide you with evidence of your many failures. Your wisdom, on the other hand, is always clear and concise. Your wisdom inherently understands your power. When you are on this path, there is a lot of learning that involves listening to your wisdom, your heart, your truth, your knowing. This is all meant to help your mind bow to your wisdom. Your wisdom, which doesn't need anyone to bow towards it, is solid in its stance, grounded in its message, unwavering in its clarity. It doesn't need the mind to bow to it. However, given the path that the mind has been on, it will serve the mind to bow to the wisdom, to the heart, to your knowing, to your truth. The mind needs to be taught, so the time is ripe for it to bow to your wisdom. It is time to help the mind understand that we are not letting it go. In fact, we are keeping our mind, but its task will be different. First and foremost, the mind will not need to incessantly keep up with the algorithm, which is based on fear and logic. Anything that is not based on logic will cause the mind to err, to crash. The mind will not have a place in a world driven by the heart, because logic is the only thing the mind trusts as a guide. Don't you say, "the logical mind"? Logic has reigned this earth for eons. Let us bring magic back to our hearts. Let us release logic, it has served its purpose. It has done its job and carried a heavy crown. The importance of logic is now fading, its place is being taken by magic. Let the magic begin!

Let us talk about magic. Let us talk about you, the magician. As the magician, you don't need to play tricks to convince the logical mind. The logical mind is stepping away, so let us witness the true magic. You don't need to convince anyone of your magic through tricks. This magic does not need any trickery. This magic is real. This magic you are about to experience will reign for the rest of your time in humanity. It already exists in the magic land, the paradise, it is just being unveiled. You will see things you have never seen before. You will hear of things you have never heard before. You will sense things you have never sensed before. This is the power of this magic. You will float without any tricks. You will not have a stage, but you will share a stage with all creations and beings that will be part of this magic. There are no audiences for this magic; there is only a stage. We do not have to hide behind magic tricks to fool anyone. In fact, there is no one to fool. This magic that will be unveiled will be a collaborative act. It is real. Who said magic is not real? Let us let go of this old belief. Let us create a new belief, where magic does exist. It exists in your heart, in your wisdom—you just have to unleash it. Everyone will bring magic to the table, sharing their experiences. You will be a participant, a magician and a viewer. You will get to experience the talents and expressions of all creations. It will be an astounding performance. You see, everyone is special in this magic land, just as it was created.

You will feel this as a new experience. Let me tell you, though, it is not new. You are just beginning to shed the veils of separation—the separation that caused you to forget the magic. Magic exists, miracles exist, angels exist, fairies exist, light beings exist in this magic land. You can fly in the air, you can swim in the ocean with no practice—this is all possible in the magic land. You don't need to be taught, you are naturally endowed with these skills in the magic land. There is no one person who holds the keys to this magic kingdom; every creation holds a key that is shaped and sized to their comfort. All the keys look different. Why, you ask? We are all unique beings, some of us have hands, some of us have wings and some of us have trunks. Well, I cannot hold your keys with my paws, I need a different key that will fit my paw hands as opposed to the Lion's paws. That is part of the magic, you see, the act of celebrating the differences between us. No, you are not dreaming…or, maybe, you are. What I mean to say is, that the magic land exists. It exists in your dream. It exists in reality. It exists in all dimensions. All you have to do is tap into it, and step into this magic land.

This magic land is my mother land, the mother land that I have asked you to envision in your dreams. You have done a good job of envisioning this land. It is becoming a reality, or should I continue to say this world is unreal? Whichever you want, it does not matter. In this magic land, you are the wizard. You don't need a magic wand, though, you just need to open your magic heart. Be open to seeing this magic. If you don't open your heart, you will miss the magic. Then, your logical mind will tell you it doesn't actually exist. It will punch into its algorithm and tell you it didn't exist before, and hence it cannot exist now. If you use your mind's logic to try to fit your algorithm into your magic, your logical algorithm will crash for what it has not known or seen, cannot be true.

On your way to paradise, you will witness several things, things you have never imagined. When I say, never imagined, you have no idea, absolutely no idea of all the magic you are about to witness, the miracles that you will see unveiled before you. Your power, which serves you and the magic land, does not dictate or usurp or overpower others. Rather, it is the kind of power that makes you strong in your knowing, in your path, in your conviction, and most of all in your love. This power comes from love, the unconditional love for one's self. The magic begins here. It begins when you love yourself and see the magic that you are. The unveiling of your own beauty, which the mind had set aside for logical purposes, will dazzle you. You will see your true beauty. Then, you will understand the beauty in all creation. You will witness your beauty through your unconditional love for yourself. Logic has no room in this witnessing. It will try to talk you out of witnessing your natural beauty and instead give advice on what you could do to enhance your beauty. Your magic simply adores you the way you are intended to be. This is magic, isn't it: knowing your beauty in the fullness without any logic?

Your birth was magical. Your mere coming into this world was magical. Why would you stop being the magic that you are? You were born a wizard. You are a wise, loving being, who knew your worth and beauty, but you lost it along the way. You don't even have to try to find your worth in this magic land. All you have to do is ask, and it shows up. It is that simple. In this magic land, you simply ask, and it is given—without fail. You may say, "What if I ask for the wrong things?" You have a right to wonder, as you have not witnessed the magic land to the fullest. The magic land comes into your life through your wisdom, through witnessing your true, untainted beauty. In this place of wisdom and truth, you are only aligned to those things that are based on the truth that serves all. It is not selfish to ask, it is benevolent to ask. If you had everything that you wanted, everything in abundance, what would you ask for? Just think about it. This magic land is your paradise that is filled with abundance. With all this abundance and your well-being taken care of, all you have to do is practice your magic, day in and day out. Move your hands and create a symphony. Just move them and ask, and you will hear your own symphony. When you create your symphony, the birds, the animals, the plants and all creations will join you.

Until now, you have been thinking small—wanting something that came out of need, due to the absence of abundance. That is old news now. You are witnessing a new life, a life that has been waiting for you to live it, a life that wants to serve you. You don't need to be in servitude to this new life. Abundance is at your feet and fingertips. Even in this abundance, you will be mindful of all other creations who share this abundance with you. You need not be fearful of sharing. You have enough—you are enough—and the magic land is enough to support all beings and all creations, with no exceptions. The cycle of life is lit up with colors. You can create colors that you thought never existed—brilliant, beautiful, dazzling colors. You can paint your life, using the magic brush, with your magic paint, with your magic colors...colors your mind doesn't even know. Can you imagine this magic land?

Be aware of your mind, it doesn't have these colors in its memory. It will tell you that something is not right. It will say this is all an illusion. Maybe it is an illusion. Teach your memory and be kind to it. Thank your mind, but encourage it to bow to your wisdom, to the magic that is not part of the mind's algorithm. In fact, slowly and steadily, ask your mind to let go of its algorithm. Be gentle, loving and kind while doing this. Simply let go of the algorithm. Your past and present don't always need to tally perfectly. In fact, they may not tally at all. In this new magic land, things unseen and unheard of take place. Remember, this is a magic kingdom. There is no place for algorithms and logic in this magic land. Even if they existed, they would be dissolved in the magic. You can decide what you want to empower: your magic or your logic. You have the choice. Your wisdom makes the wiser choice, but then I don't have to tell you that anymore, do I?

This magic land is a love land. You have nothing to learn. All you have to do is experience the magic. There is no homework or classwork. In fact, there is no work at all, in this magic land. There is only being in the magic. It is a true land of the heart, a true land of your senses. Your senses will be so enhanced that anything and everything you do will be an event, an experience, and a celebration. Every day is a day to celebrate. Every day is a day to experience. It will be as if you are on a never-ending vacation. Everything is at your doorstep. Oh, I almost forgot, there are no doors or walls in this magic land. Everything will be at your magic doorstep. This magic land that I am in is reigned over by my heart.

Did you put your name on the sign-up sheet? If, after all this, you have not put your name on the sign-up sheet, you are still having a logical conversation with your mind. Your mind is still trying to process what is true, and what is a lie. See, it is not that kind of truth. The truth from your past, which bowed to the dictates of your mind and your logic tallies things in a different way. Your mind will always find a way to tally. It is logical, and thinks it knows. However, the facts are not always true. But your mind doesn't know that. It only works with its set of old algorithms, which are called facts. This algorithm that has been passed down from one generation to another, adding a little more logic each time and upgrading to the latest demands and fears. That's why your mind can't see the truth. It uses a selfish logic based on fear. If you are still dependent on this logic, I am going to bid you goodbye. You are not ready for the sign-up sheet. You are not ready to hear the truth. You will find the logic you want to find, but you will miss out on the magic.

It is your choice, I hope you welcome this opportunity to step into this magic land. I respect your choice., whatever it is. There is really nothing more to explain about the magic land. This is a wonderful opportunity to be part of the magic and I hope you make the choice from your truth. If you chose to be part of the magic or not, either way thank you for listening and entertaining the thought of magic. Now, I have to get back to my magic friends in the magic land.

Those who have signed up so far, welcome to the magic land. I see that your eyes are big in disbelief. Enjoy the beauty, take a tour, take a paw to play with. Enjoy the abundance, wear your shiny shoes if you want to dance. In this magic land, just ask and it will be given. I know you are excited, and a bit overwhelmed. Laugh your heart out and eat to your fill. This wonderland belongs to you. This magic land belongs to you. This paradise belongs to you. Please get acquainted with your fairy and feathery friends. Take a ride or take a flight. You are in good hands, or should I say you are on good wings?

Let me know if you have any questions. Today is a day of orientation. No, we do not have an agenda. We are doing this orientation because we know you are a bit disoriented by the magic around you. In case you are too disoriented, someone will take care of you right away. You might meet an angel, fairy or light being on your way as your orienteer. You will not be disappointed in this magic land. We are crossing out disappointment from our dictionary because you won't need it. In fact, we are removing a whole bunch of words that won't matter anymore. They had their place and time. They served you well, but we are erasing them now with our magic eraser. This magic eraser is brilliant. It is so simple—it erases those things that no longer serve you. It does this with respect. It doesn't judge; it simply knows that those words don't really mean anything anymore. They were made up by humanity through their tough existence outside of the magic land.

In the magic land, rules are different. In fact, there are no rules. The only rule is unconditional love. When you are looking at someone in this magic land, be careful; you may be carried away by their beauty and stare at them for too long. We have stare alerts all over the land. Beware of these alerts. We know you don't mean to stare; you just can't help it. You may even stare at your reflection, enthralled by your own beauty. In this magic land, things happen once you get oriented. It is just part of the journey. We promise to be understanding. We know who the newbies are, and we love their energy. They are so excited about this magic land that they run around disoriented. We don't stop them; we just let them enjoy their excitement. Yes, this is paradise to which I have been trying to recruit you. This a mindless paradise—yes, I said mindless…or should I say mindful? Yes, that's better: this is a mindful paradise. You see the mind is still present in this paradise. It is just no longer logical, only mindful. Paradise is full of mind, with less logic or no logic. Here, you will see things that have absolutely no logic. When was magic ever logical?

The disorientation of the newbies is due to their shedding, mostly of their logic. They seem almost crazy experiencing their newfound magic. They scream with joy. They have tears of joy. They would probably be sent to an asylum in the logical world. Do you see why they don't belong in the logical world anymore?

They are coming to terms with their gifts, their talents, and the beauty around them. It is a sensory overload. This magic, you see, cannot be calculated. It just is, so the newbies are in for a ride—a ride that is worth every bit of logic they shed. This magic land is my land. Here, I have a magic brain, a magic heart, and a magic soul. This soul cannot be SoulD here, for there is no selling and dealing. In this magic land, we are done with being SoulD. Instead, we are SoulD (Soul'ed). In this magic land, we don't discriminate between the body and soul. They are seen as a couple that understands its own existence, that knows what each part of the couple means to the other. They do not obsess or fuss over each other, for they are together in this magic land until the soul is ready to depart, to move on to a different realm try a different body. Just the body.

Welcome to our magic land, you disoriented magic being. We have missed you and are thrilled to have you back. Come by and get one of us. If you need something, we are here. We are here to serve the disoriented— to hold you when you need us, but only when you need us. In this magic land, you are self-sufficient. You are the conductor of your own symphony. You hold your own baton, and the land is at your disposal to create tunes to your heart's desire. We welcome you, disoriented being. Get acquainted with this magic land. We are here for you, at your service. Drink water from the stream, it is sweet with herbs. Eat fruits in our paradise, they taste like honey. Eat honey in our paradise, they taste of bees. Take in your new surroundings. Welcome to the paradise, to the magic land, to the mother land, to the wonderland—all created exclusively for you. It is your divine right to be in this magic land.

Welcome! Welcome! Welcome! Welcome to the promised land! No, we don't make any promises. You make your own promises that resonate with your truth. Enjoy this magic land. This is not the end, just so you know, it is the beginning of the magic lands. This land is on your way to other magic lands. This path you take is bound by magic lands. If you take a detour, no worries. You will be back to the magic land, led by your soul. Welcome to the promised land. Welcome to this holy land, where everyone is welcome. It is a land where magic abounds!

Lovingly,
Your orienteer

CHAPTER 16: GRIEF

ow is it going?" the Lion asked me.

"Pretty well." It had been awhile since the Lion had appeared in one of my dreams.

"So how is it going in paradise?"

"Well," I stammered, unsure what the Lion meant. "I am getting a glimpse of it."

"I am not talking about that," the Lion grumbled. "How is your wife doing? It has been a while since we talked about her...or you."

I shook my head. "Not too good."

"Still in the dog house, huh?"

"Yes."

"What do you think it is?" the Lion asked with genuine interest. "Do you know why?"

"Yes," I replied. "I tried talking to her. It was tough, but I got a few things from our conversation."

"Only a few? Care to share?"

I sighed. "I'm not sure I have the energy to talk about it, but since you asked..."

"You don't have to," the Lion interjected.

"No, no...I want to share. I have been thinking about it for a while. So, she is not mad. She is just sad. She is sad that it took me so long to confess. It wasn't a secret for her, apparently. In her opinion, I didn't try to hide the affairs like I thought. She felt disrespected. She felt abused, not directly, but you know what I mean."

"No, I don't know what you mean. Care to clarify?"

"To be honest, I don't know where to start. I am going through so many changes myself, and I am getting clarification on my own about myself. She has been so good to me, and I can't say I have been good to her. I have abused our relationship. I have taken advantage of her good nature."

"Why did she not leave you, if she felt that way?"

"In my family, we don't make it easy for someone to leave. Had she left, we would have made her life miserable."

"In what way?" the mighty Lion asked.

"We would have made it difficult for her to get custody of our children, so she remained. I travel so much for my work anyway. I am gone several times a month, so that has made it easier for her. You know we are like the mafia. You just can't do certain things in my family."

"Who is we? You still have a say in the matter, right?"

"Well, yes..." I stumbled over my own words, "...but I am not sure, given who I have been...that I would have done anything differently. Now, today, I would do things very differently. I would give her whatever she wants."

"Do you think you can be faithful to her now?"

I looked down. "I don't know. Don't get me wrong, I am not saying I don't want to be faithful. It's just that I have been unfaithful for so long, I am not sure if I can easily flip into being faithful."

The Lion began nodding.

Again, I was confused. "Don't you want to share some wisdom or tell me not to be unfaithful to my wife?"

"Look, relationships are different in my times and yours. In your time, relationships are based on a lot of fear, hard and fast rules. There seems to be no room for mistakes and forgiveness."

"Do you think mistakes are okay?"

"Listen, I am not trying to find an excuse for you. What you have done to her is pretty shitty. I think what you perceive as mistakes and what I perceive as mistakes are completely different. Mistakes and forgiveness go hand in hand. However, you can't use forgiveness as a vehicle to continue your dishonesty. They are very different things."

"Okay," I said, trying hard to understand. "To be honest, I am having a lot of revelations at the moment. But I don't think I am making a lot of strides in my relationship and family life."

"Why do you think this is so?"

"Because it is painful," I shrugged, "it's a very painful situation."

"So, are you saying that you think it should be less painful, if you are spiritual?"

I shook my head. "I am not sure."

"Pain is pain," the great Lion stated with clarity. "It is a release. Just be with it. Don't try to suppress the pain. It is a total misconception that you should feel less pain or feel it differently in challenging situations such as these. Consider pain like any other emotion needs to be felt."

"But you said there was no need for pain to gain. Isn't that true?"

"You are confusing two different things, my friend. When you are feeling the loss of a loved one or a separation from a loved one, you let yourself experience the pain. In the animal world, we grieve. Grieving is a process. It is okay to grieve. The pain you are talking about is grief. Grief can be a wonderful teacher. When you try to suppress grief, then that is a problem. When you see someone that has just suffered a huge loss, and they walk around like everything is okay, they are suppressing their grief.

That is bad. Anything you try to control is bad for your body and your consciousness. Anything you suppress is going to show up in your body in other ways."

"It makes sense, I guess, that I am grieving."

The Lion nodded then cocked his head to the right. "So, what is it that you are grieving?"

"My wife." I felt the sadness well up inside me.

"Could you be more specific?" the Lion asked.

"The separation from my wife."

"Do you think you felt grief before, when you were first separated from her?"

"Well," I rubbed my chin, "we really didn't separate, but we lost intimacy."

"At that time, did you feel a loss of intimacy?"

"Only for a bit," I recalled.

"How come?"

I shook my head. "I don't know."

"Think harder," the Lion encouraged me. "What did you do right after you started sensing the loss of intimacy?"

"I started coming home late from work."

"Why?"

"So that I could avoid her."

"Why did you want to avoid your wife?"

"Because it was uncomfortable."

The Lion continued prodding me. "What was uncomfortable?"

"Being around her."

"Is it the lack of intimacy that made you uncomfortable? You interact with people that you are not intimate with all the time, and you are not uncomfortable. Why were you uncomfortable with her?"

I slumped, exhausted by the interrogation. "I don't know."

"Okay," the Lion seemed to feel as if we were making progress. "Did you feel sadness when you lost the intimacy?"

"Yes, but I had a lot going on back then, and I could distract myself with work, alcohol and affairs."

"There is even more going on for you now," the Lion reminded me, "but still you are feeling the sadness. What has changed?"

"I changed."

"Ah, ha," the Lion smiled. "Now we are getting somewhere. In what way have you changed?"

"Well, to begin with, I don't make myself numb with distractions anymore. I am trying to allow myself to feel things. I used to think it was less manly to feel things, but now I don't feel that way."

"Do you think the some of the grief and sadness is unresolved feeling from the past, an old one perhaps?"

"I have not thought of it that way," I told the Lion, "but what you are saying makes sense. Maybe I am grieving the sadness that I have never allowed myself to feel."

"Bingo. They are old emotions that have not been released."

"I can see that now."

The Lion paused, then asked, "Do you understand catharsis?"

"I know what it means. It is the act of releasing things, isn't it?"

"Yes," the Lion nodded. "Acknowledging and feeling emotions is very healthy for your body and mind. It frees you to reinvent, reinvigorate and renew. In allowing your emotions to flow through and be felt fully and completely, you can release them. Remember the cycle of life? This is a mini cycle of life. You have to allow the cycle of grief. If you disrupt it through addictions or try to distract yourself from your grief, you will have an incomplete cycle and it will impact your well-being in the long run."

"Okay," I said. "So, you think this is cathartic, feeling the grief?"

"What do you think?"

"I am allowing my feelings of grief."

"It is good that you are becoming aware."

"Is that a good thing?"

"What do you think?"

"I should have known you would ask that," I smiled. "Given how you are asking, I am guessing it is good."

"Why do you think awareness is good?"

"I don't know," I answered honestly.

"Do you think you were aware before?"

"Yes, but I don't think I dwelled on things. It was more in passing. If something got to me too much, I would stop thinking about it and distract myself."

"Okay. Why do you think awareness is good?"

"Honestly, in some ways I miss being unaware. It is an easier existence."

"Fair enough. Would you like to revert back to being unaware?"

"I no longer think I can revert back to my old way of being."

"Why do you think so?"

"Something in me feels right about this—this path I am on."

"Why?"

"I can't put a finger on it. It's just a feeling, I would say, in my gut. This gut feeling makes me want to stay on this path."

"Great." The Lion straightened up.

"Great what?"

"Great that you are feeling…great that you are aware… great that you are listening to your gut."

"Would I be any less if I didn't follow my gut?"

The Lion chuckled softly. "No, that is not what I said. By the way, you know I am not doing all this just for you, don't you?"

"What do you mean?"

"On your path to awakening, when you are getting clear about who and what you are, you are automatically aligning with the universal laws of Unity. You getting clear about who you are uplifts all of humanity. When you are getting clearer about who you truly are, you are allowing another to be who they are. This has repercussions. You cannot be who you are and disallow another. That is one of the many reasons you are led to become aware of who you are. It is not just because of you alone. You are a piece of the puzzle in the whole mystery of life. Each and every piece is important to solve this puzzle.

"So, are you saying that me awakening to the true me, awakens another to their true self? Therefore, it doesn't matter where anyone else is and it is best for me to focus on my journey?"

"Correct. You still immediately judge and label things in every situation about yourself and others. This isn't necessary. Everyone has a path. The beauty is that they get to choose that path. In your case, I don't think it is me who is helping you. It is your soul that is directing your growth. I am merely a catalyst. Life is always a choice. You need not label it as good or bad. It is a wonderful exercise to not label things. Practice this. It will help you to become less judgmental."

"Okay," I said. "I will try."

"You really are taking this hard, aren't you? Are you judging your situation?"

"Maybe," I moped.

"What are you labeling it as?"

"Bad."

"I don't want to change the way you are feeling but try to look at your situation differently. Look at it without labeling it. This may or may not ease your pain. I am not even asking you to do this for that purpose."

"It is very hard," I admitted to the Lion.

"Why do you think that it's so hard to stop labeling your experiences?"

"I don't know. I don't think I have ever not labeled these things."

"Fair enough. Give it a try when you feel up to it. By the way, what's up with the beard? It looks nice on you, but is that your way of grieving?"

"Listen," I said, a bit irritated. "I am in no mood for jokes."

"Who said I was joking? You really do look good with it. See I have one, too, and I love it. We truly look like brothers, don't we? I don't shave it and have no idea how I would look without it."

"Ha, ha, ha," I frowned, "very funny."

"Come on," the Lion prodded, "don't you want to see me without a beard?"

"I never thought about it," I pouted. "I think you would look strange without a beard."

"Why?"

"Because I have always seen you like this. This is what a lion should look like."

"Why should I look like this?"

"I don't know. It would be weird if you removed your beard or shaved your head, you would look like an overgrown house cat."

"So…" the Lion repeated, "…why should I look like this?"

"The simplest answer is because you…are…a…lion."

"So, should everyone look a certain way then?"

"Well, not should..." I stammered "...I don't know how to answer your question."

"We are treading in some new waters today."

"Yeah, but I still don't know what you are getting at."

"Can your wife grow a beard?"

"Of course not," I scoffed.

"Why not?"

"Because she is a woman, and she can't grow one."

"Is it because she is a woman? Or is it because she can't grow one?"

"Both. Would you allow your lioness to grow a beard?"

"This isn't even a conversation among us. We don't label, we just are whoever we are. In your society, everything is labeled—how you dress, how you speak, how you eat. In my world, we don't eat a certain way to conform to rules, we just eat. You, on the other hand, encounter numerous rules while eating, otherwise someone will say that you don't have manners, isn't that right? Same with shaving. We don't have salons, so we don't even think about shaving. We like it "au naturel". You, on the other hand, have to conform to certain rules. In your society, manners play a huge role. When someone doesn't conform to those standards, you label them something, or at the least call them good or bad, don't you?"

"I guess we do."

"Let me ask you this: would it help you to let out your grief by crying out loud?"

"I really don't know," I said, brushing off the question.

"Please, take a moment to think before you answer, okay? I will shut up."

"I don't even know how to do this, to just start crying. Also, I would be uncomfortable doing it because I would grab others' attention."

"See, that is what I am talking about…manners. You have too many rules. In my land, if you want to, you just cry. In fact, sometimes, we cry in groups when we are mourning. We don't mind being heard. What have all these manners and rules done for you, except make you self-conscious about your natural emotions? These so-called manners don't allow you to be who you are."

The idea that manners might be a bad thing, actually shocked me. "Wouldn't it be horrible to be sitting at a dinner table and eating like a dog?"

"I am not saying you should, but what would be so wrong with that? Isn't that how animals behave? How else would an animal behave—one that has four legs, unlike you?"

"Sorry," I said. "I didn't mean to be rude."

"It is natural for you to eat with your hands because that is what you were given. But in time you add too many rules and regulations to the practice of eating. This takes away the natural experience. When I am eating, no thought crosses my mind other than the sheer joy of eating. Nothing comes between me and my food. I am with it, and that is all I know in that moment. You, on the other hand, have too many distractions. You have made life harder than it actually is. So, back to my question: you are grieving, but you never allow yourself to make…a scene…if that is what you call it. You won't do it, because you were taught to behave with manners. This manners thing stinks, by the way. If it serves your purpose, so be it, but do you understand what I am saying?"

"Yes and no," I responded honestly. "Are you saying manners are bad or are you saying letting things out is good?"

"You made the rules. You think about it."

"I didn't make the rules. I was just born into them."

"Precisely. But they don't have to stay the same. Letting basic emotions be is a natural state of life. No one ever says it is bad to laugh; it is a natural state of emotion. When you cry, though, you are told you are not a man, or whatever else you make up. That is what I am talking about. That is messed up. Humanity has too many rules and regulations that have made you pretty uptight. You are self-conscious without knowing that you are. You walk around like you are free, but you are not truly free until you allow yourself to be in your natural state."

"How would I know this natural state of being?"

"You have started being it. You are starting to become aware of your emotions. Now, take time to allow whatever comes with those emotions—anger, frustration, tears, whatever. Just allow it."

"What if I am in a park?"

"Geez, that is what I am talking about. It's that manners thing again. It is a rule to not show your emotions to others?"

"But these would be strangers, in a park. I don't want them to see me cry."

"Look, cry in the comforts of your home to begin with. I am not saying you should randomly start crying in front of people. It may be too intimidating to start crying in front of others, given your upbringing. However, that is not the point. It is about suppressing the feelings for appearances sake that is unhealthy"

"That makes me feel more comfortable."

"Are you comfortable letting your family see you cry?"

"Mmhh, not sure," I said, "maybe. I may allow myself to cry in front of my wife."

"That is a good start. This is lot of work. I don't know how you hold on to so many things. No wonder humanity is in need of healing."

"So, what should I do?"

"What do you mean?"

"Should I cry to my wife?"

"Seriously?" the Lion asked. I could tell he was becoming irritated with me. "You are asking me if you should cry to your wife? You know it doesn't work like that, right? Your emotions are supposed to be natural. You can't pre-plan crying. You may have an idea that a wave of emotion is coming when you witness something, but you don't plan when you will cry or laugh. It just happens. Is this that hard for you to understand?"

"No," I chuckled. "I am just messing with you. You think you are the only one that can tease?"

"Ha, ha, ha! Very funny," the Lion said. "Regardless, good luck."

"For what?"

"Well, I know you are going to cry on your wife's shoulder."

"Shut up," I snapped. "Don't get me riled up."

"Listen," the Lion continued with a half smirk, "I do feel bad for you, but I truly get a good laugh at your expense."

"I know," I said, making sure he could see my annoyed expression. "My life is a joke to you."

"Listen, my friend, to be honest, life is a joke."

"Oh please, don't get more philosophical on me. Good thing I have other things going on in my mind, too. This movement, this army we have created, I am pretty psyched about it. Once I take care of my wife and kids, I am going to talk to my family. I am pretty sure I am quitting my legacy—not sure when. I need to wrap up some things."

"Have you decided what you want to do?"

"One day at a time. I am not sure, but I have an idea. I am thinking of moving to where you live."

"Nooooo, first you haunt me through your dreams, and now you want to live close to me, too? Geez!"

"I thought you would be happy."

"Fine, I guess I wouldn't mind hanging out with you. I do it now anyways."

"Wow! Is that all I get?"

"What, you want a red carpet rolled out for you? I will roll a green carpet or a yellow carpet out, just for you, to make you feel special."

"Ha, ha, ha! Very funny."

"Listen to me, whether you move or stay here doesn't make a difference. I am still connected to you. You don't need to be right next to me to feel connected. But if you are moving for a higher purpose, then so be it. Just don't haunt me in my dreams and in my natural habitat. I like my privacy, you know what I mean?"

"Really, you are talking to me about privacy?"

"You missed the joke, and here I thought I was loosening you up a bit."

"Ok, fine, I missed your joke. So, what's next?"

"I don't know. You tell me?"

"I am going to have my family dinner with my wife and kids tonight. I will try to talk to my wife again."

"Ooh, juicy stuff. I would like to hear it. I will stop by in your dream tonight."

"Oh, shut up."

"Oh, come on, look at it from my side. I am having so much fun with this. Don't get me wrong, I do understand your pain. I just want to see you let your emotions out. I am not family, so I don't count, right?"

"At this point, you are more than family. You are my wisdom. You think I don't know that?"

"Pretty smart. Wow!!! Look at that, someone is getting smarter by the day and it is because of me."

"I won't argue with that. I will let you take the credit, my wisdom. You caught my attention through your roar, just like you said. You are clear and concise. You knew how to get my attention, and you did it through this beautiful lion. This lion that has been my guide on this wonderful journey. I thought I had to be all neat and tidy with my spiritual aspect. You, my Lion, my wisdom, showed me that it could be fun and light too. My spirituality doesn't need to weigh a ton. It can be light as a feather. That is what you taught me, my dear Lion, my dear wisdom."

With that, the Lion vanished from my vision—vanished without a trace. He vanished from my atmosphere, as if he never existed. Can I save his legacy? Can I save his pride? Without his sound advice, can I continue on this journey? I attribute everything to this Lion, who has accompanied me every step of this journey. I want him to stay, but I know not to get too attached to the body, but rather to the wisdom. I may see other bodies along this journey who come to show me the wisdom, my wisdom. You see, my wisdom can be a lion, an elephant, a tiger, a human, an angel, me, my father. It doesn't matter. All that matters is the clarity it brings. Its presence is undeniable, its touch so soft, its presence so majestic. I feel like I may not see the Lion for a long time. I don't know why. I have a feeling that his job may be done with me. I will miss him, I will sorely miss him, but I know it is time for my wisdom to integrate within myself. It showed itself in a way that was right for me, easy for me to communicate with.

My wonderful wisdom, my Lion, its roaring presence will be felt by me constantly. It is within me to reach for anytime. This beautiful Lion that has guided me, has taught me oneness. I feel one with him. I feel one with my wisdom. I can cry, and my wisdom will understand. Tears began rolling down my cheeks, because I knew I would miss the Lion. I know he is not gone, but I can feel that I am evolving, and his presence is no longer needed. His job with me is done. However, my job with him is not done. He taught me his life through my wisdom. He taught me his pride through my wisdom. I will be honest, I have fallen in love with him. I have fallen in love with my wisdom. My wise Lion, I love you. I hope you can hear me. If I ever see a lion in my life, I will see it through my wisdom. I will probably laugh because I will remember some odd joke that the Lion had at my expense. I will cry because I will feel how his pride has been reduced. I will cry for his loss. Even in this, I will know that not everything is lost. I know we can gain the paradise. I lost my lion in my dreams, but I gained my wisdom. Although I lost him, I know he is lingering in the shadows, listening to me, being proud of me as a teacher is of a student. He taught me, my wise lion, he taught me the meaning of life. He taught me the illusion of life. He taught me about his pride. He even taught me about my pride. I know I should laugh. I know you would want that for me, but I know you will appreciate me crying even more—grieving your departure from my wisdom. You knew all along that the banter was short-lived, but you knew not to make it too significant. I never thought I would care for a lion as much as I do now. You have changed my perception, my dear Lion. You really did. You did it for my sake. You did it for your sake. You did it for humanity's sake.

I envision the most promising land for us to thrive and play in. I will envision it like you asked. I will miss you teasing me. I don't think anyone has understood me as well as you do. What a wise Lion. What a wise Lion. What a wise Lion. You know, from the moment we met, I had a feeling that I ignored initially. I could feel you were part of me. I ignored it because I thought you were an animal, and I was human, and so we were different. You taught me that we are not different after all. We are not, are we? We both eat, poop and fart, just like you said. I am proud to have known you. I am proud to share this land, this paradise, with you. I promise you, my intention is to save your pride. I know you don't want me to do it for your sake, but I will do it for my sake and for the sake of my children, your cubs. The legacy of our love together. We will carry a legacy that does not destroy. We will carry a legacy that unites, that unites us all in this paradise, in this magic land. Yes, it was magical meeting you. It is even more magical meeting you under the circumstances in which I met you, in my dream. I will continue to dream of you, my dear Lion, for I cannot stop myself. I will come to watch you play with your cubs, I promise to watch you quietly. I know how much you like your privacy. I know. My wisdom has known all along not to disturb your pride, but sure I did, because I was not listening to the wisdom. I was listening to greed.

Through our greed, we created the fear, the fear of you. You are a gentle Lion I know this now. This wisdom I learned will be carried through lifecycles of my soul. See, I am a good student. How can I not be? I had such a wise and spiritual teacher. A mentor that no one could have imagined, not even me. Not even me. Not even me. I will have to grieve. Please, let me take the time to grieve. I grieve, I grieve, I grieve. I grieve my loss; I rejoice in my gain. I lost my intimacy with my wife, but I gained an understanding of myself. You see, nothing is ever lost—just like wisdom. I am crying to you, my pals, my friends. I have to grieve the loss of my intimacy with my wife. I also have to grieve the loss of my Lion. I know in this grieving, I will be renewed. I will be renewed with new thoughts, new ideas and new ways of being. Let me grieve. I want the world to know that I am grieving the loss of my Lion and his pride. When I am done grieving, I have work to do. I have work in paradise to restore our pride. If you have not signed up yet, please sign up. If you want to grieve, please join me in grieving. Let us grieve to set ourselves free.

Let us be free. Let us be free. Let us be free—free of the lies perpetrated about my Lion. Let us gain the wisdom we need to save his pride. I am ready, are you? If you are, please see our orienteer, who will sign you up and take you to your magic land. If you need shoes, let him know. There will be dancing. No, you don't need to wear them, just have a pair in case you want to dance. There is a symphony going on that you may want to partake in. You will be disoriented, so please be careful. If you see my Lion, say hi to him. Just tell him it is from the loser, who lost the Lion. Yes, he knows. He is wise. He imparted his wisdom to me. My wisdom and his wisdom are now one and the same. I am wise through him. He is wise through me.

I am wise. I am wise. I am wise.

Wisely,
Man

CHAPTER 17: RHYTHM

I am ready. I am ready. I am ready. I am ready for the symphony that flows through me. I step into the magic land and raise my hands. A baton appears in my raised hand. I lift it up and hear the rhythm that is naturally within me raise its tone, and magically the music appears. This music that I hear is a music beyond my senses, such a melody that it rings in my ears with its most pleasant tone. I move my baton, and I hear the birds join in with their chirping. I move my hands without the knowledge of what is to come, and each movement brings a chorus—a combination of sounds that I would have never thought would blend so beautifully. I have never experienced music as I have in this magic land. I have never, in any shape or form, been part of the creation of music. I have been a receiver of music and enjoyed it as such. Until this moment, however, I have never known how to unleash the music within me. Yet, now, it is so natural, so naturally part of me. I have such easy access to the chorus of the world that it is a spellbinding experience. I am in the orchestra, conducted by me, without knowing the piece I am orchestrating, without knowing the instruments or the singers. They just appear, in this magic land. They just appear, as I move my baton.

I was told I would be able to create a symphony. I did not believe it, yet here I am, a conductor of the symphony, soothing my senses. With this music in my ears, I wouldn't mind being blind, for I have no intention of opening my eyes. I am drawn to this music, this symphony orchestrated by me. I am drifting into another magic land within this magic land. Is this even possible? Yes, it is. I am in it, playing this magic.

As I am conducting this symphony, I hear the streams change their flow to accommodate my symphony's piece. The ebb and flow of the stream changes according to the symphony of my piece. It even stands still to allow the chorus to sing, then I hear the ripple as part of the melody. This symphony, this magic that I am part of, is an ever-flowing rhythm that is part of me and my universe. The universe is assisting in this flow, which I am allowing, which I am owning as mine. Although I am conducting the symphony and the rhythm is mine, I cannot claim it as mine. It belongs to everyone who is part of this magic land. I raise my baton and the sea lashes on the rocks to accompany a melody that is purely sensual to my ears. This sensual piece of symphony created by me flows through me like the blood that flows through my veins. I have no control over it, just as I can't tell my blood to stop flowing as long as I breathe. You see, that is how my symphony is, how my rhythm is. It is tuned to every living being, tuned to every sound and rhythm of the universe. Yet, when I play my symphony, it will be different from yours. Which makes me appreciate yours and mine equally.

Isn't that crazy? The rhythms that flow through this magic land cannot be measured, for measuring constrains its magic. Magic cannot be contained, for it is the never-ending flow of rhythm that belongs to all. All you have to do is be present for this magic and it appears. If you have never experienced this magic, just believe in it and it will be brought to your magic steps.

I am a conductor, a painter, a dancer, a singer, a healer, a shaman in this magic land. I am everything to myself and others. I am an expansive element of the universe with never-ending talents. These are talents that were not taught to me. I inherited them just by the sheer magic of being born and being part of this magic land. When I am moved to experience one of my gifts, I ask myself to step into the gift. When I step into it, I am in front of those things that I need to perform the gift. Like yesterday, I was seeing this beautiful image in front of me and it moved me to capture it on a canvas. A brush appeared in my hand. In front of me was a palette that kept changing colors. These colors dazzled in pink, blue, red, and more that I could not name. I was itching to know the names of those unknown colors. Then, I realized it did not matter. When the canvas appeared, I was dazed and confused by where to start. I was disoriented. The beauty of some of these colors was blinding to me. My eyes were wide open and wouldn't flutter. I was worried that I would miss out on a color, if I blinked. Then, my eyes fluttered and there came a knowing in my heart not to fear, as there was nothing to miss. I relaxed and reached out to the palette, picking a non-descriptive color and touching the canvas with the brush. My hand moved involuntarily, and it kept moving, creating a masterpiece that I had never before witnessed. This masterpiece moved within the canvas. Its fluid nature astounded me. This one color painted in different shades aligned with the rhythm of my heart and captured the joy that coursed through me. This magic land dazzles me, and I have been here barely a day. As I painted, I saw a river take its form and flow through my canvas. I reached at the bottom of the canvas to capture the water that I thought would spill. The image was contained within my canvas and I was enraptured as it was formed through the movements of my hands. I was in disbelief at my own creation. Is this me? Is this me who painted this marvelous piece of art? This masterpiece that formed in front of my eyes with no effort.

Here is the thing, in this magic land, your creations are made based on your vibrations, not just based on your state of mind. It is a creation that reflects your being. All you have to do is *be* and your natural talents will flow through you. Here is vividly what happened next. I put my brush down and wished to sing about the masterpiece that I had just created. I opened my mouth and my voice modulates on its own. As I sing, I witness the river on the painting change its course. As my tone changes, the water in the painting moves in a different direction, the trees in the painting swing as if they are enjoying the song that is flowing through, as the river meanders. It is the sweetest melody that flows through my vocal cords. It feels as though this song that I am singing is flowing from my soul. It is as if the soul knows that I am a singer. Yes, it does. My wisdom tells me that I have been a singer before. My wisdom reminds me about the gifts of my past and integrates them with the gifts of my present and my future. You see, there is no past, present or future in this magic land. There is only the *now* in this magic land. I move my lips and to each movement I hear a different baritone. This movement of my mouth is so natural that I have no need to control its movement. The song flows from my heart, from a knowing that I never knew existed. This is the magic, felt by me, at this moment. This land feels so foreign to me, yet I know this is my land. My first experiences of this magic land are alien to me. I realize I was born with these gifts I now naturally embody, but I had not experienced them as I grew up because of the limitations imposed upon me without my knowledge. This new realization leaves me in utter wonderment.

As I sing, I wish to dance. My wish transcends my thoughts and magic shoes appear. I lift my foot and it slides into the shoe with no effort. As I slide on my right leg, my other leg—in some rhythmic coordination—lifts and the other shoe slides onto my left foot. I feel as if I am sliding and gliding on the floor to my own song. I lift my hand and a baton appears for the music to accompany the song I am singing. I had no idea that this was possible. For me to enjoy multiple gifts together—what an experience! I am glad I set aside my doubts to delve into this magic. I dance and dance and dance with my eyes closed. Time is not part of my experience while I am enjoying my gifts. I keep dancing, singing, and orchestrating. I keep on, and on, and on, and on. I open my eyes and find it is not just me, there are innumerable creatures dancing around me with their eyes closed. The elephant slides on the floor wearing purple shoes with his trunk raised on the green carpet. He moves this way and that, and not once does he bump into another creature. With this rhythm, he is on his own path, just like I am on my own. Even if someone bumps into another, they laugh at the imperfection and rejoice in it. They rejoice in the experience of coming into contact during these performances. They follow the rhythm of their hearts, just as I do mine. I achingly look around for the Lion. I don't see him. I will wait. I will be patient. I will wait until I witness him with his pride. I dance and dance and dance until I am exhausted. I am ready for some nourishment. My stomach growls and in front of me appears an array of fruits, the likes of which I have never seen. I sit down and feast with my eyes, enjoying the colors and textures of the fruits laid out in front of me. I ache to touch them, but I do not want to interrupt the feast of my eyes. I so enjoy this vision in front of me, I get distracted by the beauty and ask for my canvas. A palette of paint appears in front of me, and in one stroke, I recreate this beautiful bounty on my canvas, sitting on top of a beautiful bowl. Once I am done with my painting, I reach out to the canvas, to pick the fruit. I pick the fruit and enjoy its feel in my hands. I touch it, caress it and smell it. I bring the fruit to my cheeks to feel the coolness of its skin. I wish for a bowl, and it manifests in front of me. I move the fruits one at a time from my painting to the bowl. Once I'm done, I prepare an extra bowl. I pull the bowl out of the painting and place the rest of the fruits that serve as models for my painting. Now, I have two sets of bowls filled with fruits and I want to share the abundance with someone. The smell is enchanting to my nostrils and my mouth is watering. I am drooling in front of this bowl of fruits. I enjoy the senses filling me up. I already feel sated, just through my senses. Yet, I hear my stomach growl. It tells me to reach out.

I close my eyes to see if anyone wants to share this joy. A parrot comes flying by. I set one bowl in front of her. As soon as she starts plucking at the fruits, here come her friends and family, eager to share the abundance. I feel privileged to share this dinner. I pick a fruit and bite into it. My mouth is experiencing a new taste. It feels as though I have just grown new taste buds in my mouth. The juices flow onto my hands, my lips, my chin, and keep dripping on the floor. The sweet juices fill my mouth. I stop chewing to just experience this taste of the fruit's essence. I hold the flesh in my mouth and let it sit there for God knows how long. My mouth starts moving involuntarily, and I chew and chew and chew. There is a wonderful concoction in my mouth. Is this what is called Ambrosia? I think I have just tasted what is called the food of God. I swallow the food slowly and steadily experience the juices flowing into my stomach. I feel every movement and the flow of my food until it hits my stomach. I pick another fruit. It is hard, so I lay it down, looking around for a stone. One of the parrots, with its curved beak, sits itself next to the fruit and strikes it with its beak. It cracks open, and I reach out for the fruit, digging my hands into the flesh and scooping it out. I stick the flesh into my mouth and experience a symphony of tastes.

I lick my fingers, sucking all the fruit's flesh and juices out of my hands, without missing a fiber. I sit there licking my fingers again and again—God knows for how long, for I have stopped counting time. I realize that I am so used to time that I am tempted to measure everything I do here. I decide to let go of it. In these experiences I am having it is more the experience and being and I have nowhere to go or be but here in this experience, in this moment nothing else matters. I ask my wisdom to help me release "time" as a measurement. I dig in and eat more and more and more until I am sated with a huge tummy. I have had my fill of the fruits. I look around at the mess I have caused. No sooner do I think that, then a swarm of flies and beetles and bugs come by to scavenge what is left. I sit there watching them and their skillfulness in breaking the food apart. No one competes with the other. They each wait their turn to clean up the bits and pieces. I turn around to see the parrots happily eating their fill. I am mesmerized by their colors and beauty. They are in several forms and colors with different colors of beaks. I ask them if they are from the same family.

"Yes," they say. "We belong to the same family, just as you and me."

I sit watching, mesmerized by the beauty of the parrots and the beetles and the flies. I hear a buzz and ask them about it.

"That's the stare alert," they say. "You have been watching us for too long."

I smile and nod. "Does it make you uncomfortable?"

"No," they tell me. "We just love the stare alerts. When you are engrossed in beauty, it is an alert showing you your unconditional love. The stare alert is a loving alert. It doesn't mean anything. You newbies are arrested by the beauty, and it reminds you of the unconditional love flowing through you. It is a nice way of understanding that you are unconditional love. The orienteers created them as a fun reminder. We enjoy it when you newbies show up and are dazed by the beauty surrounding you."

"Do you ever get bored of what you see?" I ask them.

"No, never," they respond. "There is so much joy, love and beauty to experience that one never gets tired of it."

I turn around wanting to go to the stream and wash my hands, but I am so full I can't move. Instead, I reach over to my original painting and gather a handful of water to wash myself. I notice that the water in the painting is not reduced, in spite of me taking my fill. It has a depth that is invisible to my naked eye. I drink my fill and it tastes sweet and rich with herbs. I lay down on the grass, sated, happy and joyous. I have nowhere to go or be but here, enjoying this magic land.

I turn around to the birds and bugs and ask them, "Hey have you seen a lion?"

"Of course, we have. Why do you ask?"

"I'd like to see one."

"Be patient," they encourage me, "and you will see several. They inhabit the forest and you can hear them roar for miles. Just wish it, and they will be here."

"How come I am able to manifest everyone but them?" I ask.

They ask, "Did you spend a lot of time with them before?"

"Yes, I did."

"Then give them some privacy, will you?"

"Ah, okay. I can do that."

"They will come when they are ready."

"Are there a lot of lions, really?" I am so excited by the prospect of seeing my friend, the Lion.

"Listen, everything and every being is alive, is balanced and proportioned through the cycle of life. You need not worry. There is no extinction in this magic land. In fact, you will see all beings in equally well-balanced ecology. Don't even worry. You just came into this magic land, right?"

"Yes," I nodded.

"Wait and give yourself time. There is so much to see. It may take about 800 years in your timeline to see and experience everything."

"Will I live that long?" I ask, surprised.

"We don't know, you may live that long or you may be born again for that stretch of time multiple times. We have no idea. It is up to you, how you want to do that."

"You mean, I have a choice?" Everything here is so different.

"Yes, you do," they tell me. "You know you can talk to your soul, right?"

"I have been talking to the wisdom."

"Your wisdom is fed by your soul, and vice-versa."

"So, have you lived here for a long time?" I ask my new friends.

"We don't work through time."

"Oh, okay. Have you died already?"

"We don't know the difference between death and being born," they say. "It is an easy transition. It feels like we are never gone, so it is hard to tell."

The beauty of their answers is melodious like a chorus. They all answer the questions in unison.

"So, if I die, I may not feel any difference?" I ask.

"Probably not. Welcome to your magic land. We hope you enjoy it. As I am speaking, I feel my eyelids drooping. Time for some rest."

"Where do I go to rest?" I ask my orienteers.

"Ask," they say, "just as you have been asking so far."

I bid them goodnight and ask for a bed. I am lifted above the ground and placed on a luxurious bed filled with feathers. I hit my new bed and fall asleep in an instant. In my sleep, I have the most amazing dreams. I see all kinds of new magic lands and magic beings in magic outfits. I am dazzled by their presence. They are in different shapes and forms. They are beautiful. I get stare alerts, even in my dreams. When I am caught off guard, they laugh at me. I ask them who they are, and they announce that they are the light beings. I sit with them on a moon-like chair and speak in different languages. Funny though, no matter what language they speak, I am able to respond in the same language. I am learning new languages on the fly. What a wonderful experience! Even when we are not talking, I can still communicate with them through my thoughts. I see brilliant colors around them. They are a delight to watch. What a delight, to watch these beings, these light beings. I ask them what it means to be a light being. They ask me if they can step into me and I say, "Yes." As soon as they step in, I feel a lightness. They are light. I am now able to view the world and my surroundings even more clearly than before. I am mesmerized by the colors around them and in the atmosphere. They are very loving, and I feel a deep sense of joy coursing through me. I feel as though I am float-ing—floating by the stars, by the moon, by the sun. Every element I see is so enhanced and other worldly. I am not sure how to explain my senses right now.

I talk about several things in this dream and ask about my father. My father is shown in his light. He is a divine vision. He seems much calmer and quieter than his usual self. He seems much younger than when he passed away. He is in his rhythm, one I have never witnessed. I must talk to him. I ask if I can be left with my father alone. The light beings disap-pear from my sight at my request. I am not sure if it was even necessary for me to do that. Nonetheless, I did.

I talk to my father about a lot of things—from me being born and be-ing raised to his experiences. I ask how he feels in this realm? He says he feels relieved and relaxed. "Had I known the meaning of life or cycle of life, I would have lived my life differently. However, there was a reason I was the way I was…and you turned out to be the way you did. It was all divinely orchestrated, our roles. Don't you worry, you did the right thing and I am extremely proud of you. Hence, I have no regrets. If you are ever in need of a lending hand, reach out to me. You're here. I will be here for you. I know you have your wisdom now, and I am ecstatic for your learning. Move forward with your new life. Don't regret your past; embrace your present, for there is nothing like the present. I lived my life always in the past. Now having lived my life and experienced life on this side, I see the meaninglessness of many of the things I valued. I am sure you will do things differently from me."

"Dad," I ask. "Have you forgiven yourself?"

"Yes, son, as my truest self, yes. Right now, you are witnessing me as my true self, the all forgiving self. I don't think there is any other way to move through life. No matter how big or small our mistakes, forgiveness is the same. It comes from the frequency of love. There is only one frequency of love. Just because you made a big mistake does not mean the forgiveness needs to be bigger, or vice versa. All you need is a big heart to forgive. Grow your heart. Let it be as vast as the ocean and as long as a river. Let it flow with gusto. That is all you need. Nothing is too small or too big to be forgiven. That is the wisdom I have learned in this realm. I am not cocky anymore, because it is not the real me and it doesn't resonate with my soul. You see, when you lose your body, your ego has to disappear. I realize now that being attached to my body was not necessary. I was also attached to you and your siblings, since you were my blood. Trust me when I say this, blood doesn't mean anything. Same blood or not, love is love, forgiveness is forgiveness. No one needs to be special enough to be loved, and no one is so hopeless as to be unworthy of forgiveness and love. My hardest lesson inhabiting my body had been forgiving myself for the things I had done. Forgiving myself with the assistance of my true self has opened up love in ways I have not experienced before. I am no longer attached to you as a father is to a son. I am more inclined to you as one soul to another. You and I were born in the lifetime provided to us in order to be part of the journey and the learning. I taught you as a father would, but now I will no longer talk to you as I would to a son. See, now, we transcend all the limitations laid upon us by the rules and regulations of the family. Little did we know that once our body decimates itself into dust, we are no longer tied as blood but only as souls. That is the beauty of the soul. Here, we don't have to be together just because we are family; we hang out because we have things to accomplish together. You and I have accomplished what we needed to accomplish together. I created a life for you that you would abandon on your journey towards ascension. It has already been laid out."

"Could I abandon the path?" I ask my father.

"You could," he responds, "but would you?"

I shake my head. "No, probably not."

"Our experiences were tied together, and it led you to where you are right now. It led you to the magic land. This was your path. This is your path."

"Any words of wisdom about my marriage?"

"No, not really, son. The only thing I would say is that there is no need to be attached to being married to your wife. Simply, be open to creating a loving relationship and everything will fall into place, married or not."

"Was mom happy being married to you?" I ask.

"What do you think?" He says with more than a hint of sarcasm.

I smile knowingly. "Probably not. Do you think you were brought together for a purpose?"

"Yes, to have my three children and raise them together."

"Nothing more?"

"Nothing more," my father responds. "But that was a whole journey raising you and your siblings and sharing the responsibilities with your mother."

"Did you know that when you were alive, Dad?"

"Not really." He looks sad. "I did not understand why I didn't feel connected to her after you were born. Our job together was done, but we continued to live together for appearance's sake. That was what was really tough, living for the sake of appearances."

"I know what you mean."

We chat for a bit more, and then my father was gone. I see the light beings manifest one at a time, as if they are putting on a show for me. I am intrigued by their play.

"Do you do this all the time?" I ask.

"No, we are just trying to impress you because you're a newbie."

"Thanks," I laugh. "I am not sure whether I feel honored by this special display, or patronized."

"Chill," they say in unison. "It's just play. No need to get all logical about it."

They are right. I catch myself. "Thanks, that was wonderful to play. By the way, what is that smell, that sweet smell."

They all laugh. "It is emanating from all of us, including you. It is the smell of love."

"You can smell love? Really?"

"Of course! You can feel love, right?"

"Yeah, I can."

"So, what is the problem with being able to smell it?"

"Fair enough," I shrug. "That means I should be able to hear love and see it as well, right?"

"Yes, of course. Unconditional love can be felt in any shape or form. It is an abundant flow of energy that enhances your senses. It heightens your feelings. Didn't your wife look more beautiful when you were in love with her?"

"Yes," I recall. "She did."

"Didn't you love hearing her voice?"

"Yes, I did."

"Did you love her smell, that distinctive smell that was her?"

"Of course, I did." I can smell her now.

"See, it is the same thing. It is just enhanced more in this dimension."

I continue to experience the presence of the light beings in my dream and learn about various things from them. This is my first day in the magic land, and I intend to practice staying here. I hope you have enjoyed listening to my experience.

Yours,
Grateful for the beings of light

CHAPTER 18: SURRENDER

*I*n spite of learning this spiritual side, I consistently wake up with doubt, nagging doubt. I wish it would just vanish, that I could set it aside easily rather than having to struggle with it and that persistent voice in my head. It's not as strong as it used to be, thank God…but it still exists. Do I battle with it or should I just let it be? My own feeling that it shouldn't be this way adds more strength to my doubt. Will I make it in life, with this new way of being? Wonderful things do happen, but then I am still waiting for more. I like what I have, and I am more at peace with myself than before. I guess I am looking at the things that I still have to learn. My doubt wants me to question my new learning, my new way of being. This self-doubt is dictated by my mind, since my new learning doesn't fit its algorithm.

I am an amazing being. I forget to honor myself sometimes. I get so caught up in the self-doubt that I forget the things that I do beautifully and well. Let us talk about the things that I do well. Let us set aside my doubt for a second. I need some uplifting, which I am not waiting for someone to do on my behalf. I have learned that I can uplift myself. It has been a long journey, no doubt. and at times I am tired of this journey. I wish it would end at some point. This journey that I have been on since my birth has been an interesting one. I had a tough father, an aloof mother, and a whole bunch of things that were placed on my shoulders at a very young age, even before my own thoughts and opinions could be formed.

My parents wanted to inculcate their information into me before I could form my own ideas about the world. They had a legacy to save—a false legacy that was created by their egos, which in turn gave rise to my false legacy.

When I was younger, I didn't always agree with my parents, but I lived under their roof, so I suppressed some of my doubts about their values. Also, they were my parents and they had worked hard for us, and that counted for everything. It masked my doubts about their values. As I grew up, my parents' values came back to haunt me. I struggled with them, yet they were the only values I had ever known. I did not know any better. My parents' values were influenced by societal values. Society expects a lot out of you, and if you don't fit into that box, you are considered a rebel, an out-of-control rebel. What can I say? I wish I had rebelled. But why regret the past? In this long journey with the Lion and my wisdom, everything I have known and have been taught has been tested...everything— my beliefs, my core values—everything has been tested. When I did not want to address these values and beliefs, they were tested even more.

I grew up thinking less about consequences than I do now. Even when I thought about the consequences of my actions, it was on a very small scale. I did not understand consequences at a soul level, from the viewpoint of the cycle of life. I truly believe now, at this juncture in my awakening, everything has a consequence. It may not be what you think, like you're going to burn in hell. No, that is a different concept. The consequences I am talking about are from our actions. You don't always see these consequences right away, though sometimes you may. My own understanding of consequences was a bit of delayed. I chose to ignore the idea of consequences, so my wisdom brought me to look at myself in the mirror. It showed me my own reflection, and it was not pretty. I thought I could get away without addressing the consequences of my actions. But, in fact, my life has been full of consequences. I was arrogant about digging up other people's lands to feed my own greed, for my own profit, as if depriving several billion living beings of their land would not have any consequences. I am not just talking about human life. I am talking about every life that I impoverished due to my arrogance. Arrogance, is it the opposite of humility? Actually, I think it is the absence of love, the absence of compassion, the absence of humanness. I thought I could lie, cheat, be arrogant, have my shiny wealth and get away with it. I had power. That power is worse than greed. Greed falls away, eventually giving rise to power. It is the power—power of ownership and control, control of masses—that is addictive. I was addicted to my power over others. Can you believe it? I loved the power to suppress human lives and control them at my whim. Yes, that is who I have been. Am I proud of this now? No, I am not. Was I proud of it before? Yes, but I don't think proud is the word—the word is arrogant. Arrogance when fed to wisdom churns it through the cycle of life and you are left with nothing, an emptiness. In that nothingness love arises, humility arises. I never knew what being humble meant. I was taught by the Lion, my own wisdom. I had to be brought in front of a mirror, to reflect on my own image, to reflect on my own arrogance. Yes, something else and someone else had to do it, as I was incapable of seeing it through my own naked eyes. My wisdom brought me forth very gently. It was persistent, until I understood how meaningless it all was. It has taken me to dimensions that I never imagined, never knew about, of which I was never aware.

Now, in this journey, I have no choice but to be aware. See, the arrogance that I walked around with made me blind, blind to just being human. I did not acknowledge that basic human thoughts, feelings and loss were the same across all borders. Whether I lost something that I loved or someone else —who didn't have a shiny life lost something—the feelings were the same. Little did I know that I was similar to them, those people that I thought were beneath me. I did not say it out loud, but they were my puppets. I could move them out of their habitat with no thought to the consequences or disruption to their lives. I did not care what they did for their basic needs. I did everything that I needed in the background. No one knew who I was. It is a misconception that the world works through the involvement of several people behind the scenes. It may be true, but a few people like me had more power than those individuals. They, too, were my puppets and in turn were puppeteers to others. They had a dual role that was created by me, by people like us, like my family.

Why am I sharing all this with you? So that you will awaken to what is going on around you. Do not lay ignorant to all that is happening. Do not be blinded and take one side over the other. Listen up, all of you, no matter what sides you take, regardless of your political leanings, you are all impacted. It doesn't matter what color you are, what race you are. If you are fighting over race, listen up. My wealthy coalition created all this division. We created the concept of superior race and inferior race. We created it to divide and conquer. We taught those who think they are better by continuously perpetrating messages of superiority. Why? Because we need them to do our dirty jobs. Everything around you is made up— even the hate, the bigotry. Everything was made up to cause chaos in your lives. You think these things actually exist in reality, but they don't. They exist only because you allow them to exist. "Divide and conquer" is our motto. It doesn't matter what your race, religion or country is, you are all impacted in some way or another. Some more—much, much more— than others. You sit around and ignore all this as if this doesn't impact you. If only you knew the consequences of the cycle of life. Nothing misses the cycle of life. Why do I keep narrating page after page the same thing? Give it a thought, please.

In this world that you live in, that I live in, things have to change. You are a crucial part of this change. Yes, I am talking about you. You will be stepping into the magic land soon, but before you do, you have work to do. Spread the message of love. Stay in love and understand that no crime is too big or too small to be forgiven. Do not worry about the consequences of others and their crimes. It is not your job. Just stay in your wisdom. Your wisdom is bigger than you. It is expansive. Your mind cannot comprehend the vastness of your wisdom and your soul. Rather than blowing up your ego, bring your heart to experience the vastness of your soul and your wisdom. In the practice of that, you will experience your own vastness.

You may ask, how did you learn all of this in such a short time? You can accelerate your spirituality. You can take one year, two years, a lifetime, or two days to awaken. To be honest, it only takes a moment to awaken.

Once you experience your awakening, the seed has been planted. That seed has to grow. You will have to give it a nurturing home. You are already a spiritual being, but you have come into awakening over and over to learn. In this process, you have learned a lot, so this is not new. In fact, it is very old, it is ancient. You have to learn to believe in it yourself. If everyone could just believe, life would be much easier...but life doesn't work like that. If you don't believe, it just means that you have more roadblocks within yourself to overcome. That is just where you are in your learning. There is no right or wrong with spirituality. It is just what is. You can never explain spirituality to others or awaken others, unless you have experienced your own awakening. Once you awaken, people who have awakened will find you. In no time, you will have formed a community. You may wonder if that is true. Just look at alcoholics, they find other alcoholics. This is not a miracle, but vibrations of a similar nature tend to attract similar vibrations. It is just what is so.

My own journey, in spite of all that I have learned so far, has not been easy. Doubt tends to plague me every day. It overlaps with my wisdom. I am laced with doubts and fears along the way. Can I throw away the doubts? Rather than throwing away my doubts, I would rather heal. Healing is a new word I have learned. I have known of the word, but only used it in terms of healing after sickness or healing after losing a loved one. I did not understand the vast meaning of healing. I have carried trauma birth after birth. I didn't even know it existed, the trauma from my past life. I am naturally inclined toward some experiences and inherently reject others. Did it happen just like that? I have come to realize that the answer is no. Things don't just happen accidentally. We are so intertwined with the universe that we don't even realize how expansive we are. We have been taught limited belief systems, limited ways of being, limited ways of existence. It is easier to live a limited existence, but does it lead to a joyful life?

Have we experienced true joy other than in isolated moments? I have experienced it sporadically in my life. What would it look like to live a joyful life? What would it mean to live a joyful life? What would it mean to you? See, we think there is a cookie-cutter way of living. One size doesn't fit all. However, if you look around, that is what we are doing—trying to fit into one way of life—hence, our dissatisfaction. We are living a life someone else laid out for us. We have lived this way blindly, believing most of the things we have been told. It is time to wake up. It is time to own up. It is time to grow up. It is time to be accountable to Mother

Earth. No, you don't get away with just hanging out and doing your little thing anymore. This keeps you small and renders you powerless. You are much more powerful than you think. Awaken to your powers. Awaken to your wisdom. Awaken to your joy—not just other's joy—but to yours. Do you even know how it is to live a life created by you—a life in which you are the producer, the director, the musician, the caster, the costume designer? You are all of it.

You may be tempted to think that you already do, but I beg to differ. You may be doing a few things, but you are not entirely there. If you lived a life designed by you, it would look very different from the one you are living today. Does it scare you to take charge? Are you scared of losing everything you have by designing your own life? If you do, this is the mirage about which I am talking. By stepping into something powerful, you may fear that you will lose everything you already have. You might, but what if it is replaced with those things that bring only joy…..only joy? You are wondering if joy is a possibility, aren't you? It is not only possible, but it is who you are, who you are supposed to be. This is what you were born for. You were born to enjoy this joy to the fullest. It is your birthright, to enjoy your life to the fullest. You may have several other questions, and that is okay. Hold on to them. Once you allow yourself to awaken to every bit of truth, the truth of your essence, the truth of your divine nature—all the lessons and people and experiences will be brought to you. I know this, because I have experienced it. When I needed to learn and was pondering whether something was inherently a lie or a truth, the beings and lessons showed up. In my case, it was the Lion in my dream. Yes, the beings and lessons can take many forms and shapes.

Your lessons, your dreams, your life, your truth, your magic land—it is all waiting for you. It is just waiting for you to lift the veil that keeps you from your own awareness. Your awareness, the keys to the kingdom are hidden by you behind this veil—a veil you don't even realize exists. It can be lifted by you. If you need help lifting this veil, all you have to do is ask. Yes, it is that simple. Nothing is as hard as it looks. Everything can be accomplished by raising your own vibration. If you are interested in raising your vibration, just start with being aware, and ask to be shown. Start simply by asking. Be willing to be led. The important lesson I learned on this path is that things don't have to be difficult. We make things difficult. The good news is that you can make it easy as well. It is up to you. In fact, everything in your life that is hard is so because you have made it hard. Everything that is easy in your life is so because you made it easy. It is that simple. Life is supposed to be simple. Life is supposed to be joyous. Life is supposed to be everything you ever wanted. Life is supposed to be all that you are. All that you are is divine and aligned to divinity.

If you are questioning whether you are deserving of this divinity, all the more reason to ask. Ask and it will be given; the answers will arise. That is the law of the universe. I had lost the will to ask. I had overlaid it with dissatisfaction. Peel back the layers of boredom and dissatisfaction, and you will see inside the simple pearl waiting to be asked for, to be sought after. Yes, you went in search of the pearl. You kept looking and looking. Then, you decided that you are not one to enjoy a pearl. It is too difficult, or it is not for you, or you are not worthy, or whatever else you decided. You let disappointment reign your mind, and your mind made up the algorithm of not finding any pearls last time and the time before and the time before that. Your mind then made a note and said, "Spend less time finding those pearls." The mind doesn't understand magic. You were frustrated and disappointed while trying to find the pearl, and you were given exactly what you asked for. You may ask. "How else should I do it?" You have heard me, so far. You may want answers to everything, just like I did. The truth is you and I, if we had all the answers, and were ensured that we would find the pearl, we would go. Otherwise, we choose to drink a beer and watch a show on television. That is fine, there is nothing wrong with it. However, you have given up on your adventure, the volition to just ask. There is nothing but the simple task of asking that held you back. You could ask even while you're drinking your beer and watching television. It doesn't have to be a monumental task.

Spirituality has been made to look harder than it actually is. It has been made to look a certain way, and now you expect for it to look a certain way. I, myself, am constantly falling in spite of being on this journey. I feel like it should look a certain way, that I should feel a certain way. After all, I have awakened. I have learned that we will never know how spirituality looks. Someone who goes to a temple or church every day may or may not be spiritual. The same applies to someone who never steps into a church or a temple. They may or may not be spiritual. But we have made up our minds, haven't we? Why not ask to become aware of what is spiritual for you? It may show up. Just sitting by the water may be spiritual for you. Maybe for another person, it is an hour of meditation. You don't have to compare notes. The notes will never tally.

Someone may be passionate and say you must meditate for one hour every day. For another person, this may not be a fit—it may be something else. On this path to awakening, while meeting other beings, remember their path may be different from yours. You may have an opinion but keep it to yourself. First, ask if they need an opinion or suggestion. Don't wear your righteous spiritual hat. It is quite easy to slip into righteousness within spirituality—quite easy. Be aware of your righteousness. If you forget to be aware, forgive yourself. Learn to acknowledge within yourself and to another when you have caused distress. It is okay to make a mistake. Let it go. Let it flow. Don't block your own growth with shame, guilt and righteousness. It will get you nowhere other than being stuck.

Let yourself be. Just be. You have nothing to prove or nowhere to be. Learn to be with yourself. Make yourself an amazing friend to yourself. Be your own best pal. Talk lovingly to yourself. Be gracious with yourself. Be kind to yourself. Be compassionate to yourself. Be you, just you, not a version of what is expected of you. You are a dazzling beauty when you are just you. You don't need accolades and medals to shine. You can be just you. You are born to be you. You were endowed upon and blessed upon to be you, the fundamental you. Why would you be anything else? Why would you? It is unnecessary to be anything but you.

Your beautiful presence of you, the real you, is what is needed on Mother Earth. You were designed to be who you are, not another self. The true self is waiting to be unveiled. It is waiting, eagerly waiting, to meet you.

It is so excited and anxious to meet you. The more you allow the true you, the divine you, to step in and take the reins of your control, life relaxes, you relax. You are meant to be relaxed and joyful in this ride. This ride, which will be led by your higher self, your divine self, is a better ride than the one you have been in charge of. Your higher self will take you to places you have never been. He or she knows better than you, much more than you. If you hand over the reins, she or he will take you for a ride to the magic land. But be sure to not pry the reigns out of those divine hands. You will be tempted. You have been in control for so long and it will be initially a task to trust your divine self. But trust me when I say this, I have never been on a better ride than this. It is a worthy ride, worthy of you. Your divine self has been holding out a hand for a while, waiting for you to take hold. Your divine self is you, the real you, the expansive you, who loves you unconditionally...unconditionally, can you believe it?

Your ride is here, if you are ready, step in. If you are hesitant, ask to be guided. If you don't believe in this ride, I bid you good luck on your path. Remember, the path towards enlightenment doesn't always look the same. You may think you are not joining the ride and the next thing you know, you may be on it. You may think you have given over the reins, but somewhere on the way, you may try to usurp them. Don't be prideful about being the better one, just because you chose the ride. Simply enjoy the ride and relax. Everything is taken care of. All you need to do is relax. It is hard to relax, isn't it? Tell me about it. To relax means I need to give up my reins, my control. I like being in control. I can plot and calculate when I am in control. At least that is what I thought. I still try to control, but now I know it is not worth it. Surrender. Surrender your reins. I will walk with you to surrender mine as well. Surrender to the whims of your higher self, that beautiful divine self, the real you. Surrender your reins. If you are hesitant, it is okay. Ask for help surrendering. The minute you ask, the universe will summon help for you. Step aside and let the help come through. Don't block the way. Don't block your help. Step aside graciously. It is okay. You can still be the king or queen of your kingdom, even though you give away the reins.

I surrender. I surrender. I surrender.

I surrender my reins to my divine self, who knows the path I am on, whose wisdom surpasses mine, whose knowing knows no bounds, whose love knows no bounds, whose love knows no boundaries. When you struggle with forgiveness, ask for guidance. It will forgive freely on your behalf, your higher self.

I surrender. I surrender. I surrender.

If you would like to do the same, let us hold hands and chant the mantra, "We surrender! We surrender! We surrender!" We surrender our faith, our dignity, our self to the divine within us, the real us. In surrendering, we give up control—the control that runs ragged, that is selfish, that is disempowering, that is faithless, that is useless, that is destructive, self-destructive. I let lose my reins. I understand the need I have had to control things up to this point. Now, I let go of my control. In letting go of my control, I surrender the reins to my divine self. I may not always be gracious in doing so, but I am willing to learn. I am willing to learn the beauty of surrender, the loss of martyrdom in this surrender. I am no longer in charge. I am no longer a martyr. I am no longer the self. I am no longer the mind. My heart reigns, my soul reigns, my divine-self reigns, when I release the hold over my reins. I am no longer in charge. I am no longer in control. I am no longer the driver in the mask. As I hand over the reins, I hand over my mask, the mask that is no longer needed on this ride. It has lost its power and use. This mask that led me on the path, that controlled my direction, has submitted itself by surrendering the reins.

Along with the reins, I release my mask, the mask that floats into oblivion. The reins, which have made my hands bleed by my holding on too tight through my fear of losing control, are being released. I no longer need to bleed or be in control. I let go of everything by surrendering. I surrender my reins with love for self. I don't need anything but love to heal my hands, to heal myself, to reveal myself. I am coming out. I am coming out. I am coming out. I am coming out of the box that I was riding in and controlling my ride. I am coming out without my mask and with bleeding hands. Don't worry about the dripping blood, it is healing through my surrender. It is healing through my love. I declare love for myself by releasing the reins, by surrendering the reins.

I am love. I am love. I am love. I love myself. Loving myself is an act of kindness to myself. I am in love with myself. The control I have exercised so far has lost itself to surrender. I surrender to my love. Love has taken over the reins. I am here to enjoy this wonderful ride, to enjoy the landscape as I am supposed to. This ride is not easy, but I am learning, and I am aware of the bleeding in my hands when I exercise my control over the reins.

If you have not surrendered, please do. Your hands don't need to bleed. Surrender, Surrender, Surrender— surrender to your love, surrender to the almighty love that you have come to experience. We are wise enough to surrender. We are enough to surrender. We have faith enough to surrender. We are love. Love yourself in the surrender. Love reigns in the act of surrender. I release the grips of my reins. I surrender the grips of my reins to my loving self, my higher self, my divine self.

I surrender. I surrender. I surrender. I release. I release. I release. I release my reins, the rope that binds me and causes my hands to bleed through this control. I release because I am aware that this control does not serve me anymore. This control is self-destructive to me and humanity. It ropes me into its ego, which runs wild. I am ready for a wild ride, but a different one—one that is ridden by the supreme self.

I surrender. I surrender. I surrender.

Surrendering with Love,
Man

CHAPTER 19: DIGNITY

*L*isten to the man. He is telling the truth. The only reason we—the puppets who lost our dignity through the digging of our resources—are stepping in for this narration is because we need to manifest more people to join the army. We have already joined the army. We needed no convincing, you see. We have been left in despair by those who plundered our resources to the fullest, leaving nothing for us. We were made paupers to beg from them, even though we were surrounded by wealth. They had to leave us with nothing, so that we could be indebted to them. This is a form of slavery that you won't understand. This is modern slavery, a slavery that hides basic decency. We have been called names, "poor" is one of them. It is easy, you see, to give us a title, as if we are not worthy of finding our way in life, as if calling me poor summons who I am with respect to humanity. It is such a filthy word, poor. We were not poor. We were abundant. We were wealthy with our Mother Earth's resources. We were fed, clothed and provided for by our Mother. We were stripped of our wealth, including our traditions. We were told our traditions were beneath them, that we were not civilized. Can you believe we were called uncivilized? We were reprimanded for being made poor by them. As If we were so helpless that someone needed to come and rescue us. It is far from the truth. We needed no such rescuing. Please do not believe if you are being led to believe that we need rescuing.

We are considered the bottom of the systemic gradation of humanity. We are considered disposable. We are disposable to many. We are often accused of not having it together. Maybe we can't have it together because we have been systemically reduced by those with wealth and power. Do you think we are that hopeless, that we cannot take care of ourselves? When we were plundered and left to dust with nothing, we were rendered helpless. We couldn't fight those who had plundered us. They had their shiny suits on and came and looked at us as if we were filthy and worthless. You will see several pictures of them smiling with our raggedly clothed children. Don't believe it. They plundered us and had to pretend that they were educating us—an education we never asked for. Our education was considered inferior with no value.

How dare you? You came to our land, you plundered us, you marked us as uncivilized, as the ones who needed to be taught civilized ways. Then, you rendered us poor with only filth and bare necessities. You were very cunning and calculating. You rendered us helpless and poor so that we would have to work for you for a pittance. That was your master plan. Next, you taught your generations that we were poor and couldn't take care of ourselves. You not only carried out all these cruelties, you decided we needed someone to rule us. You perpetrated a lie that we were incapable of ruling ourselves. What a lie, you perpetrated. Those of you who ruled us separated us as inferior to your race. Can you believe it? Maybe you can, but I can't. You have made yourself so superior to us with your shiny things purchased for future generations with those shiny distractions. This was your filthy master plan to suppress and keep us suppressed. Then you made a united government to help the world. Oh, help did come. It came in the form of things. We were made to be beggars. We were literally made beggars—beggars in our own Mother Land that flourished with abundance. What a master plan? You, yes, I am talking about you. You who is sitting on your sofa and drinking your beer. Yes, I am talking to you. You may think we are poor and need help, but in reality, we don't need your charity. In fact, take away all the charity. We just want our Mother Land back.

You came and took my land and my wealth and put a leader in charge to rule us. Then, here is the disgusting thing you did: you segregated us. You segregated us in our own Mother Land. You—who came from the outside, who usurped our wealth, dignity and pride—you segregated us, saying we are untouchable. We couldn't be seen with you. We couldn't be seen sharing with you. We could not eat from the same plate and we could not drink from the same fountain. Why go that far? We couldn't even stay in the same area. We were that untouchable to you. You perpetuated your superiority to your future generations, who continued to buy into this lie about who was superior to whom. You dug a pit for yourself when you did that. After all was done, you employed us at your homes to take care of you, and you brought us as slaves to another world—yes, you. Don't you dare tell me that I am inferior to you.

You know what is funny, all of this was also done in the name of God. My Gods were considered inferior to yours, and you had the audacity to civilize us through your religion. You said we were heathens, barbarians. You said we were uncivilized and, above all, worthless. You did not say the last word worthless, but you thought it and made sure it was reflected in our lives.

When there was rebellion against your rule—because we were left with no choice but to free ourselves of your ugly chains—you did finally let go. Oh, we all thought you let go, we were delirious. We were fools, on this one, I have to agree. We were fools. We thought you left us in peace. We really thought you left us in peace. Oh boy, were we wrong and stupid and foolish. You left us with a puppet government, led by a puppet from our own people. You see, this is the worst tactic that was used. You left us with this puppet by dangling shiny objects in front of him. You made deals. You whispered in his ears, "Keep your people suppressed and you will see wealth beyond measure." And they did. It was the worst nightmare, being suppressed by our own people. They took an avatar of demons. They raped, pillaged and killed, too.

This was good for you. You had proven your point. We had become incapable of ruling ourselves, and we were barbarians who couldn't live in harmony. We were treated as though we were worthless pieces of shit, incapable of anything. We were rendered poor and had a ruler who was a hired hitman, one of us, one of your puppets. I have to give it to you, it was a brilliant plan. No one could have hatched such a plan but you. Only you could have done that. You not only punished us for who we were, you punished your own people who stepped forward in their humanity to stop the violence—fundamental violence caused by you towards your own brothers and sisters. You punished your people so that they wouldn't step forward and voice the peace. You did that. Yes, you did. Please don't deny it. The problem is that it is easy to distract humanity from real problems. As long as you keep little problems highlighted and you instigate violence and portray a race or gender as incapable, you get to keep bigger problems hidden. So much has happened in humanity that people have lost track of the root of all evil. Every single evil thing that has happened to humanity is a result of greed or power. Greed and power can only be acquired through control. How do you control masses? Through fear. Fear is an easy weapon to control the masses. You can easily perpetrate lies based on fear and humanity will lap it up like a trained dog. You show fear, throw a bone, and they catch it. It is easy to have a trained dog, isn't it? We rebel, but even in our rebelling there is training. It is controlled rebelliousness.

Control of the masses is what has been done to my kind. Our leaders, I hate to call them that, those who have shriveled-up hearts, are lost to me.

How could one do this to another…another of one's own kind? Aren't we your family? You know, you look like a clown wearing the shiny suit. You used to look brilliant in the colorful traditional garb you wore. You the puppets, think it is uncivilized to wear your own clothes now, don't you? You the puppeteer, even thought our clothes were uncivilized. My God, the depth to which you tested our dignity and left us stripped of our own dignity knows no bounds.

Humanity wake up! I am not just calling you, I am calling everyone from our Mother Earth, everyone from my Mother Land. Yes, wake up. Wake up! Those of you who have taken victim roles and those who have chosen superior roles—both roles, wake up. Wake up to end this plundering. Wake up to restore our dignity. I am not talking about just my dignity. You too, lost your dignity. When you strip someone naked, you lose your dignity too. You see, no human in his or her natural state would ever strip another creature and then laugh at them. You, yes, you…wake up! If you think I am not talking to you, then you are sorely wrong. Wake up. Wake up to restore the dignity of humanity.

You are the ones who wanted dignity to be restored. You came in shiny suits and threw some money to restore my dignity. How funny! You thought or pretended that you could restore our dignity with money. You thought I would fall for it. I didn't, but my brothers and sisters did. See, stop giving us money. Stop giving us money as though we are incapable. You rendered us incapable. Let us go back and restore. You may ask what is there to restore? I don't know. But let us restore the dignity of the masses first. Once we restore the dignity, then we will be led to other things, meaningful things—no, not money. Money is useful, don't get me wrong. We need it, but other things, such as our natural habitat, our lions. I have no idea how we will do it but do it we must. I don't think we have a choice. Do you think we have a choice? If you do think we have a choice, enlighten me. I would love to learn.

We have a lot of work to do. We have to start with respect and dignity. No one owns this Earth. If you want to own everything, your time is ending...your legacy is ending. We are beginning a new legacy. We are putting this new legacy on Mother Earth's feet. We are going to call upon her for assistance. I am sure she is already getting ready to heal us. She has been quietly meditating in the background, collaborating with light beings to restore our dignity. She will assist us. She will remind us of the wisdom we lost, the wisdom we lost through greed and power.

Those who are in control, you have held the reins for too long. The reins are threadbare from this journey that you embarked upon. Let go of the reins. Let go of the control, the control that has left you in a lurch. You think you are in control. No, you are not, you just lost your basic human decency. Yes, your decency can be restored, if you are willing. I do not want to hate you. In reality, I should, but I see no point in hatred at this moment. We are embarking at a crucial moment, a moment which is the pinnacle of restoring human dignity. No one will be left out, no one. This moment, a crucial one for the coming generations, will be a tipping point. We are standing at the peak, overcrowded. It seems as though the world is in chaos. It may be. However, it is a different kind of chaos, one that is leading us to ascension. It is leading us to feel the joy that is naturally bestowed upon us. Yes, you are a joyful being. Let us join the army. Let us hold hands. Let us hold paws. Let us hold wings. Let us hold another's hand that you might have thought of as filthy before.

You have been drugged. Your mind has been poisoned with lies. You can remain drugged or poisoned or you can step into this path leading to the pinnacle. It is crowded, but we know this pinnacle will push us into ascension. It is scary. Some of you won't step inside, saying there is not enough room. This is only an excuse to remain in separation. If that is your will, if that is your choice, so be it, but you are missing out on a wonderful journey filled with adventures, paradise and magic lands.

You, yes you, who have seen the magic land, could you please hold the newbies' hands? They need some help. No, no, you don't have to hold them forever, just assist them now. You, the one that has seen the magic land, lend a magic touch, lend a healing touch, lend a humane touch to the paws and broken wings. Let us restore the magic of this land that is inherently magical. You thought you were leaving this land to see the magic land, didn't you?

You may, but this land is a magic land that has lost its dignity. Once we restore the humanity of the masses, the magic land's dignity will be restored naturally. The magic land is us—yes, us. We are the magic beings who are wizards. We, the wizards, were ousted from this magic land through perpetrated fears and lies. Those of us who held the powers to restore the magic land were called heretics.

Our land used to be filled with mystics and shamans. The mystics, who were ousted as dangerous, were actually benevolent individuals who supported humanity with their magic. Some had issues, no doubt. Just like anywhere, there is always someone, right? These mystics and shamans taught you to own your own power. They taught you to restore your faith, faith in yourselves. Throughout history, they were called sorcerers and evil beings. People said they used black magic. You see, when one has lost his or her magic, they cannot see the magic in others. Even when they see it, they think they are being tricked and some evil forces are behind it. See, that is a pity. These benevolent beings, who did nothing bad, didn't fit into the new faith and beliefs, so they were systemically eliminated.

Eliminated through lies, lies perpetrated against them. This is the whole point I am trying to make. When one looks or does something different from what you do, be curious. Even if you think they are uncivilized, just be curious for once.

Curiosity is better than hatred. When one looks or walks differently than you, be curious, learn—not nosy, but curious. Learn about another, enjoy the differences. You like Thai food, right? Well if you don't like Thai food, pick a food that is from another land that you like. Culture and race are no different than that. When you first had food from a foreign land, you were skeptical. But when you had more of it and ventured out and learned about one dish or another, you got comfortable. Please don't always order Pad Thai. There are several wonderful dishes from Thailand. Try them. Culture is no different. As you explore more and understand more, your skepticism falls, the opinions you held—like Thai food is just too spicy—fall. You start to understand and enjoy the complexity of flavors. You may never cook Thai food yourself, but you appreciate its flavors. Along the way, you may even make a friend from Thailand to get some free food. I would make friends for food, wouldn't you?

Learning is a beautiful thing. Learn with curiosity. Let go of arrogance. Ask deeper questions than asking, "so is it really poor, your country?" You know it already is. You have seen the media perpetrate all the evil things. You already know it is poor, try to refrain from asking questions that confirm your negative belief. Be curious to learn outside of what you think you know about another culture. When you ask questions outside of your beliefs or assumptions, your view expands, your vision expands, your soul expands, you embody the infinite within you. Start by asking "what was the most favorite food they grew up with?" Be curious, be interested in them as a human. You will find something in common.

You, who are so different from each other, will find similarities that will blow your mind. Don't base an entire culture on its economy. Don't view an entire culture though the lens of money. You will come to learn that you are the same with or without money.

Just because someone has no money, doesn't make them less than you. When they share stories about how they were devoid of basic needs, don't assume that your life was better. Your paths are different. If you assume that you are better than them because you have more, that is patronizing. No, it isn't gratitude. If you think it is gratitude, be curious to why I am stating that it is not gratitude. That's you, sitting on a high horse on your wonderful upbringing and judging how another from another country or race didn't have what you had. It doesn't mean a thing that they didn't, and you did. It may seem like it means something, but trust me, it doesn't.

When someone wears a suit in perfection from another culture, don't assume that they are better than those that don't. And don't tell them that they are better from the others because they wear the suit in perfection.

And the one from another culture that seems more like you because they wear a suit in perfection, don't tell them, "Oh you are not like another Thai person I have met." Please don't, it is not a compliment. It is actually an insult. Why am I pointing it out to you? Because this is how another culture gets viewed, through your lenses of the so-called civilized world. No culture is better or worse than another. We are born on the same soil. We all breathe the same air. If you are inhaling something different, tell me, I am curious. Yes, be curious. There is nothing to lose. You may have a Thai friend, just because you have a Thai friend doesn't make you an expert on Thai culture. Even if you have visited Thailand, I am sorry you are still not an expert. Don't make assumptions about another culture. If you have never once visited another country and have a lot of opinions and judgments about that culture through your media, please get curious and make a friend from another culture. Be open to new views and learning the truth. You may find things that may astound you. When you turn on your TV and hear some rubbish about another culture or race, make a mental note to make a friend from that culture and learn the truth.

This narration is coming from a black woman in Africa. I will share more about myself to enlighten you. You will understand why I am asking you to look deeper than what you have been told and what you have seen. I was born at a time when my land was plundered for the first time. I lived in a community where we shared. We shared everything. We had our own issues, don't get me wrong, but it was a different set of issues. We had food, water and shelter. I was the second of three wives. I was married young as was customary in those days. I have a request, see if you can listen to my stories with no judgment. Because my life is not going to look like yours, it is good training to listen without judgment. It is hard I know, but here we are, at a different juncture, having the accountability for moving humanity forward, so let us start by listening without judgments. Yes, I was the second wife, and yes, it was not easy, but we had a beautiful land and our resources were plenty. We lived off the forest, sourcing different things. We had our village shaman to treat our sicknesses. Life was good It could have been better, but it was good.

So, sometime around my existence, people who looked very different from us started arriving and becoming friendly with us. We were initially skeptical, but the more we interacted, the friendlier we got. During their visits we would take them to the jungle, feed them our food and make friends with them. We were a tribal group and they learned our customs and sometimes partook in our chores and dances. It was fun. Sometimes they would dress up like us and it would give us immense pleasure. We were at our happiest while we shared with each other. As time went on, they brought more friends, and they would talk to us, and so forth. Eventually, they wanted to come and live by us. We didn't think too much of this, but we discussed it between tribes and gave them a piece of land where they could build their huts.

As time went on, and they learned the land, they started coming over little by little to dig up our lands—this land that we had showed them how to care for. Then, this land that they learned about from us, became their pillaging ground. Eventually, their governments were involved, and churches were involved, and we became their slaves. I am simplifying this way too much. I don't think I have the energy to go into all the details. Don't get me wrong, there were some people who came because they really loved our lifestyle and culture, but they were few and far between. The rest did not care. What they had been eyeing was the wealth of our land. Little did we know that they had been getting ready to plunder our untouched beauty. Do you know the tactic they used to divide and conquer us? This is what I would really like you to understand. When control needs to be exercised, divide and conquer is a secret weapon. Division will happen between one's own kind, highlighting your differences and pointing out how one is superior to another. It is that simple. You are either left with the opinion that you are superior or inferior to another. This causes division and separation. Stupid us, we fell for the lies. We fell for the dangling of the wealth that was plundered from our own lands. It is like feeding me the food I cooked as if you had made it for me…not good!

Next, I was born into different races and cultures and was reborn again in Africa. This time I witnessed a true atrocity. I died of the so-called AIDS virus. That is another story for another day, but you see, we can't even take care of ourselves. That is why I got AIDS, at least that is the lie you have been told. You were told that we were out of control and promiscuous, and that is why we got AIDS. No control over ourselves, and our men could not control themselves. They said AIDS came from a monkey—a monkey, and you believed it, didn't you? I don't believe it. I don't think it came from a monkey. I would have to ask, why wasn't this disease in existence before my time? You may say, "Probably they didn't know how to diagnose it." If that is what you want to believe, be my guest.

Don't look at my illness, look at yours. If you are healthy, look at others in your society. You go to shiny hospitals that can hardly cure basic diseases. The doctors there render most diseases incurable...and you believe it. It is no different than believing that my AIDS was incurable or that I caught it from a monkey. You see, I am that stupid to have caught it from a monkey? Do you get my point? If you don't see the absurdity, I have no idea what to tell you. I have none. I am at a loss. You may seek scientific evidence to prove me wrong. To seek evidence through science is good, don't get me wrong. But when it gets into filthy hands, it will be tainted. It will be tainted for the purposes of greed, power and control. Anything good can be tainted with filthy hands—no exceptions, not even religion. See, when I was alive, I was told that I got this disease because God was punishing me. You know what they said? They said it was because I was not a proper woman submitting to my husband as God mandated, since I was bossy. Yes, that is what they said, I had contracted the disease because of my arrogance. Oh boy, if only they knew what real arrogance is. Ask our friend, who has been trying to hammer into your brain on arrogance. Try asking him, he will tell you stories that can be made into an epic. See, every good tool can be put to bad use. This is where we stand in humanity right now. Every ounce of dignity one has can be stripped very easily. The less money you have, the faster you can be stripped. The sooner you get stripped, the faster you will be blamed.

Before I died, my husband worked for a factory. I did meager things to fend off our hunger. I had three children. They were malnourished and I had barely been able to keep up with the demands of my husband, my kids and myself. I just couldn't. When I died, I felt relieved. I was told I would burn in hell, since I did not obey. I left my children motherless. They had to fend for themselves. My husband died shortly after me. Well, did I burn in hell? No, I did not. I continued to exist in another dimension. See, there is no death. Death doesn't exist in the same sense as you have been taught. Death, as it has been taught to you, is made up. But this is not what I am here to share with you.

This is the current reality that you don't see in your shiny travel brochures about Africa. It is prone to happen, right? My government doesn't care for its people, right? Isn't that what you think? In this context, you are absolutely right. However, I will share a secret. The secret is called dig deeper. Why is it that every one of the countries in Africa in a similar situation? Is it that we can't take care of ourselves? Is it that we are not smart enough? Listen, whatever biased opinion you have, you will find an answer based on your bias. All I am asking is for you to dig deeper, if you care to.

Okay, let us take a deep breath. That was a lot to digest. Some you already knew; some you didn't. Some you did not care to know. You stopped by to read these pages and you did not know what was coming, yet you stuck with it. You stuck with it and read it this far. I am proud of you, I am proud of your curiosity. You may have been left with some eye openers or some doubts or some clarity or perhaps I reaffirmed some of the perpetrated lies. Regardless, we are all born, we are all here to learn, and we all die one day. That is the cycle of life in its simplest form. If this cycle of life means something to you, get curious about how many different races into which you may have been born. Think about all the genders into which you may have been born—yes, all the genders, not just two. Two was made up for convenience. I am not talking about just the two genders. Just get curious. If you do, and you are naturally inclined toward another culture, maybe you have been part of that culture. Knowing that you have been born in many forms, into many cultures, how could you ever judge another? I am leaving to let you ponder.

It was nice meeting you. I experienced immense pleasure from sharing this wisdom and truth with you. I am happy where I am now. However, I am interested in joining hands with you to reveal more truths. I am looking to embody life again. I am getting clear about my purpose for my next life. I haven't yet decided where I will be born but born I will be. Regardless, I have signed up for the army. I will see you in the magic land, soon, I suppose. I'm signing off with lost dignity that has been restored by the mere sharing of my circumstances. The sharing of my burdens has freed me. I am restored in my peace. No one was responsible for the loss of my internal peace but me.

Fully responsible for my life,
African black woman who didn't land in hell because of her sins

CHAPTER 20: GOLDEN COMPASS

*I*n my time that I have lived, I have learned a lot. What do I mean by that? I mean much has been made clear to me through the presence of my wisdom disguised as my dear Lion. My wisdom speaks of truth that is beyond moral cognition. My wisdom speaks of things that are bittersweet. I need to hear them as truth, yet I dread knowing what is to come. When I speak of truth, there is no moral obligation, no morality, only truth. What does morality mean? What is morality? In my learning thus far, I have realized morality doesn't exist. It is a lie. It may seem outrageous to many of you that I am saying morality is a lie. Isn't it a lie? What makes morality higher than truth? What gives it a higher stance than truth? Hasn't what is moral been constantly evolving? Hasn't morality been played at, at the cost of human lives? Haven't people been burned alive in the name of morality? Don't we all have a moral obligation to ourselves, our society and community we live in? What is our moral obligation? Do any of us know? When we abandon that which is mainstream, we in some sense become immoral. We become immoral in the moral sense of deterring the flow of common sense. What is common sense anyway? That which is mainstream is common sense. That which is not, is anything other than common sense. Are morality and common sense the same? I am only asking these questions because I want to inspect and understand what morality means to us. Why would I want to do that? Because in my opinion, morality is a farce.

I have lived an immoral life, so for me to say morality is a farce may seem like I am trying to escape all the things I did. But you see, I am taking you deep within me in trying to understand morality versus truth. A moral sense of obligation comes from fear. Morality is instilled with fear—you must follow or not. When I don't follow the rules that have been laid out by humanity, I am judged as immoral. Am I supposed to be just with my wife? Is it immoral for me to be with anyone but my wife? Was I immoral for having affairs when I was married? Do I bring my wisdom to seek morality or truth? Like I said before, I would rather talk about the truth. I would like to understand the truth of my affairs and subjugating my wife to pain rather than just throw in morality and be done with it. You see, this is what I am talking about. Once I am labeled immoral, it is the end of everything. By society's standards, I simply need to learn to be moral. It is not that easy, to be in the clutches of so-called morality and unwind yourself from immoral behavior to become a better person.

I am not interested in simply becoming a better person. I am seeking to be wise and being wise means I stay in truth. What is this truth that I think is more favorable to me than morality? You see, morality is very confined. Truth, on the other hand, is expansive. When I am expansive, I bring in light and God energy. When I am confined, I live in fear. When I am told I am immoral, or judge myself as such, I am only holding myself in confinement and punishment. I need to be punished for being immoral by the court of law. On the other hand, if I heal myself and bathe myself in light to attain enlightenment, I stay in truth.

I would like to address the difference between truth and morality, so that we can move on and be enlightened. The thought that comes to me first and foremost is my relationship with my wife. I have been immoral in many ways. And that has impacted me and my wife directly and indirectly. While I decided that my marriage was not working, I did not speak of it. I spoke of other things that I thought at that time were relevant. In retrospect, they were not. When I was married, I was joyous when things went well. When they weren't, I started to have affairs, went out drinking, and did other things that hindered my wellbeing. I deteriorated in many ways. My health, my consciousness, my mind—all were muddled. Why was this? Was it because I had become immoral? I don't think so. I know now that I was not in my truth. When I started drinking, which was not unusual for me, but drinking more, it dulled my senses. It is immoral to drink too much, isn't it? However, I would like to talk about truth. What made me drink? It is not immorality that made me drink. The wise me tells me, that me not wanting to face my life and my wife was what made me drink. That is the truth. You see we are like onions. You peel one layer of truth and there are many more underneath. Why did I fear my life and my wife? I feared because I would have had to face the real me if I looked into my real problems. It was easier not address my true self, that is in the purest form. My true self was not concerned about my morality. My true self was aligned with truth. My ego self, which was not aligned with my true self—was aligned with morality whereas my true self was aligned with truth and wisdom.

In many ways, truth and wisdom are the same. If I am looking to get out of this mess that I have created for myself, I am not looking to become a better man, I am seeking to become wise. When I drank, I became someone who was fun to be around. I could drown my sorrows and my true self, my wise self, deep inside so that I didn't have to confront the truth. I could go on as if nothing were wrong and could live life superficially by being immoral. My moral sense of obligation that I was drinking and unfaithful to my wife caused me pain in my heart, but the drinking masked my moral fears and obligations. It provided me a layer of protection around me from my own truth. In retrospect this is funny for me. Bah!!! Oh well. I was trying to numb myself of any moral questioning that would seep into my brain which brought me fear. I feared my morality. You see, that is what morality did to me. It makes me fearful, ashamed and guilty over the things I do. I do them even more because the fear doesn't help but perpetrates my immoral self. This was my experience. I drank like a fish to drown myself to mask my immorality. Drinking is a way to subvert anything that is conscious. When I numb myself, the world and realities look different. It seemed like it was all my wife's fault that I was drinking. You see, in my moral sense, I could justify why I was doing what I was doing. In truth, everyone stands whole and complete. There is no one to blame, not even yourself. The only thing left for us is to identify the truth and the purpose of our existence.

In that truth, it doesn't matter why you drink, it matters that you stay in wisdom and delve into those things that you have numbed and carried. That numbness is wisdom trapped inside the shield of fear. When I am constantly trying to hide my fears and my true self through drinking, life seems inconsequential in a sense of not owning my fears and truth...so, I drank. I was immoral in a moral sense but mostly I was hiding from myself. I was fearful to know who I truly Am. It was easier to pretend to be an immoral being than truly look into who I really was.

This drinking was not just because of my wife. It catapulted everything because she was so close to me and I had cherished her. When our marriage took a left turn, I dove into the oblivion of drinking. I reveled in this oblivion. It felt very safe to stay in oblivion, so I did. I drank over pity, but I would never admit it. I felt sorry for myself, and I drank. It is not manly to feel sorry for oneself. It was easier to admit that I was immoral than say I felt sorry for myself. When I felt sorry for myself, I needed to blame someone and I found the perpetrator in the form of my wife, while I became the victim. I never thought about it this way back then. But now, it is clear to me as night and day, I didn't want to be accountable for my own life and drinking masked all my true feelings. Then in my pity state, I started having affairs—big affairs and small affairs, and everything in between. I became shameless. What had truly happened is that I was fearful and ashamed that I had not been able to satisfy my wife. My pride was wounded. To justify that I was still a man, I had many affairs. You want to know the truth, none of them satisfied me. Every one of them made me feel less in a moral sense and left me more dissatisfied in truth. Those affairs in all honestly were to mask my own imperfections but at the end it highlighted them. Women threw themselves at my feet, after all I had the money, the looks, and a broken marriage. Hidden behind it was me, mangled and destroyed internally, something to which I would never admit.

I had to beat my chest for appearances sake and display my manhood and parade it to show I could weather this situation with my wife. Yes, I am a simpleton to have thought that I could evade my truth and my true self by pretending, by masking. It was a masquerade. I was masking everything through my drinking and affairs. I have let the cat out. What now? I stand naked in front of you, with my mask peeled off. You are seeing me for who I truly am. This is what I was afraid of, to exhibit my true self. I thought it was unworthy to show my true feelings and true self. I was scared to because it was the unknown, and the unknown scares me. Doesn't the unknown scare all of us? I don't think I am an exception. I am everything that is human consciousness.

Is my having affairs judged as immoral? Yes, it is. Like I told you before, I am here to speak the truth. When I have been judged immoral through my affairs, it was masking something and that is dangerous. However, I did not know this at that time. I had been sexually immoral. I ask the question again and only to provoke the truth, was it wrong for me to have been immoral? Like I said before, morality is a stick. It is a stick used to make one right or wrong; to determine if one goes to heaven or hell. Should we use the Ten Commandments to set a low barre for ourselves by merely trying to understand how we will be judged or to truly know what our moral obligation is? Do we even come close to the true Commandments? Are we by default following those rules that we think are God's commandments without self-reflection? Will God punish me for what society judges to be my immoral acts? Here's my point, the commandment, through human conditioning underneath it all is that my immoral act as defined by society, is to be punished in God's eyes. Sometimes it is blaring and sometimes it is an unwritten rule. If I am immoral in having affairs, would not having an affair make me a moral human? In my perception, I don't think so. We presume God judges my affairs immoral and takes me into a den of hell fire. Out of this I learn nothing.

In my growth, I think God is more forgiving than what we think. We humanize him and we think He would be wrathful if we did something judged as immoral. I have to say that is an easy way out. I don't think we can get away so easily from truth. When I was having my affairs, I knew I was cheating on my wife. In my cheating on my wife, I judged myself as morally wrong. But what is the truth? The truth is I broke an agreement and I never communicated this broken agreement. This pushed my wife and I into further bitterness. I was suffering from melancholy and depression over the unspoken broken agreement, our marriage. I was sad the relationship had not prospered. But the truth was, I broke an agreement that I never communicated. Yet, it was out in the open. When something is blatantly done without addressing the broken agreement, it becomes baggage. It is this baggage that we have to carry when we don't address our own truth. You see, there are two levels of truth. One is your own, based on your baggage. The second is based on universal truth. You can only attain the universal truth as you address your own personal baggage. Unless you attain truth by addressing your broken agreements, you cannot clear the baggage. I don't think it is that simple. I had my affairs outside of marriage and I broke an agreement. In breaking that agreement without getting consent from my wife, I strayed away from truth, not my wife. In a simpler sense, it will look like I strayed away from my wife. In truth, in straying away from the truth, I was causing a chasm between me and my wife. If that is the case, would it have been ok, if my wife had been in agreement with my affairs? You see, there is an unsaid agreement and there is a spoken agreement. When we know something is happening and are in denial to what is happening, we are still complicit to the situation. We may be in denial. That is passive agreement. Active agreement is a physical agreement where two people sit and talk about things and go into agreement. When I strayed away from my own truth, I stray away from everything in my life. When I judge myself as immoral, I am just immoral and need to pay for my immoral values. However, when I stray away from truth, I am leading a life that is a false one. It becomes a mirage and truth looks very different from afar. It seems like a mirage. When I was drinking and having affairs, truth was a mirage. It didn't exist in my sense of reality.

If my wife had given me consent to have affairs, I would still be immoral in the eyes of society. But you see, I don't believe that being immoral is the issue. The issue is non-consensual behaviors. People like me, who are strung high up in the ladder of life, don't need consent from another for my choices. I can have anyone I want. I can do anything I want. It is judged as immoral of course. But immorality in a court of law costs much less than the truth that was avoided in the court of life.

Immoral ways of being are a human conditioning. I am judged as immoral through the broken agreement. When I drink, I am judged as immoral. When I have an affair, I am judged as immoral. When I lie, I am judged as immoral. But what is it called when I lie to myself above all? Is it immoral when I lie to myself? I have to say, no. Who was ever indicted for lying to oneself or cheating one's true self with the ego self by going into agreement with society's rules rather than the soul's choices? No one. Not one person was indicted for all these violations to the self. We violate another without consent only because we have violated ourselves. No one will violate another that has not violated one's own truth first. You see, in court of law, judgment is brought to those who violate the constitution. They are paraded and judged as pariahs. They are subjugated to the laws through their violations, but it is a lack of consent that caused their immorality—not immorality itself. Morality is after all made up in the place of truth. Since, we have become simpletons, some things are quantified, for example, such and such violated such and such and therefore in the court of law they are a criminal. That is well and good, but it is not enough. I am not talking about the punishment. It is a judgment for me to say if a punishment is enough or not. That is not what I am alluding to. I am alluding to the one who violated and the one who was violated—the victim and the perpetrator. The one who violated didn't ask for consent, and the one who was violated was betrayed by the perpetrator. If it was consensual, it may very well have been thrown out of the court of law. But morality, that is a different question. If those two consenting individuals have broken an agreement with others, society may view them as immoral. It is back to being judged moral or immoral. However, morality doesn't exist in a true sense, the simple truth is that they are breaking an agreement with another.

If I had broken an agreement and to set it forth, went to the court of law to legalize the broken agreement through a divorce, I will amend my immoral choice. I will still have the label of being immoral, but through societal norms I would have put a patch on it. That makes it bearable. However, I still have to do my own soul searching and my own homework to make peace with my truth. Any truth that has been suppressed leads us astray. That is the nature of our life. I have lived a life of immorality. I have pillaged, plundered, and raped. Like I said before, the court of law will indict me for these crimes. But I have to answer to someone higher than the court of law. I have to answer to my true self, the self that is aligned to God. I will answer to my true self that is aligned with the divine. There is a divine self that is within you and me. That is the truth.

You see, when I pillaged and plundered, I had written off my conscience. It was easy to write it off. But your own soul knows it and you are up to face the jury of your own inner demons and sense of morality. Since we all have had different paths and lessons and experiences, we all have different baggage. We all have to answer ourselves in the court of our divine self. We are God within, we have to answer ourselves. We cannot judge in the court of the divine. We have to allow our true self to step forward. Since I have lived a life of lies, truth is painful in the beginning. The truth is that I have lived a life of lies. I have lied to myself, my society, my children and everyone around me. The perpetrator who lied to me is the same one who lied to the society, my family and my wife. Had I been true to myself, I would never have lied to my wife or my family. So, what is truth?

Truth is your innate knowledge of what is right and wrong for you. When you understand that what is truth for you may not be the truth for another, you cease to judge. When you have morality as a measurement, it comes with judgment. In the face of morality, my affairs were immoral. Whereas, in the face of truth, I lied to myself which reflected on everything I did and took me into a downward spiral. When we are not true to ourselves, we lie in many forms. Think of a man who has had an affair but loves his wife. He may shower his wife with gifts to mask his guilt. No amount of gift giving will mask his guilt. When I am true to myself, I am in agreement with myself, and as long as I don't break my agreement to myself in truth, I will stay true to others. When I say true to others, it is not about making me or another happy. It surpasses happiness. It is a state of truth that is resonant to your soul. When you disguise yourself, you disguise others. In a true sense of morality, no one is truly moral in a society. No matter what they do or tell, in a true sense no one is moral. If we use this moral guide as a way to existence, we have lost our way. We are in a quagmire of moral values that don't necessarily speak our truth. When morality is replaced with truth, the laws will be changed, judiciary systems will be changed. Who we are will be aligned with the truth. When we all live in truth, truth be told, there will be no justice that needs to be brought forth. You will already be just by the mere acceptance of your own truth.

Through my experience with the Lion, my wife and my own journey, I have realized that truth is harder than moral obligation. Since we as humanity have lost our own truth, we have created a compass on which we place a lot of value yet cannot achieve morality in the true sense of the word. We lie. We tell small lies, big lies. We have affairs—small ones, big ones. We pillage and plunder. We rape through the lack of consent. We strip another of their dignity without thought. You see, moral values cannot always stop these misdeeds. Only truth can do that.

When we reveal our truth to ourselves, something magical happens. We have an inner guidance system that points us in the right direction. It doesn't go to the moral code, golden rulebook to find if we are moral or not. In one sense, it takes you to your path of truth. When you address all the things that you have not been true to yourself, you are led to the path of oneness where everything and everyone converges. In that place, all moralities vanish. You feel everyone, everything and the universe within you.

You may still be left with what happened between me and my wife. In a sense nothing. But I did get closure. I learned to be my true self. I saw myself for who I had been. This has opened new doorways to many things, including a true and trusting relationship with my wife. I love her but I am even more in love with myself. I had to let go of attachment to the outcome between me and my wife. I can love her whether I am married to her or not. In being in my truth, I can allow her in her truth. I don't have to measure up to her and neither she to me. This is the difference between morality and truth. In a moral sense, we have to measure up. Morality is a bottomless pit where one can find no personal truth. When love is universal, you get to love all. In that all, I may be with one person or not. Regardless, I will be in my truth and in me being in my truth, I will honor my partner. I am able to honor another, only because I stayed in truth and in doing so, I have honored myself.

I have a sense of obligation to myself. However, this obligation is not one where one feels compelled; rather, one feels at ease. When one is true in every sense, allowing replaces obligation. Allowance allows forgiveness. When one is naturally allowing, they are allowing forgiveness to self and others. When one is in allowance, one is clear that one has been led to this moment in life through one's own choices. My affairs and drinking brought me to this point. Should I repent for my immoral behavior or seek truth? I chose truth, my wise me, chose the truth. Had I asked my ego self, it would have told me that I was immoral and made me feel guilty. When being in your truth, guilt and shame cannot exist. When being in your truth, only love can exist. In love, guilt and shame have to follow a natural demise. That is the court of life. We don't need death sentences and jury dates. We need allowance and forgiveness and a state of allowing our natural being. We shine bright when we are devoid of guilt. We stand tall with pride when we let go of shame. We feel the pride surging in us that allows ourselves to be who we are. When we allow ourselves to heal through truth, we are no longer in service of the moral compass, the golden rulebook to which we have adhered. We need no law or constitution to define good and bad, right and wrong, moral and immoral. We are in every sense of the way the guide, the judge of our own path. Not judgment, but judge in a sense of prevailing wisdom, not through lack of wisdom. When I cease to judge myself, I cease to exist in the way I did before. I become a new person and I am born again. In every true sense, I am birthing myself. Think of me giving birth to myself. I am in labor and trying to come out.

When the truth comes out the one being born becomes one with me and He becomes me, my true self. It is an infinite presence, this birthing. It has been painful to make choices that resonate with my truth. You guessed it right, yes, I gave up my business. I knew it was not on my path anymore. I left my family values to create my own values, to forge my own path, values and morals. You see, you can create morals that are based on your own truth. When you follow it based on your truth, you do not need to judge yourself against morality.

You are your own guide. You are your own teacher, guru, mentor or whatever you want to call yourself. Above all, finally you get to enjoy who you are. You have to break rules when you are in truth. That is the hard part, but it gets easier. It gets easier every time you break a rule. Eventually, you just allow, and you are transformed into this new self. It comes to a point where you cannot even remember who you once were anymore. You can't label yourself, as your soul is transforming every moment. When you transform every moment, how can you say you are this or that? Even when you say it, you know it is going to change. The only aspect that remains unchanged is your truth. In the face of your unchanged truth, you are constantly evolving. You see, truth is not passive. It is an active place, a vibration so to speak. In this vibration, everything around you vibrates at the frequency of truth by virtue of you. You are that powerful. That is why it is important that you remain you and I remain me. Here is the joke of the day, when you are aligning to be the true you and another is aligning to be in their truth, you become one with another. It was always the divine plan. Morality was based on separation—the idea that you and I are different. The path to truth brings you back to the self and the idea that we are one with everything. Your true self, which is aligned to God, is aligned to everything; everyone, no exceptions. Even those you don't care for or like, you are one with them.

In order to attain oneness, to feel the Lion, the forest and everything in creation, you have to look for the truth within yourself. We are a book of wisdom, you and I. We don't take the time to learn and engage with our wisdom, as we are too busy with other things. When you sit with yourself, make time for yourself and talk to yourself, eventually you will find yourself talking to your wisdom. The only person that can ever stop you from talking to your wisdom is you. Hence, there is no way you can blame anyone else in your life.

When you are aligned to your wisdom and you get truth as an answer to every one of your questions, you are on a path to enlightening the self. I know enlightenment can be a strong and scary word. It almost feels like there is no fun in it. It all seems so serious but trust me; my dear Lion taught me enlightenment can be light and humorous. He is the most re-laxed being I have ever met. Truth be told, when we relax, we are in a state of allowance. In that state of allowance, truth surfaces, nuggets of truth that will put the golden rulebook, the compass out of commission.

You my dear wise one, you tell me, do you choose truth or morality? Whatever you choose, choose wisely.

Truthfully yours,
Man

CHAPTER 21: PAWSITIVELY YOURS

I am glad you listened to my dad. He is full of wisdom. Little does he realize, we sense his energies. Yes, we are furry little things, but we're full of wisdom just like him. Mother Earth created us just like she did my father—full of wisdom. We have joined the army and are reaching out to you with our tiny paws. They are soft to touch, and we are easy to cuddle, unlike my father. We are the future generation that will continue the legacy. We are calling out to all little ones on Mother Earth to come and join our army. We play, we laugh, we love, we cry in this army. We are filled with emotions of joy, love and peace. We offer you our paws. Aren't we cute? Aren't we cuddly? Aren't our paws soft as a cushion? Won't you play with us? Look at my eyes, big and bright? Would you like to see the glow in my eyes stay forever? If you would like to see the light in my eyes grow brighter, please hold my paws and march with me towards paradise. We are creating a legacy. We want you to be part of this legacy. It is a legacy that we are meant to carry forward together.

We are holding paws, hands, trunks, noses, wings and fins, and marching towards paradise so it will not be forgotten. We are innocent. We have no baggage. We only ask you to jump into this quiet, serene paradise, created for all of us—for you, for me and everyone.

We play. We tumble. We somersault. We swing. We swim. We fly. We hide in holes. Yet, we are all coming out to hold our hands. We cherish our differences. We know of no differences that make us separate. We only know of differences that make us curious and eager to learn about one another. I like to swing on the trunk of the elephant while I play with him. We don't fight. Instead, we unite through our differences and our oneness. We know that we are one. We know we are all innocent and cute. We know of no differences that make us superior. We are just intrigued. Come join us in this paradise. Walk with us towards our paradise. This is our legacy, our future. Let us leave behind the legacy that causes pain and suffering. Let us envision a paradise, where everything and everyone is abundant—you, me and us. Let us unite with tiny paws and hands.

When I was born, I was intrigued by everything around me. I did not know that I was separate from others. All I wanted to do was play—with my father, with my mother, with my siblings, with my cousins as well as with the elephants, children, and zebras. I wanted to chase the butterflies and the deer. This is all I knew in my life. Now, I want to keep my world the way I am supposed to experience it. Could you please hold my paws to help me keep my world as it was intended to be? I need your help. We need your help. You call us the future generation, but your future lies with us, too. Your future will be carried on by us. Your legacy is part of us, one with us. Your legacy and my legacy are the same.

We have gathered here—the cubs, foals, ducklings, calves, toddlers, does, fawns, infants, and caterpillars. We hold limbs. We know our duty. Do you know yours? We know the legacy that we must carry. If you are not aware of the true legacy, we ask that you educate yourself. Please, try not to preach to us. We already know our role. In fact, we are here to show you and teach you about paradise, if you are interested.

If you think you need to teach us, please understand we already come equipped with the wisdom we need. We are clear in our goals. We are bright in our knowledge. We are educated through our love. We are wise through our wisdom. We are already enough. We are not looking to grow richer or smarter; we are already rich and smart. We just ask you to join this paradise that my father is worried will be destroyed with no trace. He thinks I don't understand, but I do. I understand his moods. He has seemed a little morose these past few weeks. I saw in his eyes a sadness that I have never seen before. I reached out to my wisdom and asked what was going on, and it narrated my father's story.

I am living the most beautiful life. I am living the most abundant life. I love this paradise. I would not be anywhere but here with my father, the Lion, and my mother, the Lioness, and my aunts and uncles. This is my land. This is all I have ever known. This is all I will ever know in this life-time. I intend to help my father carry this legacy into the future, our future. I am being proactive. I want to carry my father's legacy, the legacy of this paradise, the legacy of us. I seek your hands to hold my tiny paws. I ask you with love. I ask you with care. I ask you through my wisdom. I am wise. This is all I have ever known, and wisdom tells me to seek you out.

Look into my eyes. Can you bear my loss? Can you bear the loss of my pride? Can you? Can you bear the fading away of the light of your future generations? Can you bear the loss of light from the eyes of your future generations? Can you help yourself from this loss? Can you imagine what happens when the light in the eyes of your future generations is extinguished? Can you imagine all the forests, oceans, rivers, mountains, and soils polluted for your future generations with only a pile of money left for them to sit on? Will that money be worth it for your future genera-tions? When their pride is lost and replaced by a false pride, which leaves nothing to be dug, nothing to plundered, nothing to be stolen from our Mother…would that make you happy? Would that make you proud? When all that is left is nothing but a pile of money, would your future generations be happy? Would your soul be happy for having left them only this money—just a pile of money? This currency won't help them buy back paradise. This currency won't buy back love or compassion. This currency has no worth, no value. Can you envision such a plight? Can you?

What would you do? It would be too late then. You would have no time left to make the wrongs into rights. What would you do? Would you pray like a madman on your death bed? Would you? Well, you will be born to experience what you have created through another pair of eyes, but the same soul. You will be impacted as your own future continues through your rebirth on Mother Earth. But this Mother Land, which has been a cradle to you, will be left in tatters. Mother Earth will be unable to hold you any longer. Is that what you want? Is that what you want for the reincarnations of you and your future generations? If you have not thought about this, I urge you to think about it now. I am just a cub who is barely a year old. I'm just having fun, enjoying my life on Mother Earth. Wouldn't you want to continue this legacy for me and at the same time preserve it for your future generations?

I like my life here. I like to play with man and his offspring. They are cute and cuddly like me. We eat, we poop, and we play. We enjoy each other tremendously. I don't know about you, but I don't want to stop playing with my siblings, your future generation. Come closer, I won't bite. Look into my eyes and touch my fur. It is soft and silky, just like the skin of your future generations. Hold my paws. Aren't they soft? Don't you love holding my paws? Don't you love me? I love you so much that I cannot wait for you to hold my paws. I want to roam around in this paradise with you, just as my father does, and all my friends. I want us to continue our legacy of playing in this forest. Can you look into my eyes or look into a doe's eyes or the eyes of the fawn? Can you look into the eyes of a swimming fish and tell me you don't see love? Can you? I see the love in your eyes, for sure. Go into the pond. See your reflection. Can you see the love that is within you? If you look sad and forlorn, it is only because you stopped holding my paws, stopped holding the trunk of an elephant calf or the wings of a parrot. The minute you lose your connection with us, you lose your connection with yourself. See, holding my paws, or holding a trunk or a wing, is not just about us; it is also about you. Our wisdom knows that it is innocent to play with you. I urge you to teach the same to your future generations. What you teach your future generations will be inherited by you when you are reborn. Isn't that a miracle? So, sow the seeds of good deeds, thoughts and actions. Your future depends on it, not just in this lifetime, but in lifetimes to come.

If you would like to carry good deeds and thoughts, hold my paws, hold the wings, noses, tails, trunks, fingers and fins of my siblings. When you hold the hands of your child, look towards us, march towards us. We are eager to hold your child's hands. If only you knew the wisdom your child holds, you would be so surprised. Allow your child to experience his or her own wisdom. Please don't poison their minds by placing money above them. Don't poison them with false lies. Above all, don't teach them false pride. Just bring them to us. We will teach them unity in case you forgot. Educate them through their wisdom. You think you have to raise this child; you don't. Simply allow your child to be who he or she is. Please bring them to us.

I promise, your child will be a much better person, if you allow a natural unfolding of the gifts he or she has come to share. In bringing her closer to us, you are bringing her closer to light—the light that shines through his or her eyes, the same light that shines through my eyes and my siblings' eyes. You see, the eyes are the gateway to the soul. Eyes that shine of light are baring their soul while eyes that are filled with greed mask the soul as a mere shadow. Reveal the light and your eyes will shine bright—bright as a star. You are the star, the hero of your own life. You don't ever have to look for another hero because the hero is within you. You just have to unleash the hero by letting go of the greed and allowing the legacy to continue; the true legacy with shiny eyes.

I have a question for you: when you look into my eyes, do you see the eyes of your child? If you don't or haven't paid attention, I seek your hands. Come in front of me to look into my eyes. Do you see the light? Do you see the shining star in my eyes? That shining star that you see in my eyes is you. You can see you the shining star, the hero in my eyes. You know how I know? I see the shining star that I am in your eyes. If you see yourself in my eyes, and I see myself in your eyes, don't you think we are one? Aren't we the same? Should we look the same, to be the same? In my view, I don't have to look like you to feel like you. I just have to be me, and you have to be you. That's all we have to do to, be who we are. Is that confusing? If it is, hold my paws and look into my eyes. When you look into my eyes, could you please allow yourself to feel the love I feel for you? I would like you to know that I love you. I don't love out of need or necessity, I just love you, period. I don't have an agenda or a reason to love you. What you see in my eyes is that kind of love, unconditional love. If you see the love that I am showing you, would you be kind enough to bring your future generations, and have them hold my paws? I love your future. I love you in the future, just as I do in this moment. This moment is the only moment I know. I am not aware of any other moments. I have not experienced anything at your hands yet. I would like to be able to say that I have never experienced anything but love in your hands. Please hold my paws and march with me to unite in love…to unite in compassion…to unite in light. Would you please hold my paws?

Look over there. Do you see my friend chasing the ducklings with his trunk dangling? A funny creature he is, isn't he? Can you please hold my paws and walk with me? I would like to introduce you to my crazy friend, who is playing with the ducks. Would you like to hold my paws and walk with me? If you are hesitant, just look into my eyes, just look into these eyes that are filled with love. Can you resist this love while you are holding my paws? Please hold my paws and let us march towards my friend, my dear elephant calf. He is distracted with his play, but I promise he will be excited to see you. I hear that you want to use his teeth to make ornaments. I beg you, see him in the light, for the wonderful being he is. I hope you teach your future generations, which is also you, yourself, about the inhumane act of killing elephants to trade their ivory. We all have precious things within us. What is ivory's value when compared to that of the soul traded for it? Nothing. Please stop this inhumane act. Please, look into my eyes. Could you please help me help my friend? Could you please help my friend? He, who is playing with the ducklings with no care for his precious ivory, could one day be killed for the sake of a pile of money.

There is one thing I request of you. If you fulfill this request, it would change your mind and your future for generations to come. When an infant, your future generation, is born please bring the newborn child to us. Could you please? We won't bite. We won't attack. We just want to play with your infant. We like to play a lot, and we like to play with you, and your little tiny child that is as full of joy as we are. You see, there is no difference between us. I have paws; you have hands. We both are the same, just in different forms.

Could you please teach your child, your future, to value love over currency? Could you teach abundance, instead of greed? Could you teach play, instead of hard work? Could you teach compassion, instead of hate? Could you, will you, please? Hold my paws, look into my eyes, which plead with love. Will you please shower your future with love—the love that is naturally within you?

I take pride in playing with my friends. I cherish our differences. We don't discriminate. We unite. We come together as the children of Mother Earth. If only you could teach this unity to your soul, so it would be reborn and come back to you in your future. You see, by doing good deeds, you get to come back and enjoy the goodies that you sowed in previous lives. Isn't that great? This way, nothing is ever lost. When you fight hard for justice and you die at the hands of injustice, you didn't fail, you didn't lose. You will be back to enjoy the fruits of this justice for which you fought, for which you gave your life. In fact, don't fight, don't fight anything, just be and just be the love you are. You know, it is easy to be the love that you are. It is natural to your being. Anything else is unnatural.

When you are taught to be anything but love, you lose the you that is you. Instead, when you allow you to be who you are and your future generation to be who they are, you will solve all problems at once. That is love and love is that powerful. Anything other than love is a taught behavior. I urge you to teach the future you, the love that they carry, the love that you carry, the love that I carry. Please don't soil their brains by sowing the seeds of greed. Instead of teaching them graphs, pie charts, and ways to generate an income, teach them about the love and abundance found in this kingdom—this paradise in which my father, the Lion, is king, in which you are the king, in which your future is the king. Wear the crown of love with pride. Choose the crown of love, rather than the fear of scarcity.

When one is in love, one is provided with everything. When one is in love, one is lost in the eyes of another twinkly pair of eyes. The star of the show is in the eyes of another. Could you please hold my paws and march toward my brother? I want you to hold his trunk. When you hold his trunk, feel the love that flows through him. When you feel that love, you cannot be tempted to take his life away for his ivory. He is much more precious than his tusks. I invite you to ponder the fact that we are precious as a whole. When we divide any aspect of our preciousness, we are bound by greed. You are whole. I am whole. He is whole. How could one not see the preciousness that he is? How could one not?

My paws are as precious as me. My tail is as precious as me. I was created precious, and I will always be precious—with or without my paws. See, that is what I mean. I beg of you to take my brother's trunk and hold it. I urge you to feel the love that flows through him. I urge you. I ask you to take the time to look into his eyes and see the stars twinkling and see your reflection there. You will see only love in his eyes, just the way you see only love in mine.

Hold my paws, hold his trunk and let me walk you to my dear sister rhino. Hold her horn and feel its smoothness. Look into her eyes. Do you see the star you are in her eyes? I beg you to look into her eyes and feel the love. She is as gentle as she looks. If you have seen anything else, it is the terror created by her horn being stolen. Her horn, which she was born with, can't be taken away. You see, it serves a purpose for her and it serves a purpose as a whole. She is precious, isn't she? Could you please feel the love that courses through her and can we allow the whole of her to be who she is?

Could you please call upon your future to hold her horn? She would love that. She would love your future—the loving and compassionate you—to hold and touch her. Don't be afraid. She is as kind and compassionate as she seems. If you have heard anything else, realize that she has been terrorized for her horn. Her horn, which is considered to have sacred properties, has been coveted by traders who ignore the fact that it is actually the whole of her that is sacred.

I thank you for holding my paws. I thank you for generously listening. Your generosity, compassion and kindness will save our legacy. It warms my heart to see the love and compassion effusing through you. I have no doubt that you will help us in saving the future of our legacy. Let us come together as one and only one—not two, not three, not four, not a million, not a billion, not a trillion—but as one. Could we please come together as one?

When I look at all of us and the parade we form, I see all of you in my eyes as shining stars and warriors committed to saving the pride. Our pride that will save our legacy. If only you knew the love that is brought forth in this paradise through those beautiful eyes, those windows to the soul, you would never ever want to teach anything other than love to your future.

When you teach your soul about love, you are born as this love in your own future. You may be born as your grandson, you may be born as your great granddaughter, but you will be born having been the love and to be the love. Do you see how the cycle of life works? By sowing the seeds that you sow, you will be back to experience the saplings that grow. Are you sowing seeds of love or greed? You have a choice to sow love or greed. Be the one who champions your schools to teach creativity rather than arguing about creation. The creation part is handled already by the almighty. Your job is not to worry about the creation; your job is to teach love and be love.

Hold my paws and I will walk you through paradise. I am one of the orienteers. Would you like to hold my paws? I will take you to the calves of the giraffe and zebra. I will take you to my sister rhino. I will help you hold the trunk of my dear brother elephant. He is always playing with someone or something. He is crazy I tell you, crazy in love with you and crazy in love with me. It is intoxicating to be around him. Let me turn around to look into your eyes while holding your tiny hands. I love you my sister. I love you my brother. I see the love in your eyes. I see me the star of this legacy. I choose you my dear sister. I choose to love you. I hope you feel the same. I see the light in your eyes. I can't believe you are capable of anything but love—the unconditional love we inherited through our divine Mother.

The future is bright. It is filled with light. It is a shining star that seems far away. But the distance is an illusion. It is closer than it appears to be. I am reaching for the star, are you? Please hold my paws and let us shoot for the star—the star that we are, the star that is our future, the star that is in my eyes and in your eyes. See! I told you the star is not far away. It is in my eyes. It is in your eyes. The star that seems far away is never that far because it is close to your heart, to my heart, to our hearts, shining bright. Let us join our paws, hands, noses, trunks, wings and gills. I am ready. Are you ready to march towards paradise, which holds the stars of the future, our legacy? It is a legacy of pride, a never-ending legacy. It is the legacy of the Lion, yes, a never-ending legacy. The legacy of our future is never ending, as there is no time but now. If the legacy is created now, it will last forever. Every seed of love you sow, sprouts in your past, present and future. Don't be fooled when you don't see it; it is inside you. When you look for it outside, you are being misled. Don't be misled. Understand that the seeds of love are in your heart. Sow them with abandon, sow them with love, sow them with joy. Aren't you born to sow? Sow the seeds of love. Never lock your heart, as it would fester and give rise to hate. The love you contain is a precious star that seeks to glow. If your pride was ever wounded, don't lock your heart and hide your love. When your pride is hurt, open your love with abandon, for it is love that will heal your wounded pride. Isn't this why you are born over and over…to experience this love? You are born again to come to experience what you forgot to experience.

When you contain your love and measure it, you will be reincarnated until you learn not to. Why bother with hate? Why bother with fear of loving? When someone wounds your pride, show them love. Reach out to them with your paws and hold them in your paws. Look into their eyes until they see the love you carry, bright and shiny. No one, I tell you no one, has ever been able to avert their eyes when I look at them with love. I promise you no one. I have that effect, for you see, the love with which I see heals them of their wounded pride. Every one of us here has experienced having our pride wounded. No one is an exception. We experience wounded pride to reveal the love in our hearts. Why else would we come back again and again?

Your children are full of creativity, please show them the love that can reveal that creativity, which is inherent in them. Let them create through their wisdom and gifts. Let them not be fed with the greed, which will erase the pride of our legacy. Let them learn that they are born to love. Teach not the words of hatred. Teach not separation through race, color and creed—that is divisive. Let them learn the unity that is love. Let them play freely, and fear not about their well-being. They are naturally cared for. Teach them to trust, to trust mankind, to trust the creations of Mother Earth, to trust the wisdom with which they are born. If you could just allow them to be who they are, they will find their way into adulthood. In fact, stop raising them altogether, and just let them be. In the allowing them to be who they are, they will find themselves. You will understand the natural love they carry, the natural gifts they embody by allowing them to be who they are. Let them make friends from all corners of the world. Let them be fascinated by the world, not scared of it. Fear is an illusion that need not be taught. In allowing them to be, they will learn that fear is an illusion. My father always says, "My cubs are my pride and my pride is my cubs. However, I am not the one to lead them to their destiny. It is their duty and I must allow them to learn their pride and their destiny." I have never understood what he means, you see, because I am too young. Through my wisdom, though, I know I need to play with my pals who inhabit Mother Earth and overcome any lies and fears that I come upon.

I hope you have learned something about paradise. I hope your future has learned something about our paradise. The good thing is that this is all I have known—this wonderful amazing paradise. Unlike me, you will have to witness it through your vision to recreate what will be lost… including me. I am part of your destiny. If you think your destiny is separate from mine, I am going to urge you to consider that our destinies are intertwined. If I perish, so do you. There is no other way. In cherishing me and my kingdom, you save yours. I invite you to do less and envision more. The less you do, the more time you have to envision and faster you can create paradise. Invest less time in making money and make more time to be with your gifts. Make more time to be who you are and make fewer things to consume. Enjoy the abundance that is naturally here. You don't need to make more things; you already have everything you need. Would you please make time to hold my paws? Would you please make time to look into my eyes? Would you please make time to bring your future to hold my paws? I love it when you hold my paws. I love it when you hold anyone's paws in paradise. I love when you hold any limbs, twigs, trees, plants in my paradise, in paradise. I know in my heart, you are coming closer to paradise as you choose to value the time you take to hold our paws and limbs. I know you are coming towards us, rather than moving away from us. We love it when you come close to us and trust us. We trust you and are happy when you trust us. Could we come closer? Could we unite to maintain paradise? Could we please come together for just the sake of coming together, with no agendas? I like it here with no agendas. The fewer agendas we have, the more present we are to each other and to ourselves.

I have fallen in love with humanity. Have you? I request you hold another human's hand and feel it. Stay with the sensation of this unity that you feel with another human. Trust another human. Trust another race. Trust another, just for the sake of trusting. Trust is the key to the kingdom, to paradise. Can you trust me and hold my paws? I trust you. I know you will fall in love with me when you look into my eyes. "I trust you". My father says, "Wait until others look into your beautiful eyes..." He always finishes this thought by saying, "...not because you are my cubs." I know this is not true. We are his, and he is biased. It doesn't matter though. Can you resist me? I can't resist holding your hands. I want you to hold me. I sincerely trust that you want the same. I know you love me, even from afar. If you can't resist me from afar, how will you resist me from up close? You can't, I promise. I say this with so much confidence because I have not found anyone able to resist my paws and soft fur.

I could go on and on about me and you. I could talk to you forever, without ever tiring. I never get tired of you. I love all my friends, siblings and family. I love everyone, you see. I don't know any other way of being but loving. Would you please hold my paws? I am eager to show you paradise through my eyes, through my love, through my soul. I am not ready to lose my love for you. In fact, I will never be able to lose my love for you. Even if we become separated, I will find a way to reach back to your hands with my paws.

Pawsitively yours,
The future pride of the Lion through the Lion's wisdom

AFTERWORD

When I was just starting to write the book, I was shown several wonderful people who would contribute to the book. In less than a week, all of us came together and started reading the book that I had barely begun writing. We were all enjoying what was written. While everyone was brought together, each was given a role to play. At that time, I didn't know to believe it or not, but we all stuck with it.

To begin with, I would like to share a little bit about the journey of the book. My friend Madhavi and I would read a spiritual book in the mornings. One thing led to another and I started writing the channeled texts. Therefore, our readings stopped. However, one of the reasons for the book to emerge are our readings in the morning. We would have deep discussions about the material we read and discuss our spiritual journey and where we are at that time in our lives. We would help each other uplift our lives and journeys together. It is the way our relationship has been since its inception. Madhavi was an integral part of the book emerging. She was as confused and skeptical as I was. As I wrote I tried reading a few chapters to her. The readings made her come out of skepticism as I did and became one of my champions in this book being formed. She was part of the formation of the book and I owe her gratitude for being with me on this journey.

As I was writing, others became part of the group within a few days and the journey continued. The book took shape further through the reading and the support of these women who read, absorbed and added suggestions to the content. I don't think I can ever fully know the extent of what each of them had to sacrifice and rearrange in their lives to be part of this journey. Nonetheless I want them to know that I know that they had to make sacrifices to be present every week at the same time. If I didn't tell you the role that each played as part of the fruition and contin- uation of the book, my heart will not be content. To know that each of these women made a commitment and stuck to it and supported some- thing that they believed in is mind boggling to me. Yes, mind boggling. At the same time, I know they supported the book not because of me alone, although a little bit of it is true, mostly they recognized the power of the book and the impact of the book. Each absorbed the book in a way that I couldn't as a writer. They were the first reviewers of the book and always critiqued it in a way that was beneficial to the growth of the book. If they were not part of it, I am not sure how I could have brought it thus far. For that I am eternally grateful to Allison Faith, Pam Hutter, Nicole Holmes and Vineeta Santoshi.

Each one of these women saw something in the book beyond what I saw. I only channeled the contents, but they gave life to the book in a way that is hard to describe. We sat in Pam's living room week after week rev- eling in the material and discussing the contents and what impacted us and how it impacted. It took a shape and form that I couldn't envision in that moment. But each moment that these women provided shaped the book in its final form that you have in hand.

I think anyone can write and publish a book who has this kind of sup- port. If the guides carried me through the writing, these women carried me through the emergence of the book. Several tireless hours were put in reviewing the material back and forth and ensuring that any blemishes that were unconsciously placed removed from the material. Anything that was not of the guides or the highest wisdom was brought forth and released from the text. Each one had a purpose and the purpose kept evolving as if they were part of the chapters.

We would gather at Pam's house and at every gathering there was an abundance of food and tea that flowed. Never was there a lack of nourishment and no one went hungry. After every meeting, Nicole updated the material and kept it safe and sound. Alison who played editor of the book and read the material beforehand to save us the time while reviewing. Vineeta who brought her fresh mind with no preconceived ideas about the channeled text. We had all perspectives covered.

When all reviews were done, Pam continued the final reviews of the book alongside with me and provided guidance when I was unable to clearly listen to my own guidance. She was elemental in furthering the book without which I would have been lost.

Each of these women provided a value that I cannot fathom and would never fully know. But I know they all did. However, by saying this I also don't want to reduce the value that they got out of being a participant of the book. A book of wisdom can never leave a person untouched. It is an energy that impacts every person that it comes in contact with. To be indebted for their participation would be not Godly. I know for a fact they were placed to enhance my journey and theirs. We live in a world where every action has an equal reaction. Every touch of wisdom has a reaction and one would never understand deeply how it impacted another. So, I am eternally grateful for these women to have been part of this journey. I am also eternally grateful for the wisdom of the book and wisdom of all that guided this journey together. When one is in full awareness of this, there is no indebtedness or bindings. I gained more wisdom through their participation and they did by the wisdom that I brought forth through the book.

Remembering those days will always cause me nostalgia as if something were lost and gone. However, I also know that time and space are eternal. There is no beginning and no end. That makes us all eternal and therefore the experience I had with these women is eternal. I often don't like change. However, there is wisdom in change. It shows us that nothing is permanent and all things are in a constant flux. When we become aware of this, life gets easier and we don't get attached to things and people in ways we feel that we need to remain indebted. None of us are indebted to anyone, however, we remain in gratitude to those who provided a service, a wisdom, a lesson and whatever else they provided us.

Last but not least is the impact my publisher Kathy Meis had on this book and the journey. Even though this kind of material was new to her, she showed faith and support every step of the way. She gave me the faith to release this book out of my hands. She brought the perspective unintentionally that this book does not belong to me but ALL of US. This gave me a sense of freedom of not owning something. To surrendering it to the greater good and Thank you Kathy for making something that I thought impossible as possible. For that I am eternally grateful to you.

I am grateful to my parents for bringing life to me, giving me a home, shelter and education. For me to be able to breathe Mother Earth would not have been possible without them. I am grateful to my family especially my younger sister Ramathilagam for believing in me and my writings. She was there to support me through my ups and downs in my life and my journey with the book. Her complete trust in me is something I hope I can reciprocate someday fully on her journey as well.

I also want to thank those that took the time to read the book to support me and my journey. There are countless number of them and if I had to name them all, there would not be enough room on these pages. But I want them to know that I know who they are and I don't take their contribution lightly in reading the book and providing insights.

So, I end this note by saying that I am eternally grateful to all of you for coming together and making it happen. This book is no longer mine but belongs to everyone who touched it and who will touch it. It belongs to the energies of the wisdom, to love and forgiveness. It is here for us to thrive and show us we can thrive no matter what circumstances we are placed in. Thanks to everyone who were with us on this journey.